North for the Harvest

MINNESOTA
HISTORICAL
SOCIETY
PRESS

JIM NORRIS

NORTH
for the Harvest

Mexican Workers, Growers,
and the Sugar Beet Industry

www.mhspress.org

The Minnesota Historical Society Press is a member of the Association of American University Presses.

Manufactured in the United States of America

10 9 8 7 6 5 4 3 2 1

∞ The paper used in this publication meets the minimum requirements of the American National Standard for Information Sciences—Permanence for Printed Library Materials, ANSI Z39.48-1984.

International Standard Book Number
ISBN 13: 978-0-87351-631-1 (paper)
ISBN 10: 0-87351-631-0 (paper)

Library of Congress
Cataloging-in-Publication Data

Norris, Jim, 1949–
North for the harvest : Mexican workers, growers, and the sugar beet industry / Jim Norris.
    p.   cm.
Includes bibliographical references and index.
ISBN-13: 978-0-87351-631-0
    (pbk. : alk. paper)
ISBN-10: 0-87351-631-1
    (pbk. : alk. paper)
    1. American Crystal Sugar Company.
    2. Sugar beet industry—Red River Valley (Minn. and N.D.-Man.)
    3. Mexicans—Red River Valley (Minn. and N.D.-Man.)
    4. Migrant labor—Red River Valley (Minn. and N.D.-Man.)
    I. Title.
HD9109.A42N67 2009
331.5′440089987207769—dc22
                        2008044238

For my loves, Claire and Phoebe

*The publication of this book was supported,
in part, by a gift from the Bean Family Fund.*

CONTENTS

Photographs follow pages 60 and 164

Acknowledgments

WHEN I SET OUT ON THIS PROJECT, I had to significantly retrain myself as a scholar. My graduate work had prepared me to be a colonial Latin Americanist; my area specialty was in the often nebulous region of the Spanish Borderlands. My dissertation and first monograph focused on missionaries and power in eighteenth-century Spanish New Mexico. When I was hired at North Dakota State University (NDSU) in 1997, I realized how important the land-grant mission was to the institution. Several colleagues suggested I might want to look at the fastest-growing segment among the region's population: Latinos. I was intrigued; what were all of these Spanish-speaking people doing so close to the Canadian border? The answer, I soon discovered, began with sugar beets. For reasons I am still not sure of, the idea of doing this history grabbed me. I had to admit quickly, however, that I was ill prepared for this work, especially in two areas—American agricultural and rural history and twentieth-century Mexican American history.

Therefore, my first thank you must go to the scholars and publications that grounded me in the basics. For agricultural history this core curriculum came from Hal S. Barron's *Mixed Harvest,* my colleague at NDSU David Danbom's *Born in the Country,* Pete Daniel's *Breaking the Land,* Gilbert Fite's *American Farmers,* Deborah Fitzgerald's *Every Farm a Factory,* Cindy Hahamovich's *The Fruits of Their Labor,* Frank Tobias Higbie's *Indispensable Outcasts,* Carey McWilliams's *Factories in the Fields,* and David Vaught's *Cultivating California.* My scholarly mentors in Mexican American history were Armando C. Alonzo, *Tejano Legacy;* Sarah Deutsch, *No Separate Refuge;* Juan Gómez-Quiñones, *Mexican-American Labor;* David G. Gutiérrez, *Walls and Mirrors;* David Montejano, *Anglos and Mexicans in the Making of Texas;* Vicki L. Ruiz, *From Out of the Shadows;* Dennis Nodín Valdés, *Al Norte;* and Emilio Zamora, *The World of the Mexican Worker in Texas.* Of course, a brief look at my bibliography confirms my debt to many others.

Archivists were absolutely vital to this manuscript, and without their advice and assistance, this project would never have gotten very far. I owe an enormous debt of thanks and appreciation to Terry L. Shoptaugh and Korella Selzler at the Northwest Minnesota Historical Center (Minnesota State University Moorhead); John Bye, John Hallberg, and Mike Robinson at the North Dakota Institute for Regional Studies (NDSU); Patrick Coleman, James Fogerty, and Deborah Miller at the Minnesota Historical Society; David Clark, Sam Rushay, and Randy Sowell at the Harry S. Truman Presidential Library; David J. Mycue at the Museum of South Texas History in Edinburg; Michael O. Hironymous at the Benson Latin American Library (University of Texas at Austin); George Gause and Janette Garcia at the Lower Rio Grande Historical Collection (University of Texas–Pan American); and Rebecca Sharpless, at the time of my research visit, head of the Oral History Project at Baylor University. North Dakota State University's interlibrary loan staff was absolutely indispensable. My thanks to Wendy Gibson, Lorrettax Mindt, and Deborah Sayler.

I received financial support from several sources. The North Dakota Humanities Council provided significant monetary assistance through a Larry Remele Research Fellowship award. In addition, I received several travel grants from NDSU's Sponsored Programs; the College of Arts, Humanities and Social Sciences; and the Department of History.

Numerous scholars and friends read, commented on, and advised me on the text. David Danbom, Jan Jenkins, Terry L. Shoptaugh, and David Vaught read an early version of this manuscript and provided me with editorial assistance, extensive comments, and detailed advice. Jerry Garcia, James A. Garza, and Jeffrey Kolnick commented on papers presented at history conferences that were derived from this research. Marilyn Ziebarth, Debbie Miller, and Anne Kaplan at *Minnesota History* provided early encouragement and guidance. Several of my graduate students at NDSU were helpful with their insights, especially Yolanda Arauza, Anthony Dutton, and Amanda Eder, and undergraduate Matt Larson did newspaper research for me. Another student, Sara Egge, reviewed the final draft and wrote the index. In addition, several other colleagues at NDSU were also supportive, especially Gerald Anderson, Mark Harvey, Ineke Justitz, and Larry Peterson.

I would like to express my appreciation to the editors and staff at the Minnesota Historical Society Press. From the beginning, Ann Regan viewed this project as important and helped me in conceptualizing the work; Michael Hanson has cleaned up the text and steered the manuscript to completion admirably.

My parents, to whom I dedicated my first book, have continued to be my biggest cheerleaders. My daughter and friend, Phoebe Strom, has been an inspiration and a joy. Her booklet, *The Farmers Who Turned to Sugar Beets,* has constantly reminded me to proofread closely. Claire Strom, my beloved wife and companion, has advised me throughout this project, read every word more than once (she claims fifteen times), edited the manuscript, and, in general, kept me on track. Without her, this project would not have been nearly as much fun to complete.

Any errors within, of course, are only mine.

North for the Harvest

Introduction

LLOYD WAS BORN ON A FARM in the northern part of the Red River Valley near Fisher, Minnesota, in 1927. His family produced a variety of crops, such as barley, oats, wheat, corn, and "a few potatoes," and raised some cattle. This diversified farm fit a pattern common in the region after World War I, as the wheat monoculture for which the valley was famous no longer provided a satisfactory income. Indeed, about the time Lloyd was born, his father received his first contract from the American Crystal Sugar Company to grow thirty acres of sugar beets. One of Lloyd's earliest memories was riding with his father during the mid-1930s on a horse-drawn wagon to deliver harvested beets to American Crystal's nearby piling station. His father died in 1936, however, one of the driest years of a dry decade in the region. As his father lay dying, Lloyd's mother lied to her husband in order to comfort him, saying that the sugar beet crop was better than it actually was. Shortly thereafter, she moved her family into Fisher for a few years while she leased the farm to another sugar beet grower.[1]

The family did return to their land just before World War II, and an older brother and Lloyd once more planted a variety of crops, including sugar beets. Lloyd entered the army in the waning days of the war, but he was home on furlough in the early summer of 1945, hauling German prisoners of war held in Crookston, Minnesota, out to work in his family's sugar beet fields. An agricultural labor shortage throughout the region forced sugar beet growers to scramble for workers during the war years. Lloyd returned to the family farm in 1948 and received his first contract with American Crystal that year. Together with his brother's allotment, they had about 150 acres of sugar beets—a fairly large operation at that time. With wheat prices high just after the war, Lloyd recalled that their neighbors "laughed at [them] for monkeying with sugar beets." But when wheat prices sagged in the 1950s, those same people "were begging to raise beets."[2]

The larger operation required Lloyd and his brother to employ more and more Mexican migrant workers, most of whom came from South Texas. By the early 1960s the brothers relied on three Mexican migrant families to cultivate over two hundred acres of sugar beets. When his brother died in 1965, Lloyd took over his allotment and eventually expanded the sugar beet operation to over three hundred acres. Two Mexican migrant families became year-round employees at that time to help maintain the farm, which still included acreage devoted to wheat, barley, and oats. The Mexican families occupied his brother's former house and some mobile homes that Lloyd equipped with "hot and cold water and all that good stuff." When other valley growers decided to form a cooperative and purchase American Crystal in 1973, Lloyd borrowed $24,000 to participate in that venture. That move paid off for Lloyd as his income from beets increased dramatically, so much so that he incorporated his farm two years later. When Lloyd retired in the early 1980s, he turned the farm—now with allotments for over six hundred acres of sugar beets—over to his son. Lloyd and his wife moved into Fisher, although he still helped his son from time to time. When asked what had made his farming career so profitable, Lloyd replied that it was sugar beets "by far."[3]

WHEN JESUS CAME TO THE VALLEY to work in the sugar beet fields with his family, he discovered that the local people could not pronounce his name correctly. So he had them call him Jesse, a name he continued to use when he was among Anglos. Jesus was five years old when his family first migrated to the region. His father, Jesus Sr. (born in Texas on Christmas Day in 1926), had attended school in the Lower Rio Grande Valley near McAllen through the fourth grade, yet he could not speak English. Marrying in 1945, Jesus Sr. began a life of migrant labor almost immediately. Jesus Jr., his second child, was born near Lubbock, Texas, where the family had gone to pick cotton. Eventually, there would be ten children, although a girl born in 1964 in the Red River Valley died within a month and was buried in Moorhead, Minnesota. The family first worked as *betabeleros* (sugar beet workers) when Jesus's maternal grandfather encouraged them to migrate to the region in the early 1950s; he told his son-in-law that the pay was better than any other seasonal agricultural labor available. That first year Jesus's father cultivated sugar beets on his knees with a short-handled hoe.[4]

Thus began a pattern of migratory work that the family followed over the next decade. They were at home near San Juan, Texas (south of McAllen), from early November to early April, working at whatever might be available—packing fruit, harvesting spinach, or clearing irrigation ditches. They journeyed north to the valley in the late spring where they cultivated sugar beets into July. Jesus joined his father in the fields at age ten, despite the federal law that stipulated sugar beet field laborers be at least fourteen years of age; an older sister started when she was twelve. Fortunately for them, the children did not have to work with a short-handled hoe. Better seed varieties, mechanization, and herbicides had made the short-handled hoe obsolete by the late 1950s. In July the family journeyed to Wisconsin, usually near Madison, to harvest cucumbers. Around Labor Day they were back in the valley to work the sugar beet harvest. Since the harvest was mechanized by the mid-1950s, Jesus's father drove truckloads of beets to piling stations. In these years the family usually worked for the same farmer during both the growing season and the harvest. In fact, Jesus's father worked for one grower for over twenty-five years. Once the beets had been harvested, the family returned to Texas to begin the cycle anew.[5]

In the early 1960s, however, Jesus's father started making a concerted effort to keep the children in school longer, and Jesus and his siblings all graduated from high school. Most of them also attended college; Jesus received a teaching degree from Pan American University (now University of Texas–Pan American) in Edinburg, Texas. In 1975, he started coming to the valley again with his father, but he cultivated sugar beets only briefly. Most of the season he taught in one of the many schools serving migrant children that had proliferated throughout the region during the 1960s, something he continued to do for fifteen years. Jesus viewed these migrant schools as a manifestation of the improvement in the betabeleros' circumstances. His family's first migrant house had been only one room without dividers or insulation. The stove was wood-burning, and the privy, outdoors. By the 1960s their migrant house had many rooms, insulation, indoor toilets, and other conveniences. To Jesus something historic occurred for his family in the valley: "We broke the chain there."[6]

Their achievement was not without adversity and humiliation, however. Jesus encountered prejudice, although he thought it to be rather minor. He remembered going into a restaurant and overhearing a youth ask his parents whether Jesus was "a Mexican," and at a valley fair he heard someone ask if Mexicans should be there. And, of course, he continued to be called Jesse.[7]

EMMETT WENT TO WORK FOR AMERICAN CRYSTAL SUGAR COMPANY in 1949 when a friend had asked him, "Are you looking for a job?" The next day American Crystal hired Emmett as a fieldman, a job he held for forty years. Like Lloyd, Emmett was born and raised on a farm in Clay County, Minnesota. His grandfather was one of the early Anglo settlers in the valley, obtaining a homestead in 1872. Like Lloyd, Emmett's family grew a variety of crops—wheat, barley, potatoes—and raised some cattle. Unlike Lloyd, Emmett planned to avoid the life of a farmer. He enrolled at North Dakota Agricultural College (now North Dakota State University) in 1938, intending to become an engineer. World War II interrupted his education, and after being discharged from the military, he attended the University of Minnesota and received a degree in business in 1946. He decided soon thereafter to return to the valley.[8]

The job of fieldman generally consisted of three tasks. First, Emmett recruited farmers to grow beets. The company assigned him to Traill County, North Dakota, an area into which American Crystal was expanding at that time. The postwar boom in wheat prices made it difficult for him to entice farmers to grow sugar beets, but once grain prices sagged in the 1950s, Emmett found recruiting easier. The second major responsibility for fieldmen was providing technical assistance for growers. Emmett advised growers on American Crystal–approved seed varieties, specialized sugar beet farm implements, pesticides, and herbicides. Since he had no prior experience in the cultivation of sugar beets, nor a degree in agriculture, Emmett had to devote considerable time to educating himself. And third, Emmett and the other fieldmen served as intermediaries between growers and Mexican migrant field laborers. For the most part, Emmett categorized this portion of his duties as more time consuming than problematic. It was his responsibility within his territory to assign new betabeleros to growers and to oversee their orientation to sugar beet field work. In addition, he inspected migrant housing and their living conditions, and he was to resolve the disputes that occasionally arose between the grower and the worker. Emmett later described these mainly as "misunderstandings," usually over how clean (free of weeds) a field needed to be or how much pay the betabelero should receive.[9]

In order to help recruit betabeleros, Emmett spent three months during the spring of 1951 in Austin, Texas, representing American Crystal Labor Agency—a licensed business that American Crystal had established in order to recruit migrant workers legally in Texas. Some fieldmen went to Texas more frequently to help obtain workers for the valley, but since Emmett did not speak much Spanish, he went only that one year. To fulfill these three primary responsibilities, Emmett worked twelve hours per day in 1949, took care of sixty to seventy growers, helped coordinate the placement of three to four hundred betabeleros and their dependents, and drove over thirty thousand miles within the valley; for his services American Crystal paid him two hundred dollars each month.[10]

By the time he retired in 1990, Emmett was working eight hours per day, assisting about ninety growers, rarely interacting with migrant workers, and driving a bit less—around 25,000 miles per year. He was earning $42,000 each year. Clearly, Emmett experienced dramatic change within the sugar beet industry, but when asked how he felt about his years as a fieldman, he simply replied, "It's been a living."[11]

THE LIVES OF LLOYD, JESUS, AND EMMETT intersected in the sugar beet fields of the Red River Valley in North Dakota and Minnesota. Sugar beets, together with sugar cane the major sources of sucrose for human ingestion, had long been grown in Europe to feed livestock. In the 1700s German chemists learned to extract high-quality sugar from certain varieties of beets, and the first sugar beet extraction factory started operation in Prussia in 1802. German immigrants brought sugar beets to the United States during the early nineteenth century, but large-scale production did not begin until after the Civil War. By the 1870s factories were processing sugar beets in California, Colorado, and Nebraska. When American sugar consumption rose during the early 1900s, sugar beet production increased rapidly to help fill that demand, and cultivation spread into other areas, especially in the Midwest and Great Plains states. The sugar beet industry commenced in the Red River Valley shortly after World War I because sugar company scientists believed that the soil in the region would be very conducive to high-quality sugar beets.[12]

Indeed, the Red River Valley of the North, as it is sometimes called to distinguish it from the river dividing Texas and Oklahoma, has some of the most fertile soil in the United States. The various glacial eras profoundly contributed to the region's agricultural potential. As the ice sheets advanced, they pulverized and deposited ahead of them large amounts of silt, clay, and sand. This glacial till reached depths of up to three hundred feet in the region. At the conclusion of the last ice age, and as the glaciers retreated, a vast lake—Lake Agassiz—pooled over the region. Lake Agassiz helped to flatten the region by further compacting the soil, while stream tributaries carried more sedimentary deposits into the lake, adding another sixty-foot layer of soil. Thus, the fecundity of the area, sometimes called the Nile River Valley of America, developed through these prehistoric periods.[13]

The Red River formed after the glaciers finally disappeared and Lake Agassiz drained. The confluence of the Bois de Sioux River and Otter Tail River near the border of North Dakota and South Dakota creates the Red River, which flows northward into Canada and, eventually, Lake Manitoba. The present-day valley is over three hundred miles long and between forty and fifty miles wide, gradually tapering toward its southern end. Because of the relatively small size of the river (in most places less than one hundred yards wide), the high water table, and the very slight gradient, the Red frequently floods— often dramatically, as in the 1997 flood that ravaged Grand Forks, North Dakota—and disrupts agricultural operations. These floods have, though, left behind alluvial deposits that have further enriched the soil. The Red River also forms the boundary between North Dakota and Minnesota, hence the history of the valley's sugar beet industry includes developments within two separate political entities.[14]

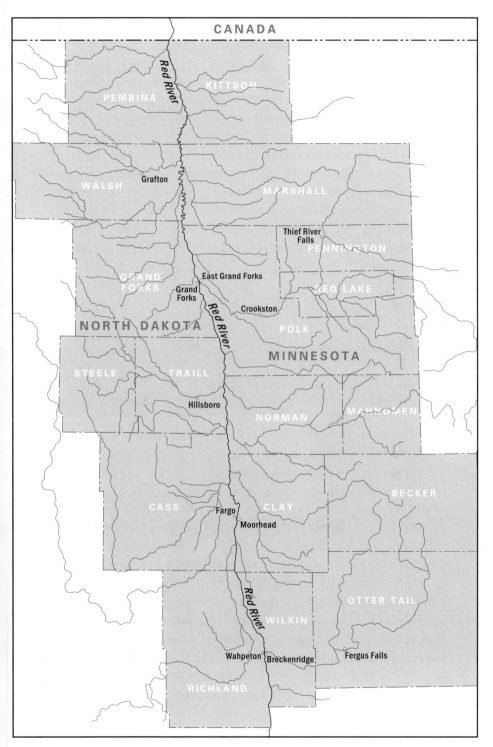

The sugar beet–producing counties of the Red River Valley region

The climate in the valley where Lloyd, Jesus, and Emmett worked can be extreme. Winters are long and cold, and snowfalls average over forty inches per year. Temperatures of –30 to –40 degrees Fahrenheit are not uncommon, and storms called Alberta Clippers can create blizzard conditions quickly, sometimes with little warning. Conversely, summers are usually short, warm, and humid. Average temperatures in July and August range over 80 degrees, and days of more than 100 degrees may occur. Hence, the temperature can fluctuate up to 140 degrees during a year. Moreover, frequent spectacular thunderstorms are often accompanied by damaging hail and tornados. The often wet conditions also provide excellent breeding grounds for mosquitoes, for which the valley is famous, and the insects torment whoever ventures outdoors. Therefore, while the valley is rich in soil and has sufficient precipitation for sugar beet cultivation, the physical conditions in which people toiled were often taxing, especially for the betabeleros.[15]

THIS HISTORY WAS NOT THE STORY I IMAGINED when I began research in 1999. I had a fairly extensive background in labor history from my graduate school training, so I assumed I would follow that methodology. In addition, I am the grandson of an Anglo migrant worker; my father grew up following the cotton harvest between Texas and Missouri until he was a teenager and my grandfather was able to settle down somewhat as a cotton sharecropper. My father managed to graduate from high school, though he recalls attending more than twenty schools in the process. My family and its history inculcated within me an inclination to root for the underdog. To support César Chávez and the United Farm Workers, I did not eat a grape during the 1970s.

Therefore, I assumed this book would be a simple narrative of conflict and adversity as Mexican migrant workers battled sugar beet growers for, essentially, their dignity—a class struggle, those that have against those that have not. Obviously, this was a portion of the tale. Poor, often illiterate, betabeleros did battle at times with wealthy landowners for better opportunities in wages, working conditions, and housing. Yet that was only a part of what occurred in the sugar beet industry in North Dakota and Minnesota between the end of World War

I and the 1970s. Sometimes it was the farmers who suffered and failed economically. Sometimes they developed close personal relations with their Mexican workers and treated them with respect. Moreover, it was not just a story of growers and betabeleros. American Crystal Sugar required the services of both. The company interacted with the migrant workers and the farmers, at times to their benefit and at other times to their detriment. Therefore, the relationships among these three entities were rarely simple. As in most instances, historical investigation showed life to be more complex and nuanced than supposed. At least, that was what I was forced to acknowledge from my findings.

Historically, sugar production, whether for cane sugar or beet sugar, has required backbreaking, exhausting field work. Such toil, shunned by those who could avoid it, most often has been performed by the economically desperate. In the Midwest and Great Plains regions of the United States, German-Russians and Japanese immigrants did most of the early sugar beet field work, but by the end of World War I most of these sugar beet–producing regions relied primarily on workers from Mexico.[16]

For many Mexicans, sugar beets represented one of their best economic chances as their own country's economy struggled to recover from the ravages of the 1910 revolution. To be sure, sugar beet wages were poor, but employers usually offered contracts to entire families. Therefore, a Mexican family's aggregate earnings from sugar beets provided the best alternative for many, at least until something better beckoned. In turn, sugar beet companies and growers welcomed the control they gained by hiring family groups. Moreover, since the companies brought the betabeleros from the border in trains, they insured that these migrant laborers arrived when needed and departed when finished. This transitory structure helped to guarantee a docile workforce in which betabeleros had very little leverage.

The development of the sugar beet industry in the Red River Valley did not follow, however, quite the same pattern as elsewhere in the Midwest for several reasons. The valley was very remote from the usual migratory routes, leaving workers little access to other seasonal agricultural jobs. The area's climate limited the sugar beet season to a single planting cycle, whereas other regions often planted two or even three times a year. This meant that field laborers in the valley were needed for only six to eight weeks early in the summer and then were not required again until the harvest two months later. What would be done with migrant workers in the interim? And finally, sugar beet production had barely established itself in the valley before the difficulties associated with the Great Depression and the 1930s drought arose.

Once the sugar industry stabilized, primarily from federal government assistance shortly before World War II, the American Crystal officials and the growers found it necessary to look elsewhere for migrant workers. Many of the groups that had performed the labor, such as the German-Russians, had moved into urban, industrial employment or, in the case of workers from Mexico, found entry into the United States hampered by the 1930s repatriation campaign. Relatively quickly, Mexican residents from Texas formed the backbone of the valley's migrant labor force, a pattern that endured for the next half century. (Hereafter, the term "Mexican" will be used to describe the Hispanic population of Texas, whether citizen or legal or illegal resident of that state. These migrant workers most often identified themselves to other people as Mexican. Betabeleros brought in from Mexico will be referred to as Mexican nationals or, where appropriate, *braceros*.)

The growers in the valley were another unique factor in the evolution of the sugar beet industry. Certainly, the region's farmers suffered through the general malaise in agriculture that was endemic in the nation throughout most of the twentieth century. Many sugar beet growers failed and left the life of farming for other careers. As did farmers in other sugar beet regions, the growers in the valley eventually organized themselves into an association. During the 1930s they formed the Red River Valley Sugarbeet Growers Association (RRVSBGA), a body that became a powerful advocate for the growers in their relationship with American Crystal and the federal government. Indeed, the RRVSBGA eventually purchased American Crystal and all of its holdings in the 1970s.

Therefore, the history of the first half century of sugar beet cultivation in the valley involved two rather powerful organizations—the RRVSBGA and American Crystal, which was ranked third overall in national sugar production. Both of these groups were significantly dependent, however, on Mexican migrant workers from Texas, and their need for betabeleros provided the migrants with some important leverage. Mexican workers, though, were not simply lured *al norte*. Political, economic, and social developments in Texas, especially along the state's border with Mexico, combined to push them northward, too. Fully appreciating the circumstances of Mexican migrant workers in Minnesota and North Dakota requires an understanding of their lives in Texas. Indeed, over the decades the balance of power among growers, American Crystal, and Mexican migrants fluctuated in response to state, national, and international political events. New beet-growing technology further influenced their interactions with one another. Dependent upon each other in a relationship that often seemed anachronistically paternal, neither the betabeleros nor the growers nor the American Crystal Sugar Company held all the advantages all of the time. Jesus, Lloyd, Emmett, and the thousands of other participants had to constantly adjust their actions toward each other in this three-corner game of advantage and necessity.

CHAPTER 1

Coming Together

NECESSITY TURNED FARMERS IN THE RED RIVER VALLEY to sugar beet growing. Necessity brought the sugar beet industry to the valley. And necessity linked Mexican migrant workers to those farmers and that industry. Necessity laid the foundation for a three-way, multifaceted relationship among these groups that endured for much of the twentieth century. Throughout the Red River region in the early twentieth century, farmers searched for new sources of income to bolster their declining economic status. Sugar beets appeared as an attractive option because of growing sugar consumption worldwide and because sugar beet contracts at this time included guaranteed earnings. To the sugar beet industry, scientific tests on soil nutrients in the Red River Valley indicated that beets grown there would produce very high sugar yields and a company's operating costs would be low. And finally, Mexicans, both from South Texas and from across the Rio Grande in Mexico, viewed sugar beet field work as a viable occupation to address their own economic problems. A violent revolution in Mexico and a profound social and economic upheaval in South Texas had displaced thousands of Mexican people from their traditional means of earning a living. Thus while growers, sugar company executives, and Mexican families had different motives, necessity brought them all together in the Red River Valley during the decade after World War I.

THE NEED FOR RED RIVER VALLEY FARMERS to find alternate crops was rooted in the region's history. In many respects the first half century of Anglo agricultural development in the Red River Valley mirrored the boom and bust economy usually associated with rural societies dependent on a single commodity. Beginning with what historian Elwyn B. Robinson called the Great Dakota Boom, the period from 1878 to the mid-1880s was an era of remarkable economic growth spawned by two developments: the arrival of railroads, especially the Great

Northern Railway and the Northern Pacific Railroad, and the emergence of the flour-milling industry in nearby Minneapolis–St. Paul.[1]

The two transcontinental railroads that reached the Red River Valley in the early 1870s were significantly different in their economic foundations. The Northern Pacific Railroad (NP), which essentially traversed the southern portion of what would become the state of North Dakota on an east-to-west axis, had been awarded enormous land grants. In Minnesota this amounted to alternating sections thirty miles north and south of the track; from the Red River westward the NP grant doubled. This land represented a great economic foundation for the NP and, indeed, as a result of the railroad's financial woes associated with the Panic of 1873, became the impetus for the first Bonanza farms. In contrast, the St. Paul, Minneapolis, and Manitoba Railroad (which evolved into the Great Northern Railway, or GNR) did not receive any land grants west of the Red River. The GNR did, though, put down significant miles of track on a north-south line from Fargo to Manitoba, giving that company virtual control over rail transportation in this fecund valley. While haulage was important to both railroads, developing markets were most crucial to the GNR, and it took the lead over time in promoting growth in the Red River region.[2]

The second important development concerned the flour-milling industry established primarily in Minneapolis and St. Paul in the 1870s. Relying on the excellent energy source of the Falls at St. Anthony, the flour mills had a capacity to turn an almost unlimited amount of wheat into flour. The Twin Cities were strategically placed at the headwaters of the Mississippi, which allowed them to take advantage of the relatively cheap shipping rates on that body of water. In addition, Minneapolis and St. Paul were important junctions for both the NP and GNR railroads. If wheat could be brought to the Twin Cities, growers, railroad executives and stock holders, and flour mill owners could all prosper; the matrix for the Great Dakota Boom was in place.[3]

The farmers in the Red River Valley provided the wheat. Dominated by the vast landholdings of the Bonanza farms, the valley prospered dramatically during the late nineteenth century. Bonanza farms ranged in size to over sixty thousand acres and in important respects were forerunners of the modern agribusiness associated with the twentieth century. With their heavy dependence on mechanization and their employment of thousands of temporary wage laborers during the harvest, the Bonanza farms had significant similarities to the sugar beet industry seventy years later. The Great Dakota Boom was, however, about more than huge farm operations. It attracted a wave of settlers into the valley, and smaller landholdings dotted the landscape. While the popular image of the Bonanza era was the vast estate, within the twelve counties that comprised the Red River Valley (six on each side of the river), the average farm size in 1880 was only about 240 acres.[4]

The economic boom created from the linkage of Bonanza farms, the region's smaller wheat-growing farms, railroads, and flour mills lasted about a decade. After rising steadily in Minneapolis–St. Paul in the late 1870s, the price for wheat began to fluctuate significantly after 1882. From eighty cents per bushel that year, the price fell to forty-six cents by 1884, rallied to sixty-three cents the following year, dropped again to fifty-two cents in 1886, and then continued to gyrate wildly in the early 1890s as a result of overproduction and the 1893 economic depression. Moreover, the weather became problematic, as 1881 and 1889 were especially dry years, and the winter of 1886–87 set low-temperature records that still stand in the region today. In addition, excessive cultivation without crop rotation reduced the productivity of the land, and as farmers turned over more soil, weed infestations plagued the wheat lands. For these reasons, among others, such as overspeculation in land prices, the Great Dakota Boom came to a halt in the late 1880s.[5]

The collapse of the wheat boom, coupled with the Panic of 1893, set the stage for the region's economic depression and subsequent efforts by valley farmers, scientists, and business leaders to diversify and improve agricultural production. For example, James J. Hill, the head of the GNR, promoted several diversification schemes, especially cattle raising, in order to increase traffic on his railroad. Both North Dakota and Minnesota state governments supported attempts to improve drainage in the region, a recurring problem, and by the end of World War I, over 200,000 acres in the twelve counties had been reclaimed. The University of Minnesota opened an agricultural experiment station in the valley in 1895; North Dakota Agricultural College in Fargo created farmer institutes in the 1890s, a forerunner of the college's extension service. The Better Farming Movement, which encouraged diversification, emerged during the second decade of the twentieth century, supported by railroad companies, banking institutions, politicians, and others. Through these efforts, growers in the Red River region produced increasing yields of alfalfa, clover, corn, flax, and potatoes. Moreover, valley farmers invested in more pigs, sheep, and cattle, especially dairy cows.[6]

These developments all contributed to the so-called Second Boom that occurred between 1898 and World War I. Many farm families who would become sugar beet growers in the Red River Valley struggled to diversify their agricultural enterprises. One family remembered that by the 1920s they grew wheat, corn, and potatoes and they also raised cattle. Another family, which would add sugar beets after World War I, grew various grains and potatoes, had dairy cattle and sold the milk to a creamery, and operated a small general store. Area farmers searched for profitability from varied commodities.[7]

These efforts to diversify the region's agricultural production spawned the initial interest in sugar beet cultivation in the valley. In fact, sugar beets were grown in the valley as early as 1872, but popular support for such a crop lagged until World War I. Primarily, the harsh climate discouraged the idea of sugar beets, although one of the main proponents of diversification, James J. Hill, rejected the notion of beet farming for another important reason. In a letter to the president of North Dakota Agricultural College, Hill opined that Americans would not work for the low wages customarily paid to European sugar beet field workers, and therefore the price of the sugar produced in the region would never be competitive. Hence, Hill correctly recognized what would be an important barrier to sugar beet cultivation in the valley: securing a workforce. Nonetheless, local community boosters, politicians, and university scientists in the years leading up to World War I promoted experimentation with sugar beets.[8]

Yet despite these various diversification efforts, the valley's farmers continued to depend heavily on grain production, a problem brought home even more as a result of World War I. Once that conflict broke out, growers attempted to increase wheat production for export to European countries, and in fact, North Dakota broke its existing record with a harvest of almost 160 million bushels in 1915. When the United States entered the war in 1917, the federal and state governments encouraged the region's farmers to do even better. Ironically, efforts to increase production did not translate into wealth for these farmers. In 1916, 1917, and 1919, the wheat harvest was below the area's norm as a result of drought, and 1918 was only an average year in wheat production. Moreover, the government established price controls on wheat but did nothing to control the cost of most commodities purchased by farmers. Thus, inflation cut into the growers' earnings. In addition, wartime speculation in agricultural land led to a spike in land values, up nearly one-third throughout the valley, which increased mortgage debt considerably for those farmers who purchased more land. When the price of wheat dropped at the end of 1919, conditions were ripe for another farm depression in the valley, and the region joined other agriculturally dependent areas of the country in the subsequent economic slump.[9]

Along with the downturn in wheat prices and a return to hard times for farmers, the year 1919 was a watershed for the sugar beet industry in the valley. For one thing, sugar prices were still high: more than triple what they were in 1914. In addition, the wartime surge in demand and prices for sugar had led scientists at the Northwest Agricultural Experiment Station (University of Minnesota at Crookston) in Polk County to experiment with two types of sugar beet seeds after they had induced a few growers to cultivate test plots. After the 1919 harvest of these test sugar beets, officials from the experiment station sent samples to a sugar mill operating in southern Minnesota. The technicians at the mill found the sugar content of these beets to be very high, and officers of the Minnesota Sugar Company, which operated the facility, turned their attention to the possibility of producing sugar beets in the Red River Valley. Two major problems had to be solved, however, before sugar beet cultivation could become a viable agricultural enterprise in the area: a sugar-producing facility had to be erected, and a labor force, secured.[10]

THESE PROBLEMS WERE PART OF THE PURVIEW of the second agent that necessity enticed into the valley: the sugar beet industry. The industry in the United States underwent significant growth in the early decades of the 1900s. After being introduced into the United States by German immigrants during the 1830s, sugar beet cultivation had spread slowly through the Civil War years. In 1870, the first successful sugar beet plant opened in Alvarado, California, and cultivation quickly spread throughout the West, assisted by two important developments. First, American sugar consumption almost doubled during the last two decades of the century, brought on by a combination of a rapidly increasing population, the growing popularity of sweet foods and beverages, and technological methods that resulted in cheaper sugar. In fact, the price of refined sugar had been prohibitive for a majority of American consumers in the early 1800s, over twenty cents per pound. By 1890, however, refined sugar sold for less than seven cents per pound. In addition, the federal government boosted domestic production when Congress passed the McKinley Tariff (1890), which for two years levied a bounty of two cents per pound on domestic cane and beet sugar, and then the Dingley Tariff (1898), which placed a tariff on imported sugar. These tariffs began a trend in government support for domestic sugar production that has endured into the twenty-first century.[11]

Most of the early sugar beet companies, such as the Chino Valley Beet Sugar Company, the Iowa Sugar Company, and the Amalgamated Sugar Company, were relatively small enterprises. Their methods of operation established the procedures that the bigger corporations of the twentieth century followed. These companies entered into contracts with farmers that stipulated the techniques the growers would use to plant, cultivate, and harvest the sugar beets. In return the farmers received a minimum base price for their beets, plus additional monies determined by sugar content and the price of sugar on American commodities markets that year. Farmers could often use the earning potential from these contracts as collateral for bank loans, which they viewed as an additional benefit. Moreover, if growers wanted field laborers to cultivate or harvest the sugar beets, the companies usually procured these workers. Sugar beet field work was very difficult, and farmers avoided doing it if they could.[12]

A small company headquartered in Chaska, Minnesota, introduced the sugar beet industry into the Red River Valley. While not the first sugar beet company in the state of Minnesota (an earlier operation's processing facility had burned down around the turn of the century), the Carver County Sugar Company was incorporated in 1905 and processed its first crop grown on farms in the Minnesota River Valley two years later. In 1911, with several thousand acres of beets under contract, the company changed its name to the Minnesota Sugar Company. It was this company that had received the sugar beet samples from the Northwest Agricultural Experiment Station after World War I. Impressed with the valley's potential, Minnesota Sugar began contracting with area farmers to send their harvested beets to the Chaska factory. This arrangement was costly, however, since the beets had to be shipped several hundred miles by rail. Furthermore, the time lag between the harvest and the sugar beets' arrival at the factory diminished the sugar content of the beets. These factors compelled Minnesota Sugar to announce in 1923 that it would build a sugar beet factory in the Red River Valley at East Grand Forks, Minnesota, but only if area businesses would contribute at least $500,000 to the operation. The following year, with the local funds secured, Minnesota Sugar created the Red River Sugar Company and began construction on the facility with the goal of processing sugar beets by 1926. Before that event occurred, however, another company, American Beet Sugar, took over the venture.[13]

The American Beet Sugar Company, as it was known at that time, began in 1897 when the Oxnard family decided to open a factory in Ventura County, California. The Oxnard brothers came from a family long familiar with sugar processing, both in the sugar cane parishes of Louisiana and in processing factories along the East Coast. Actually, one of the brothers, Henry, already operated two sugar beet facilities in Grand Island and Norfolk, Nebraska. The brothers formed American Beet Sugar Company from the Ventura County factory, the recently purchased Chino Valley Beet Sugar Company, the two Nebraska factories, and a sugar beet factory construction firm owned by them. The Oxnards chartered these companies into the American Beet Sugar Company in 1899. Over the next seven decades, it was usually ranked as the third-largest sugar beet company in the United States.[14]

The American Beet Sugar Company expanded aggressively in the first decade of the 1900s, especially into Colorado. The company found the Arkansas River Valley near Rocky Ford, Colorado, especially conducive to sugar beet cultivation. In 1905, it opened a factory at Lamar and another two years later in Las Animas. American Beet Sugar also relocated its corporate headquarters to Denver at this time. By the end of World War I, American Beet Sugar increasingly turned its attention to production possibilities east of the Rocky Mountains. California land prices, the urbanization of Ventura County, and lower transportation costs made the Midwest much more attractive than the West Coast to the company's directors. In the summer of 1924, shortly after Minnesota Sugar Company announced its plans for the East Grand Forks factory, Herman Zitkowski—a German immigrant chemist, longtime associate of the Oxnard family, and the operation manager for American Beet Sugar—visited the facility in Chaska and toured the Red River Valley to ascertain whether those areas might be worth acquiring.[15]

What Zitkowski saw must have impressed him, as did the holdings of another small sugar beet company, the Northern Sugar Company, near Mason City, Iowa. American Beet Sugar entered into negotiations to buy both the Northern Sugar Company and all of the holdings of Minnesota Sugar, including the Red River Sugar Company. In November 1924, American Beet Sugar's directors authorized the purchase of all of these properties. The parties involved reached agreement on Christmas Eve 1924; the sale closed in March 1925. American Beet Sugar selected L. E. Flink, the former vice president and general manager of Minnesota Sugar's Chaska facility, to supervise the construction of the factory and establish operations in the Red River Valley.[16]

Building the East Grand Forks factory proceeded after some delays. Part of the slowness resulted from American Beet Sugar's decision to close the Chino factory and ship some of its machinery to the new facility. The engineers designed the East Grand Forks factory to handle at least 1,200 tons of beets per day and to process, overall, 150,000 tons of sugar beets each year; by comparison, American Beet Sugar's Ventura County factory processed only about 60,000 tons. At its completion in 1926, the East Grand Forks factory represented the state-of-the-art in sugar beet refining.[17]

The basic operation of a sugar beet factory has remained the same over the last century. After the beets are delivered to the factory by either truck or railroad car (wagons, too, in the 1920s), they are washed in tanks. The sugar beets are then thinly sliced and moved into diffusion tanks where the sugar (in a liquid state) is separated from the pulp. This liquid sugar is treated with milk of lime and carbon dioxide to remove additional impurities and then is passed through filtering screens. The solution is next pumped into evaporation tanks and filtered again. Now clean, the liquid is boiled to remove most of the moisture; what remains is put into a centrifuge to dry completely, leaving only granulated sugar ready for packaging.[18]

The dedication ceremony on October 6, 1926, for this newest sugar beet facility was a festive event. The invitation, in the shape of a sugar beet, announced "another link in the chain of prosperity of the Red River Valley." Speakers included American Beet Sugar's chairman of the board, president, general counsel, and vice president; the governors of both Minnesota and North Dakota addressed a large crowd "of townspeople and country folks who had been so anxious" to see the sugar beet industry get started. Musical selections were provided by St. Paul's Great Northern Quartette and the Grand Forks Municipal Band, and the dedication program closed with all in attendance singing "America." Company officials, including Herman Zitkowski, offered informational tours of the factory that afternoon, and in the evening the company sponsored a dance for the general public that drew "a huge attendance." Amid such hoopla, American Beet Sugar launched its operation in the Red River Valley. One significant problem remained, however: the valley lacked the large labor force needed to cultivate and harvest the sugar beets.[19]

AGRICULTURAL EXPERTS CONSIDERED SUGAR BEET FIELD LABOR, whether cultivation or harvest, to be as arduous as any farm labor at this time. Thus, one of the challenges sugar beet corporations faced was how to get this work done. Certainly, the valley's wheat farmers might look askance at the nature of sugar beet field work. Sometimes called the lazy man's crop, wheat essentially involves planting a crop and harvesting it. The latter was hard work, but when compared to sugar beets, growing wheat and other grains was not so physically difficult. Of course, hiring someone to toil in the beet fields diminished the profitability of the crop. Based on cost analysis, sugar beet companies advised growers to do the cultivation themselves if their contract was for twenty acres or less, otherwise their earnings would be insufficient. For acreage above that, companies calculated, growers would be better off hiring field laborers if they did not want to do this exhausting work themselves. Furthermore, as an inducement to growers, the companies usually arranged to bring the field laborers to them. The growers had to pay the workers and to house them if the laborers were migrants.[20]

The difficulty with sugar beet field labor began with the very nature of the plant itself. What the grower planted in the spring was actually a lump or a ball of small seeds. As they grew, numerous plants emerged clumped together. If the sugar beets remained entangled for very long, their sugar content declined significantly. Therefore, it was imperative to thin the plants early when they were only three to four inches above ground, leaving about twelve inches between each sugar beet. After thinning, sugar beet field labor primarily involved keeping the fields free of weeds. This required at least one and as many as three hoeings, until the plants were tall enough to choke out any weeds that emerged.[21]

One of the best descriptions of sugar beet field labor in the 1920s comes from a report drafted by representatives of the National Child Labor Committee who were investigating children's work in the sugar beet fields of Nebraska. It describes work done by both adults and children:

> In thinning, they removed by hand all the beet plants from the bunch except one. The thinner selected the healthiest plant in each bunch to be left, placed his thumb and forefinger firmly against it to prevent it from being disturbed, then with his free hand took out all other plants and weeds. It was necessary to use both hands at the same time. This required the worker either to walk in a bending position with both hands on the ground, his head hanging down, or to crawl along the ground on his hands and knees.

Workers frequently used short-handled hoes to remove weeds during the initial hoeing, once again toiling stooped over the plant or on their knees. Consequently, a statement by a sugar beet company official that "every beet plant must be kneeled to" was literally accurate. One Mexican migrant worker from this era, who was interviewed fifty years later, recollected: "I think my bones are still healing from [that] work. I must have gone and come back from Mexico on my knees."[22]

Subsequent hoeings usually could be accomplished standing upright with a normal hoe unless a weed was too close to the plant. Such weeds had to be removed by bending down and pulling them out of the ground by hand. Weed infestations were often a problem if it had been a particularly rainy spring, a condition not infrequent in the Red River Valley. The American Sugar Beet Company provided growers with instructions on how to convert a regular hoe to a short-handle and then back to a regular size by installing removable rivets. Mechanization could make field work somewhat easier, though most growers lacked the means in the 1920s. A horse-drawn mechanical cross-cultivator existed that could thin stands of beets or weeds into twenty-inch bunches, thereby reducing the amount of finger thinning required. Whether growers cross-cultivated or not, American Beet Sugar officials calculated that each worker could cultivate only ten acres in the valley during a six- to eight-week period in a normal season.[23]

The job of harvesting the mature sugar beets in the fall was equally taxing. Farmers first used a mechanical lifter, adapted from the potato harvest implement, to loosen the beets, which now weighed four to eight pounds. The workers then pulled them from the ground by hand, usually one in each hand, working two rows at a time. They slapped the beets together to knock off as much dirt as possible. Workers threw the beets on the ground in rows with the tops facing the same direction. The beets were then topped by laborers using a unique knife with a hook on it. Harvesters lifted the beets from the ground with the hook, grasped the leafy part of the plant in one hand, and, holding the beet out, attempted to cut off the leafy part in one stroke with their knives. They tossed the beets onto piles, which were next loaded by hand onto wagons or truck beds to be either taken to piling stations for shipment to the factory or driven there directly. The pace of work was hectic, usually from dawn to dark over a four- to six-week span, both to ensure the highest-quality sugar yield and to finish before the onset of winter. Frequently, Upper Midwest harvests took place under adverse weather conditions, such as freezing rain or early snowfalls. With these kinds of working conditions, whether kneeling at each sugar beet plant or pulling beets from the ground in frigid weather, it was little wonder that most farmers avoided this labor if possible. If sugar companies wanted growers to produce the beets, it was necessary for them to find the least expensive temporary workers for the farmers.[24]

During the 1890s and through World War I, sugar beet companies, including American Beet Sugar, relied on several sources of field laborers. At times the companies encouraged local groups, especially high school students, teachers, and housewives, to form work gangs. Asian workers were used, mainly Japanese and Filipinos, until prejudice against Japanese curtailed their immigration by the Gentleman's Agreement between the United States and Japan in 1908. By far the most common group employed as beet workers in the Midwest before World War I were German-Russians, although other immigrant sugar beet workers came from Romania, Poland, and other eastern European countries. Some sugar beet areas in the Midwest relied on Native Americans to be at least a portion of their workforce. Increasingly, however, after World War I the sugar beet companies turned to Mexican workers, either Mexican Americans or Mexican nationals.[25]

Several factors caused more and more Mexican workers to become betabeleros. First, local work gangs, especially teenagers, usually toiled only a few seasons at most. Looking for other opportunities, they left the fields as soon as they could. Hence, local workers constantly had to be trained. Second, World War I curtailed European immigration, and in the early part of the 1920s, the United States imposed severe restrictions against immigrants. The Immigration Act of 1924 (also known as the Johnson-Reed Act) established very low quotas on European immigrants, especially those from eastern Europe. Moreover, many of the prewar European immigrant groups increasingly found other economic opportunities, especially industrial employment, which paid higher wages. In Colorado, Iowa, and Nebraska, significant numbers of German-Russians had become landowners through sugar beet company incentive programs and, therefore, needed their own source of workers.[26]

In addition to reducing the number of European immigrants, the Immigration Act of 1924 also provided an impetus for sugar beet companies to increasingly turn toward Mexicans as their labor force. Partly to improve the U.S. image in Latin America and equally, if not more, important to insure an adequate supply of agricultural labor in the Southwest, the 1924 immigration legislation placed no numerical restrictions on legal immigrants into the United States from nations in the Western Hemisphere. Sugar beet growers, along with other agricultural interests, lobbied strongly to make sure Mexican workers could enter the United States easily. In Sidney, Montana (an area of the Holley Sugar Company), during the 1924 hearing on the immigration legislation, the local American Legion chapter published a resolution stating that Mexican workers were "a necessary part" of the beet industry, "no less law abiding... not a burden to tax payers... and deprived nobody" of a job. To be sure, some regulations and procedures existed: Mexicans had to apply for admission, pay a head tax and visa fees, submit to a medical examination, and undergo bathing and delousing procedures if ordered to do so. One future betabelero and his family who came across during the 1920s remembered that, after they paid the eight-dollar head tax for each member, he and his family were "washed like cattle" and weighed and measured, had their pictures taken, were given a receipt for the head tax, and were then allowed across the border. In this manner over 200,000 Mexicans legally entered Texas between 1920 and 1930.[27]

While many Mexicans did enter the United States legally, thousands also came across the Rio Grande without undergoing the official process. One reason so many eschewed the head tax and physical examination was that there was nothing to stop them from crossing the river into Texas except for the river itself. Before the 1920s the U.S. government paid little attention to the Mexico border. Indeed, the U.S. Border Patrol did not exist until it was created as part of the Immigration Act of 1924. The following year the Immigration Service began hiring "former cowboys, skilled workers, and small ranchers" as border officers, but as late as 1927 in the El Paso district, which encompassed hundreds of miles of river and rugged terrain, the border patrol numbered only thirty-four officers.[28]

Besides the fact that no one could stop them, the other reason so many Mexicans crossed the Rio Grande, legally or not, involved economic necessity. In the second decade of the 1900s, Mexico had been wracked by violence and destruction. Along with costing the lives of hundreds of thousands people, the Mexican Revolution (1910–20) significantly damaged the country's economic infrastructure. While relative calm returned during the 1920s, another spasm of mayhem occurred from 1926 to 1929 with the Cristero Rebellion, and thousands of Mexicans entered the United States, driven by economic need. As one future sugar beet worker remembered, "The Revolution did not leave [us] anything, [e]verything was lost, so that is why I came to the United States."[29]

Of course, not all Mexicans entering the United States through Texas in the early twentieth century came as betabeleros or even as agricultural workers. Many came to work on the railroads throughout the Southwest or Midwest. Drawn by higher wages, experienced Mexican railroad workers could earn twice as much per day in the United States as they did in Mexico. In the major railroad hub of Kansas City, over half of all track workers were Mexican by World War I, and the city was home to four thousand residents of Mexican descent by 1920. Thousands of Mexicans came to the United States from 1917 to 1918 as part of a World War I temporary worker agreement between the United States and its southern neighbor. By 1920, large numbers of Mexican workers also worked in the meatpacking industries in Chicago, Minneapolis–St. Paul, Kansas City, and Omaha. In addition, the steel and automobile industries around the Great Lakes began to hire more Mexican workers during this era.[30]

Many Mexican citizens living in the Southwest also became betabeleros at this time. Before World War I, the industry had already employed thousands of the Mexican American field laborers living between California and Texas. In the early 1920s both the Great Western Sugar Company and American Beet Sugar hired betabeleros from New Mexico to work in their growers' fields in Colorado. But most sugar beet companies turned to Texas as their primary source for Mexican workers. As early as 1900, trains took Texas betabeleros to Colorado; in 1909, 2,600 toiled there. By 1922, in the Midwest sugar beet regions over 30 percent of all field laborers came from Texas. Even in the northern Rocky Mountain states of Idaho and Montana, in 1922 over 15 percent of sugar beet workers journeyed there from the Lone Star state. During this period the sugar companies either sent their own agents to Texas or subcontracted with private employment recruiters. The vast majority of betabeleros traveled from Texas by train to the sugar beet–producing regions. One Mexican migrant recalled, "The train started in Laredo. They started with about a hundred families in two train cars. From there, they would pick up people in San Antonio, Dallas, and Fort Worth. They would add on extra cars as needed. . . . They would give you food and everything."[31]

Significant changes in the economic and social structure in South Texas during the early 1900s forced many Mexicans living there to become betabeleros. As railroads penetrated into the Nueces Strip (the area between the Nueces River and the Rio Grande) and irrigation systems were developed, what had once been a livestock region gave way to an infant agribusiness economic structure. Many Anglo cattle ranchers sold off parcels of land to developers as land prices soared. In the process Mexican *vaqueros* (cowboys) lost their livelihood, and other small Mexico landholders lost their land because of higher tax assessments. Nueces County, with Corpus Christi as its county seat, was indicative of how the region was changing. In 1890, the county ranchers grazed 193,000 cattle and 73,000 sheep; thirty years later the county held only 19,000 head of cattle and 313 sheep. In the place of livestock, cotton production jumped from a little over 1,000 bales per year to over 73,000 bales. Vegetable output (mainly cabbage and onions) increased from 125 railcars in 1909 to 404 in 1920. As a consequence, the assessed value of land skyrocketed from $1.92 per acre in 1890 to $17.13 per acre by 1920, and good cotton acreage fetched over $50 per acre. Unable to pay higher taxes, many Mexican residents were forced to give up their land.[32]

The case of Crystal City, Texas, in Zavala County, represents an even more extreme picture of the changes occurring in the Nueces Strip. The town was chartered only in 1907, named after nearby artesian wells. The area had been a cattle-ranching region for both *Tejanos* (Mexican American families in the area since before statehood) and Anglo landowners, but during World War I a few acres of spinach were test grown and did very well. From that point and accelerating through the 1920s, Zavala County became the heart of the so-called Winter Garden, with Crystal City as its capital. In 1920, Crystal City had a population of about 800 residents with 520 irrigated acres of vegetables cultivated in the area. Ten years later the population had grown to over 6,600, of which over 5,100 were Mexicans; growers cultivated over 11,000 acres of spinach and onions. Most of Crystal City's Mexican inhabitants entered from Mexico, only fifty miles away, lured by jobs clearing the land, constructing irrigation ditches, and toiling as seasonal laborers in the spinach and onion fields. Anglo farmers encouraged as many Mexicans to settle in Crystal City as possible to keep wages low for field work. As one Anglo Crystal City resident later recalled, "All this town was ever intended to be was a labor camp." Many of these Mexicans eventually became part of an army of betabeleros in the Red River Valley.[33]

The Anglo farmers arriving in the region at the turn of the century, drawn from the Midwest by railroad and land agents, made little effort to continue the paternalistic employment relations characteristic of the ranching system. Ranch owners, both Anglo and Tejano, had maintained to a remarkable degree the Spanish tradition of *patronismo*—the reciprocal social and economic exchange between *patróns* (landowners) and their laborers. Mexican workers employed on the cattle ranches might be allowed garden plots, free grazing for a few cows, and medical attention when needed. Perhaps the patrón socialized with his workers at dances or on a feast day, and he served as godfather to a worker's child. In exchange, the Mexican worker and his family performed various services for the landowner, such as the worker's wife's cleaning house, which went beyond any specialized, wage-based employment. Often this special relationship had a political dimension, with the worker voting for the patrón's candidates of choice. Now Mexicans in South Texas increasingly found themselves in an agribusiness wage system with a more impersonal relationship with the new landowners. Indeed, since many of these new Anglo growers preferred to live in town, Mexican workers might never know their employer. It is important to note, however, that the patronismo system did not completely die out; vestiges of the paternalistic relationships remained into the 1960s and helped shape the interactions between sugar beet growers and betabeleros in the Red River Valley.[34]

The Mexican population of South Texas, both Tejano and new immigrant, experienced adverse changes in the early decades of the 1900s.

The crops being grown in the area, whether cotton or winter vegetables, offered only seasonal employment. The ever-growing influx of Mexican immigrants from across the Rio Grande kept wages depressed. In addition, the new economic structure, with its landowners unfamiliar with Mexican people, promoted a more comprehensive climate of racism than had existed before. The discrimination previously in place against Mexicans had been based more frequently on legends and folklore regarding such events as the Alamo and border outlaws. Thus, prejudice had more of a national than a racial basis. With the influx of newcomers from the Midwest not versed in Texas history, discrimination more often was associated with the idea that Mexicans, as a race, were dirty. The new arrivals found validation of this characteristic from such facts that diseases like tuberculosis and dysentery were more common among Mexicans in Texas or simply that Mexican field laborers were soiled from the agricultural work they performed. Whether based on history or hygiene, by 1930 Mexicans in Texas found themselves confined to certain areas of town, denied entry into many theaters and restaurants, and assigned to separate schools. For example, in Crystal City, Mexican children attended an elementary school located away from the Anglo part of town. The school was poorly funded and maintained since school officials assumed Mexican children would not need more than a fourth grade education. The abusive Jim Crow system in place in Texas provided a further incentive for Mexicans to leave their homes for a less restrictive environment in the North by the end of the 1920s. Therefore, just as the sugar beet industry in the Red River Valley required a large, dependable pool of workers, Mexicans in Texas looked for an opportunity to better their living conditions.[35]

IN TWO MAJOR RESPECTS, American Beet Sugar served as the link between the Mexican sugar beet field workers and the growers in the Red River Valley. First, the company entered into a contractual relationship with their growers regarding the manner in which sugar beets were produced. During the latter half of the 1920s, this contract stipulated the number of acres of sugar beets to be planted, how much seed was to be used on each acre, and that the beets be "cultivated in good workman like manner," including blocking, thinning, and hoeing at least twice. The sugar beets could be planted only on acres fallowed the previous year. American Beet Sugar representatives, known as fieldmen, could enter the sugar beet acreage at any time to check on the work being done. The grower had to deliver the harvested sugar beets when and where directed by the company, "free from dirt, tops, leaves, or weeds." In 1926, the grower was paid a minimum of $5.50 per ton of beets. If the price of sugar was more than $6.00 per hundred pounds, based on the average price in New York between October 1 and the following January 31, the grower received more on a sliding scale. In 1928, American Beet Sugar increased the minimum price to $6.00 per ton of beets, which then grew incrementally higher based on the market price of sugar. This 9 percent jump in minimum price reflected the increased demand for sugar during the decade and encouraged other farmers to cultivate sugar beets. The company did deduct from the growers' earnings the price for the sugar beet seeds that it had supplied to them.[36]

Second, American Beet Sugar arranged for field workers for those growers who needed labor, and in the Red River Valley that presented a daunting task. The valley's climate provided for a growing season of barely five months for sugar beets. In milder climates within the Midwest, as well as in California, sugar beet growers staggered their planting. Thus, they could keep field laborers continuously employed for longer periods of time, an important motivation for any seasonal worker. American Beet Sugar tried this strategy in the valley but soon discovered that beets planted too early or late in the growing season contained lower sugar content. Valley growers adapted to a single planting that was carried out, depending upon weather conditions, between late April and early June. Therefore, growers needed labor for cultivation primarily from early May to mid-July. The harvest usually began in late September and required four to six weeks. Insuring an adequate number of workers, over twelve thousand by 1929, for two relatively brief periods each year presented the valley sugar beet industry with a significant challenge.[37]

Of course, the residents of the Red River Valley were not totally unfamiliar with the comings and goings of a transient or temporary workforce. Starting with the Bonanza farms and continuing through

World War I, thousands of outsiders descended on the region each year to harvest the wheat crop. These workers were overwhelmingly white males and sometimes relatives or neighbors. Still, the valley's inhabitants had not been completely welcoming to these "indispensable outcasts," as historian Frank Tobias Higbie has referred to them. Indeed, many of the valley's farmers became alarmed when the Industrial Workers of the World began to organize the birds of passage during the war. Therefore, the prospect of relying on an outside workforce must have given pause to some prospective sugar beet growers.[38]

During the first few years, as the sugar beet industry took hold in the Red River Valley, American Beet Sugar tried a variety of sources for field labor. To be sure, since the typical beet contract between valley farmers and American Beet Sugar ranged from sixteen to twenty-eight acres during the 1920s, many growers performed the field work themselves. For instance, Edward Knudson's first contract in 1927 involved barely nine acres near Manvel, North Dakota; Leslie Sullivan had fourteen acres outside of East Grand Forks. The company also hired local work gangs, using as many as seven hundred high school students one season. Some German-Russians were brought to the valley from American Beet Sugar's operation at Grand Island, Nebraska, to help with the field labor. The company experimented with bringing in male Filipino workers from the West Coast, but that effort was discontinued quickly because, as one company official complained, "they had a tendency to drift after hoeing, as they were all stags." Mexican workers came, too, brought to the valley by trains from Texas. In fact, the company promoted a colonization scheme briefly in East Grand Forks in order to attract some permanent Mexican workers. More frequently, it relied on private employment agents to arrange for its Mexican workers, although American Beet Sugar paid to bring the migrants up by train. Company records do not reveal how many workers were Mexicans during the 1920s, but an estimate for all of Minnesota in 1928, including American Beet Sugar's Chaska operation, was about seven thousand betabeleros. By the end of the 1920s, American Beet Sugar characterized the workforce in the valley as about 60 percent "local white," about 35 percent Mexican, and about 5 percent "drift-in whites."[39]

The wages received by these workers were potentially fairly high, at least when compared with other agricultural field labor during the 1920s. Industry-wide, in the late 1920s, sugar beet field workers were most often paid on a piece-rate system based on acres cultivated. Migrant workers received on average between twenty and twenty-three dollars per acre for thinning and hoeing. The typical experienced worker handled ten acres, although some more proficient laborers worked upward to fifteen acres. Of course, workers who were inexperienced, infirm, or for some other reason less adept might fall short of cultivating ten acres and earn less. During the autumn harvest, wages were paid on an hourly scale, and these varied significantly. The average paid was, however, usually around forty cents per hour. What made the wage more attractive for migrant laborers was that companies usually contracted with an entire family. Based on these wages, a family of four could earn over $1,200 for six to eight weeks of field cultivation and three to four weeks of harvest labor. Of course, contracting with a family exacerbated the problem of child labor. No records exist on the numbers of child sugar beet workers, whether Mexican, Anglo, or German-Russian, in the Red River Valley during the 1920s, but investigators in Nebraska in 1923 found that 52 percent of all sugar beet field workers ranged in age from five to fifteen. Besides their earnings for field work, betabeleros received free transportation to and from the valley and free housing.[40]

Since the company relied significantly on attracting workers from great distances, it attempted to foster a good working environment. In the company's publication, *The Sugar Beet*, every issue during the 1920s addressed grower-laborer relations. The company admonished farmers to provide clean housing, proper supervision, and praise to good workers. An April 1929 article titled "Your Beet Labor" was indicative of American Beet Sugar's efforts. The article, which referred to both "Mexican and white beet workers," encouraged farmers to have "the shack" clean and in good condition when workers arrived. Despite the company's advice, migrant housing typically was abysmal in the 1920s (and beyond), although few records concerning the quality of the valley's housing exist. One sugar beet grower family described their migrant housing in the 1920s as "very poor," with low ceilings and only one or two rooms and with migrants required to haul their water in pails from a cistern near a barn. Investigators in Nebraska's sugar beet fields, including those of American Beet Sugar, deemed about only one in four migrant houses as "adequate." The company further urged its farmers to provide workers with space for a garden. If the fields were not ready for work or if bad weather set in, growers were instructed to provide other work opportunities, such as chopping wood or cleaning barns. Most of all, farmers were advised to remember that laborers "respond to kind but firm treatment." The company used its fieldmen to resolve problems and disputes between growers and their workers. And finally, the company provided cash prizes for field workers who cultivated the most acres.[41]

Among the workers brought to the valley by American Beet Sugar, some Mexicans chose to stay in the region from the beginning. One family came up for the first time in 1927 and resided continually in East Grand Forks over the next fifteen years. By 1930, the U.S. census identified over 600 Mexican residents in North Dakota; Minnesota's population climbed from less than 250 in 1920 to over 3,600 a decade later. Among the valley's counties, Polk County had the greatest concentration, with 237 Mexican residents. Most of the valley's betabeleros who chose to remain in the region wintered in St. Paul, however, where winter employment opportunities were more abundant, and they helped cement the Mexican community there. Over 600 Mexicans were counted in that city in 1930, but these numbers likely did not include those who might have had reasons to avoid census takers, especially if they were in the country illegally.[42]

By 1929, American Beet Sugar's operation in the Red River Valley had become fairly well established. While the company was probably not satisfied that it had secured a permanent source of labor, so far no shortage of workers had plagued the operation. The number of acres planted had almost doubled between 1926 and 1929, from about 11,500 to almost 20,000 acres. In the last year of the 1920s, the company contracted with 688 growers in the valley who harvested about 94,000 tons of sugar beets, although the sugar content was disappointing because of dry conditions during the prime growing period. Still, most factors indicated that the production of sugar beets would increase steadily in the valley. However, 1929 ushered in significant changes in how American Beet Sugar operated and in the relationships among the company, its growers, and the Mexican migrant field workers.[43]

THE STOCK MARKET CRASH IN THE FALL OF 1929 set in motion important developments for the sugar beet industry. While the ensuing Great Depression and New Deal legislation profoundly influenced the structure of the valley's sugar industry, a lesser known event in Texas that year also altered, just as significantly, the nature of sugar beet production throughout the Midwest. During the late 1920s farmers in Texas, especially cotton and vegetable growers in the Nueces Strip, became increasingly agitated about the migration of Mexican workers out of the state. Dependent on seasonal workers, too, Texas farmers resented the growing competition for Mexican migrant workers. The farmers directed their ire mainly toward the sugar beet companies that recruited thousands of Mexicans each year; Great Western Sugar Company moved as many as fourteen thousand seasonal workers, mainly Mexicans, out of Texas annually. Farmers in Texas claimed that this recruitment created farm labor shortages. Moreover, because of criticism by labor unions and other groups fearful of the increase in the Mexican population, the U.S. Department of State in 1929 moved to curtail legal immigration from Mexico by directing consular officials to enforce immigration provisions regarding contract labor, literacy tests, and other requirements. While this measure had little effect on illegal immigration, it did fuel Texas farmers' claims that the labor pool in Texas would dry up if outside companies continued their recruitment of Mexican laborers.[44]

In May 1929, in response to pressure from growers and other commercial agricultural interests, the Texas legislature passed a law requiring, among other measures, that out-of-state labor recruiters pay a $7,500 occupation tax. Challenged by the sugar beet industry, a federal court responded quickly by granting the companies an injunction against this prohibitive fee. The Texas legislature returned, however, to the issue later that year and passed the Emigrant Labor Agency Law. This statute, which remained in effect into the 1970s, decreed that labor recruiters or agencies purchase a license, post a five-thousand-dollar bond, and pay an additional yearly license fee, an annual occupation fee of one thousand dollars, and a county tax based on each county's population. This measure raised the cost of bringing Texas betabeleros to the sugar beet regions. Moreover, the state of Texas could control sugar beet companies' recruitment through the granting of licenses. During the turbulent 1930s Texas officials granted relatively few of these documents. Therefore, as the 1920s closed, American Beet Sugar, growers in the Red River Valley, and Mexican migrant workers faced a unique environment that created dramatic changes in their relationships with each other.[45]

CHAPTER 2

Depression Years and Transformation

IN 1934, in the midst of the Great Depression, the American Beet Sugar Company abruptly changed its name to American Crystal Sugar Company (American Crystal). Perhaps nothing was more representative of the major restructuring taking place in the sugar beet industry during the decade of the 1930s. Identifying the company clearly with the purity associated with granulated sugar, the new corporate name signaled the growing strength of beet sugar in America's sugar industry and acted as a symbol to entice more farmers to grow beets.

The period between the stock market collapse in 1929 and the beginning of World War II witnessed significant transformations in the method of operations and the relationships among the company, its Red River Valley growers, and the Mexican migrant workforce. While the early 1930s were extremely trying for all concerned, New Deal legislation, especially the Jones-Costigan Act (1934) and the Sugar Act of 1937, reconfigured the sugar industry in the United States, while creating new opportunities and support for corporations, growers, and even betabeleros. More than just adopting a new name, American Crystal expanded its operation in the Red River Valley and into new regions. Receiving government subsidies for sugar production, valley growers invested more and more resources in mechanization and other technological advances. They also organized themselves into the RRVSBGA and, through that body, began their ascendancy as a major economic and political force in the area. Driven from the valley's sugar beet fields by unemployed local whites in the early 1930s, Mexican workers began to return after 1935 and became the largest group within the labor force by the time the United States entered World War II. Jones-Costigan and the Sugar Act of 1937 guaranteed minimum wages for field work and helped initiate a noticeable decline in child labor in the beet fields. Moreover, betabeleros gained some control over who they worked for in and out of the valley. In essence, the sugar beet industry evolved during this period into the basic shape it maintained for the next forty years. The advantage rested with the company and its growers, but by 1941, Mexican migrant workers had obtained some leverage in their employment and living conditions. Indeed, once the United States entered the war, the sugar beet industry became utterly dependent on Mexican migrant labor, and betabeleros asserted even more control over their work, despite resistance from growers and American Crystal. Thus, although the 1930s started on a difficult note for all three groups, by 1942 all had improved their situations in the valley.

THE FIRST YEARS OF THE GREAT DEPRESSION were difficult for all agriculturists in the Red River Valley. Farm prices tumbled to extremely low levels, thereby threatening the profitability of growers and American Crystal and leading to lower wages for field laborers. All of the crops valley growers had adopted in their efforts to diversify earlier in the century earned less money in the early 1930s. In 1932, at the depths of the economic crisis, wheat earned just thirty-six cents per bushel; barley and oats, less than fifteen cents; and potatoes declined to twenty-three cents. Sugar brought less than four dollars per hundred-pound bag, down from over six dollars in the late 1920s. Per capita income in North Dakota sank to $145 (nationwide $375). In such an economic environment, many farmers went broke; perhaps as many as one-third in the region left agriculture completely or found themselves reduced to farming as tenants.[1]

Environmental problems compounded the region's economic woes. As in much of the Midwest, the Red River Valley experienced severe drought throughout the 1930s. Between 1929 and 1933, only in one year—1932—did the valley receive an average amount of moisture. In 1931, drought conditions were hit-and-miss in the sugar beet–growing areas, as some counties reported generally fair levels of rainfall, while others received virtually nothing. Heavy rain delayed planting in 1932, but drought prevailed throughout the valley by July. This pattern repeated itself the following year. Temperatures soared above normal levels, as well. J. B. Bingham, the new American Crystal manager for the region, described the summers of 1932 and 1933 as "extremely hot." In 1934, the drought blanketed the valley "to an almost ruinous extent," and hot windstorms raked the region during May and June, causing the emerging beet plants to wither in some areas. While not part of Bingham's reports, field labor conditions must have been even more miserable in such heat. High temperatures continued to be severe during the remainder of the decade. For two weeks in July 1936, the mercury soared to over one hundred degrees each day.[2]

Grasshopper infestations during the 1930s reached near biblical proportions, too. The voracious insects appeared first in the northern end of the valley in 1931 but in the following summer spread throughout the area. In 1934, Fargo's newspaper announced "Hopper Horde Hatches Early," while the state of North Dakota ordered seven thousand tons of poison, requiring over three hundred railcars to deliver. By 1936, North Dakota had created a State Grasshopper Control Committee, and Works Progress Administration groups devoted their attention to preparing poisoned bait. The grasshopper menace continued to be an enormous problem through World War II. Other insects added to the misery, with webworms and cutworms devouring numerous varieties of plants, including sugar beets. One daughter of a sugar beet grower remembered picking the cutworms off the plants by hand: "We children had to go along the rows and pick those cutworms by hand. We could pick up the worm and just throw it in the pail and keep on going, and then they killed them later. But that saved the crop."[3]

The nationwide economic slump and environmental hardship in the Midwest severely hurt American Crystal. In 1930, despite increasing its sale of bags of sugar, the company lost 1.3 million dollars. Between 1930 and 1932, American Crystal's total losses ran to over 3 million dollars. The company's financial setback meant a change in the way it contracted with growers. In 1932, American Crystal reconfigured its agreements with farmers in all regions, except California, from a contract with a fixed price guarantee to one of payment based on the quality of the beets harvested. In other words, an important source of collateral for growers—guaranteed earnings—was replaced with the uncertainty of quality, especially in the environmentally troubled regions of the Midwest. The company cut back its operations, too. Throughout American Crystal's beet regions, contracted acres declined from 117,000 in 1930 to 94,000 two years later. The company made the reductions proportionally throughout its territories, although the valley's cut was not so deep: from 22,100 acres in 1930 to

21,900 in 1932. During this period the number of growers dropped more significantly in the region, however, from 684 to 631. Through these reductions, different contractual terms, and other cost-saving methods, American Crystal managed to show a profit in 1933.[4]

The Great Depression also forced American Crystal into new directions with field labor, although the company had clearly intended to rely more and more on Mexican workers before the economic downturn occurred. In 1930, while preparing for the 1931 season, American Crystal published in a bilingual edition *El cultivo del betabel: manual para los trabajadores.* The thirty-eight-page guide, accompanied by numerous photographs showing decent housing and workers on their hands and knees, offered a description of the nature and conditions of field work, methods of payment, relationships between fieldmen and growers, and terminology and generally attempted to answer virtually any question a prospective betabelero might ask. In the section on the East Grand Forks region, the company advised field workers that other employment, such as wheat shocking and railroad track repair, could be arranged by the company once the sugar beets had been cultivated. The manual contained, however, one very erroneous statement for betabeleros: "Those who chose to work with us can count on employment year after year." Indeed, the numbers of betabeleros in the valley fell drastically as the Depression deepened and unemployment rates rose.[5]

The social mood engendered against minority groups by these hard times aggravated ethnic and racial prejudices throughout the nation, and the Red River Valley was no exception. In some counties signs appeared proclaiming "Only White Labor Employed." Prejudicial sentiments forced American Crystal to hire more local whites and fewer Mexican migrants. In 1931 and 1932, Mexican workers still comprised about 30 percent of the field labor in the valley, although the company clearly felt under some pressure from area residents to hire more locals. The East Grand Forks manager's report for 1932 noted that the company "could not take care of the requests made by local whites for beet work." J. B. Bingham hoped that for 1933 "we can increase considerably the percentage of white labor." Apparently, he was successful, as American Crystal employed local whites as 80 percent of its field workers for that year, and in 1934 whites performed virtually all of the work. Bingham noted that, as more growers relied on mechanical cross-cultivators, which reduced the amount of stooped labor, the work had become more appealing to valley whites. That field work was somewhat easier may have given the company a rationale to slash wages. From an average of twenty-three dollars an acre in 1929, field labor paid less than eighteen dollars by 1933; harvest wages declined from seventy cents per ton to fifty cents. Mexican migrant workers' suffering in the early 1930s was not limited to just the loss of employment opportunities and reduced wages in the valley's sugar beet fields. The circumstances of their existence, independent of beet work, deteriorated as well.[6]

THE REPATRIATION OF Mexican residents in the United States, including some citizens, was one of the most odious events associated with the Great Depression. Just as many unemployed white Americans resented African Americans working in the 1930s, Mexicans, whether U.S. citizens or immigrants, were also targets of hostility and discrimination. This sentiment eventually led to a program to force Mexicans out of the country, justified by claims that "real" Americans would gain employment, welfare rolls could be trimmed, and even that repatriation to Mexico would be better for Mexicans in the current economic climate. Supported by the Hoover administration, the State Department, the Immigration and Naturalization Service, and state and local governments, this program pressured Mexicans to leave the country. Though in many cases Mexicans were deported voluntarily, in that they accepted the transportation services arranged for them, others left under more duress. Many illegal residents were caught in the repatriation campaign, but the authorities also forced the removal of legal residents and even American citizens. In some cases husbands and wives became separated, and Mexican children born in the United States were forced out along with their noncitizen parents. While the total number of Mexicans removed is disputed, the figure at minimum exceeded 400,000 people.[7]

Although no figures are available for the Red River Valley—and some evidence suggests that sugar beet companies throughout the Midwest and Great Lakes areas tried to shield their workers—many betabeleros in St. Paul and other regional cities were certainly snared in the forced exodus. About 15 percent of the Mexican population in St. Paul departed. Other concentrations of Mexican sugar beet workers, such as those in Omaha, Kansas City, and Chicago, were significantly reduced in number. Even if not repatriated, those who remained in the Midwest experienced high rates of unemployment, as high as 80 percent, throughout the 1930s because of prejudice and the continued stiff competition for jobs.[8]

Though authorities in Texas did not pursue repatriation as intensely as those in other parts of the country, economic developments and discrimination during the 1930s brought significant hardship to the state's Mexican population. As farm income declined in the state, wages paid agricultural workers plummeted. In the cotton sector, where so many Mexican workers toiled, wages for picking cotton declined from about $1.10 per hundred pounds to $0.60. Moreover, mechanization in cotton further reduced the need for migrant workers. The demand for farm labor in Texas among all commodities nose-dived, declining almost 50 percent by 1932. As the number of agricultural jobs shrank, the competition for them increased. Unemployed Mexican urban workers joined the migrant stream, which exacerbated the situation further. In San Antonio, 475 Mexican city workers were laid off. Likewise, those dependent on that city's pecan-shelling industry became more impoverished when pecan companies reduced the already paltry wages paid to their workers by 50 percent. The Texas coal industry declined, and many Mexican miners lost their jobs, some turning to seasonal agricultural employment.[9]

The conditions in the Nueces Strip were no better. The citrus industry, which had expanded considerably in the Lower Rio Grande Valley during the 1920s, paid as little as twenty-five cents per hour for jobs in packing sheds that typically lasted only three or four days each week. The planting of orange trees slowed, but those who were lucky enough to be hired for that task received as little as $3.75 per week for very hard work. To make matters worse, in September 1933 a massive hurricane devastated the Lower Rio Grande Valley and disrupted the economy for several months. When the Public Works Administration started a flood control program on the Rio Grande in Hidalgo County, partly in response to the destruction from the hurricane, supervisors insisted the jobs be done by only American, meaning Anglo, workers. One bold official told the *McAllen (TX) Monitor* that its readers "will see something on this project you have not seen before—Anglo-Saxons working as unskilled labor." Mexican workers received at least one break, as the repatriation program significantly curtailed Mexican immigration into South Texas. Consequently, the labor pool was not further enlarged, which would have forced wages even lower.[10]

Thus, a significant degree of suffering afflicted all of those involved in the Red River Valley sugar industry during the first years of the 1930s, the nadir of the Great Depression. The election of Franklin Roosevelt and the implementation of the New Deal sparked wholesale changes within the sugar beet industry and created alterations that had an enormous impact on betabeleros, growers, and American Crystal.

ONE OF THE MOST FAR-REACHING PRIORITIES of the New Deal during Roosevelt's first administration was to reform the agricultural sector of the economy. Since the end of World War I, farmers in virtually every area of the country had experienced hard times brought on by overproduction of agricultural commodities, increased prices for consumer goods, and a widening gap between industrial and agricultural earnings. Therefore, Roosevelt and his advisors argued that fundamental change was vital to restoring the farm economy. The Agricultural Adjustment Act (AAA), enacted in May 1933, during the first hundred days of the Roosevelt administration, profoundly impacted U.S. agriculture by providing monetary subsidies to farmers willing to limit production of specific commodities such as corn, cotton, rice, tobacco, milk, hogs, and wheat.[11]

One farm product conspicuously absent from the AAA regulations was sugar. In essence, Congress and the Roosevelt administration found sugar interests to be too varied and contentious to be reformed easily. First, numerous powerful American corporations, such as United Fruit and Hershey, owned valuable sugar-producing plantations outside the continental United States in Central America, Cuba, and many Caribbean islands. American territories, especially Hawaii and Puerto Rico, were rich sugar cane–producing islands. Second, important Democratic Party states in the South included sugar cane–rich Florida and Louisiana, and national politicians from those states zealously protected their constituents throughout the New Deal. And finally, there was the rapidly growing sugar beet sector in America. The needs of these conflicting interests were not easily satisfied, and Roosevelt's intention to improve relations with Latin America as a Good Neighbor made a national sugar policy only more complicated. The sugar beet industry did not, however, completely avoid New Deal regulations and scrutiny in 1933. The National Recovery Administration developed labor policies in October regarding the sugar beet economic sector, at least as far as factory operations were concerned. In addition, the Roosevelt administration appointed the Dinwiddie Child Labor Committee to investigate the use of child workers, especially in sugar beet fields.[12]

In the spring of 1934, Senator Edward P. Costigan, Democrat from Colorado, introduced the Sugar Control Act, which would later be known as the Jones-Costigan Act. Edward Costigan and his wife, Mabel, both had long histories with sugar operations in the United States, especially sugar beets. Of course, Colorado was one of the centers of sugar beet production and an area of heavy investment by American Crystal. During Woodrow Wilson's administration, Costigan had served on a tariff commission that had been especially responsible for developing America's foreign and domestic policy concerning sugar. Mabel Costigan had been a social activist for many years, attempting to get children out of the sugar beet fields in Colorado. Therefore, both Costigans, in their own manner, shaped the Jones-Costigan Act of 1934.[13]

The Jones-Costigan Act restructured and reformed the sugar industry at many levels. Representatives from the federal government, national consumer groups, and the sugar corporations themselves would annually estimate the consumption needs for the country. Then Congress and the Department of Agriculture would allocate quotas based on those assessments for both foreign sugar importers and domestic sugar producers, the latter group divided by sugar beet and sugar cane corporations. For growers the legislation offered separate support payments, channeled through the AAA, based on the tonnage harvested from their fields. And for sugar beet field laborers, Jones-Costigan mandated a process that established regional minimum wages for cultivation and harvest work. The act also forbade employment of people less than fourteen years of age, unless they were the children of the landowner; youths fourteen to sixteen years of age could not work more than eight hours per day. Violation of these child labor provisions disqualified a grower from receiving government support payments. Thus, Mabel Costigan's influence and the efforts of the Dinwiddie Child Labor Committee at least partly prevailed. As a concession to the sugar industry, the legislation was to expire in 1937. Therefore, if elements of Jones-Costigan proved to be too onerous or disruptive, they could be altered at that time.[14]

Passage of Jones-Costigan had immediate ramifications for the Red River Valley sugar beet farmers. Sugar beet growers received a $2.75 per ton subsidy on the 1934 crop, and they were paid between $1.13 and $2.00 per ton during the remainder of the 1930s. For example, the average grower produced about 160 tons in 1934, which meant that a farmer received $440 in government subsidy, not an inconsequential bonus in the 1930s economic atmosphere. In addition, as the sugar beet industry nationally was granted a larger market share than that of the domestic cane industry, American Crystal moved rapidly to expand its operation in the valley. By 1936, contracted acres between the company and valley farmers rose about 15 percent over 1933 levels, as American Crystal contracted anew with many of the growers cut off during the deepest part of the Depression. By 1937, the East Grand Forks District, as the valley sugar beet producers were referred to in the company's 1930s organizational chart, became American Crystal's leading sugar beet territory. Of course, Jones-Costigan paved the way for valley growers to become more involved in, as well as susceptible to, federal government developments.[15]

American Crystal under Jones-Costigan began to enlarge its operations nationally. Total beet tonnage harvested for American Crystal almost doubled between 1934 and 1937. The company opened new areas of operation in California and Nebraska in the mid-1930s. Coupled with expanding a sugar beet territory it had developed around Missoula, Montana, during the late 1920s, American Crystal positioned itself to profit significantly in the coming years. As was the case with the growers, however, the affairs of the federal government now had a greater influence on company policies.[16]

Jones-Costigan established the foundation for the federal government's oversight of the treatment of sugar beet workers. To be sure, the industry had more of a say in determining wages for field work than did the laborers themselves. Indeed, during the 1930s sugar beet laborers had virtually no input into how much they were paid, as government and industry officials dominated wage determination meetings. Sugar beet field labor rates, compared with those before Jones-Costigan, began to improve, however. In addition, the act's child labor provisions did make a difference. As an AAA press release announced in 1935, "Full compliance with the child labor provisions of sugar beet production adjustment contracts must be checked and certified before the final 1934 and first 1935 adjustment payments can be made." While not completely eliminated, the number of children doing stooped labor cultivating sugar beet plants began to decline noticeably. Government had also helped focus attention on the plight of migrant workers in general, through such measures as the creation of the Farm Security Administration camps, which would have important ramifications in the future.[17]

The federal government renewed virtually all the fundamental provisions of Jones-Costigan in the Sugar Act of 1937, although in other New Deal measures the Roosevelt administration failed agricultural laborers. Bowing to pressure from grower associations and politicians from key farm states, the Wagner Act (1935) and the Fair Labor Standards Act (1938) excluded farm laborers. Similarly, farm workers were not covered by the Social Security Act. Thus, important advantages given to industrial workers in their relationship with their employers during the 1930s were denied to betabeleros (and other farm laborers) as they returned once more in greater numbers to the valley's sugar beet fields in the latter half of the 1930s.[18]

AS NEW DEAL PROGRAMS—especially job creation measures—took effect in the valley in the mid-1930s, fewer local whites remained interested in the difficult working conditions associated with sugar beet field labor; therefore, American Crystal once again needed to secure another source of field workers. The company turned decisively to Mexican workers, and the shift occurred rapidly. Whereas about 80 percent of field workers were local whites in 1935, the following year Mexican workers numbered over twelve thousand, or about 58 percent of the valley's hired sugar beet labor. The percentage rose steadily through the remainder of the decade: 61 percent in 1937; 68 percent in 1938; and fully 70 percent, out of about seventeen thousand hired, in 1939.[19]

These Mexican workers came more and more from Texas, rather than from across the Rio Grande, drawn from the pool of Tejanos or the newly naturalized citizens who had immigrated from Mexico into Texas during the 1910–29 wave. Conditions in Texas, especially in southern counties, had been difficult for Mexican people since the early period of the Depression, and these hardly improved through the 1930s. The preferential treatment accorded local whites in Texas New Deal programs continued unabated. The Texas coal sector steadily declined and forced many Mexican miners to seek other jobs. One betabelera recalled that her father turned to migrant labor because his job in the coal mines "was very irregular," and "my father was very tired. We didn't have anywhere [else] to go." Agricultural opportunities worsened as the 1930s progressed. Cotton output continued to dip as many Texas landowners found it more profitable to take acreage out of production in order to receive New Deal subsidies. Moreover, a sizeable number of displaced whites from the Dust Bowl cast their lot with seasonal work in South Texas, thereby taking jobs once handled by Mexican residents.[20]

One of the hardest-hit Mexican communities in South Texas was San Antonio. Pecan shelling had actually rebounded in the mid-1930s as Mexican workers were willing to work cheaper than machines could be run. In 1934, pay had dropped as low as two cents per pound, and weekly earnings, as calculated by one National Recovery Administration investigator, averaged less than $1.30. By 1938, over twelve thousand Mexicans worked seasonally shelling pecans. In March of that year, however, about one-half of the pecan workers in San Antonio went on strike, organized by the Congress of Industrial Organizations (CIO) and the affiliated United Cannery, Agricultural Packing and Allied Workers of America (UCAPAWA). The work stoppage eventually earned the workers a wage of five cents per pound, and later, pecan workers came under the umbrella of minimum wage regulation in the Fair Labor Standards Act. Unfortunately, these advantages quickly decimated employment opportunities among the pecan workers;

machines became a cheaper option for the pecan companies, and by 1940 the number of workers hired had declined by 90 percent. San Antonio became a center of betabelero recruitment in Texas shortly thereafter.[21]

Conditions were equally bad in the Winter Garden area, especially in Crystal City. Referred to locally as the Spinach Depression, the economic misery of the town had many causes. Consumption of spinach, favored by urban palates, dropped with the onset of the Great Depression, as some saw it as a luxury item. The subsequent decline in prices was dramatic, from forty-seven cents per bushel in 1929 to thirty-four cents by the mid-1930s. Serious weed infestations brought on by overcultivation and higher costs for irrigation (as artesian water levels dropped) further hurt the spinach industry. Competition from other areas of Texas now growing spinach and the expansion of spinach fields in Virginia further reduced income. Therefore, wages for spinach field labor, an occupation that employed over 90 percent of the adult Mexican population in Crystal City from November to March each year, paid barely three dollars per week in 1938. No wonder then that 95 percent of the population of Crystal City was forced into migrant labor that year; 50 percent of those became betabeleros.[22]

Like most sugar beet companies, American Crystal did not set up a labor agency in Texas during the 1930s. The company judged the restrictions and fees required under the 1929 Texas Emigrant Labor Agency Law too onerous. Rather, American Crystal relied on a combination of private labor employment agencies throughout Texas and other Midwest states, word of mouth, and *troqueros* (crew leaders) to supply its sugar beet areas with field labor. A troquero was often the head of an extended family or group of Mexican workers, owned transportation, especially trucks, and served as an intermediary between sugar beet growers and the work crew.[23]

This manner by which American Crystal obtained field workers also indicated a fundamental change taking shape in worker mobility during the 1930s. Where once the company brought Mexican workers to the valley and other regions in trains, Mexican workers now arrived with increasing frequency in their own cars or trucks. A 1938 study found that 50 percent of betabeleros from Crystal City traveled in their own vehicles. Worker-owned vehicles certainly reduced some company expense, and it meant growers did not have to arrange for their workers to go to town for supplies and recreation. But it also resulted in some loss of control over betabeleros. As long as workers remained dependent on American Crystal to get to the valley and return home at the end of the season, they were less likely to leave when dissatisfied with working conditions or if a better opportunity beckoned. Now, as more Mexican migrants came with troqueros or, better yet, in their private vehicles, they had some leverage with American Crystal and the growers if they were unhappy with the working or living arrangements. As one Texas farmer complained during this time, "The Mexicans own cars; that is one thing that causes trouble. They are independent and always wanting something better."[24]

Whether coming by train, car, or truck, Mexicans made the long journey to the valley in greater numbers in the late 1930s specifically because of the potential earnings sugar beet work offered. Under Jones-Costigan-mandated wage structuring in 1936, payment for field labor including thinning, blocking, and hoeing amounted to eighteen dollars per acre; harvest wages were seventy-five cents per ton. By 1938, field cultivation wages had climbed to nearly nineteen dollars per acre maximum, and harvesters earned ninety cents per ton. Although still lower than the pay levels of the 1920s, when compared with the paltry earnings of pecan shelling in San Antonio or harvesting spinach in the Nueces Strip, sugar beet work was very attractive. While economic developments forced more Mexicans from South Texas into the migrant stream to the Red River Valley, they now had more control over what they did with their lives while there, and they made better wages than they did earlier in the 1930s.[25]

AS MEXICAN MIGRANT SUGAR BEET WORKERS experienced significant employment shifts in the second half of the 1930s, the growers, who were increasingly dependent on betabeleros, also had to alter their operations. One of the most important areas of change involved technological and mechanical developments. While in 1930 most growers still relied on horse power, in 1932 International Harvester developed a tractor, the F-12, that had an adjustable axle system for use in sugar beet rows, and by the end of the decade, these tractors and similar models were common in the valley's beet fields. Tractors offered another benefit to growers in that acreage set aside for the horses' fodder could be converted to another cash commodity. In addition, a checkrow planter became available that allowed growers "to drop several seeds in 18 inch intervals"; the checkered pattern that resulted made cross-cultivation easier. Because grasshoppers remained a problem throughout the 1930s and webworms increasingly represented an even more destructive pest to sugar beet plants, valley farmers turned to newly developed chemicals, such as Paris Green and Parathion, to minimize damages from these insects.[26]

One of the key motivators for implementing these developments centered on the wage increases mandated by Jones-Costigan and the Sugar Act of 1937—that technology could offset higher labor costs—or so American Crystal argued to its growers. Area farmers received this message with considerable ambivalence since many growers also relied on migrant labor for their potato harvest and did not want to run the risk of not having workers available then. American Crystal likewise sent out mixed messages as the company encouraged growers to adopt technological advances in order to eliminate dependence on betabeleros while urging them to correspond with migrant workers during the winter months to draw those laborers back to the fields.[27]

The most important development for growers was, however, the creation of the RRVSBGA in 1935. Grower associations emerged throughout the 1930s in Midwest sugar beet areas for several reasons. In the new political relationship between the industry and the federal government brought on by Jones-Costigan, grower associations increased the political power for sugar beet interests. In addition, grower associations were effective in pressuring and otherwise promoting state institutions, such as land-grant universities, to devote more attention to sugar beets. And finally, sugar beet grower associations allowed the farmers to pool their assets in order to reduce the expense of recruiting migrant workers from Texas after the Emigrant Agency Law was enacted.[28]

Grower associations could also form, however, as a result of adversarial relations between a sugar beet company and its growers. Indeed, acrimony occurred between growers and American Crystal around Chaska, Minnesota, and Mason City, Iowa, during the 1930s. The basic incentive for these growers to organize themselves into the Minnesota-Iowa Beet Growers Associations involved sugar beet contracts. As noted previously, American Crystal restructured the contract it offered growers from an agreement that guaranteed a minimum price to one that was based on quality of the sugar beets harvested. In response, the sugar beet growers around Chaska and Mason City organized in order to pressure American Crystal to offer better prices for sugar beets and to induce railroads to offer lower shipping rates, although with little success during the 1930s.[29]

The creation of the RRVSBGA occurred more amicably. Indeed, it appears that American Crystal executives in East Grand Forks and some of the company's fieldmen provided the initial energy to organize the growers. Historian Terry L. Shoptaugh concluded that American Crystal wanted to avoid the problems it had experienced with the Minnesota-Iowa Beet Growers Association, and by taking the lead, East Grand Forks company officials thought they would gain influence over the organization. In addition, coming in the year after the passage of Jones-Costigan, American Crystal viewed the RRVSBGA as a powerful political tool for seeking increased acreage allotments from the federal government. While during the 1930s relations between the company and the growers' organization generally were good, the RRVSBGA would eventually challenge American Crystal's operational methods in the region.[30]

The increasing interaction between the sugar beet industry and the federal government spawned another organization in the area. The Minnesota-Dakota Sugar Beet Association represented not just American Crystal and its growers but, reflecting the increased importance of the crop in the valley, included community, political, and business leaders. The association's purpose was "to secure more favorable regulations" under the Sugar Act of 1937, and its formation revealed the position the sugar beet industry had attained among diverse economic and political interests in the region.[31]

Not everyone in the valley was as enthusiastic, however, about all aspects of the growing importance of sugar beets, especially the industry's increasing reliance on Mexican workers. In Grafton, North Dakota, a center of sugar beet production located close to East Grand

Forks, the local welfare board in 1938 passed a recommendation intended for American Crystal to "exclude the annual influx of Mexicans seeking jobs" on the sugar beet farms. The welfare board officials argued that betabeleros and their families strained relief budgets, "fostered the spread of marihuana," and brought tuberculosis into the region.[32]

For the most part, though, the latter half of the 1930s saw expansion, improvements, and increased support for sugar beet growers. In 1937, valley beet growers produced their best yield crop (10.2 tons per acre) to that date, and while the 1939 harvest had lower yields because of the extreme drought that year, federal subsidies, increased mechanization, and more acres per farmer (the average contract was now over forty acres) pointed to a better future for the growers than the early 1930s had indicated. The outbreak of the war in Europe that fall and increasing U.S. involvement with that conflict caused further important adjustments in the valley's sugar beet industry.[33]

THE START OF WORLD WAR II in Europe and the U.S. entry into that conflict quickly caused two important developments to occur in the valley's sugar beet economy. The first development was, of course, significant expansion of the sugar beet industry in the region. Between 1939 and 1942, contracted acreage in the valley increased about 10 percent while the number of growers actually declined slightly. Thus, average contracted acres climbed about five acres for each grower by 1942, a year that also saw a record yield of 12.44 tons of sugar beets per acre. For those growers involved, earnings from their beets jumped noticeably. Including government subsidies, valley farmers earned $5.79 per ton in 1939; in 1942, they earned $8.67, an increase of about 35 percent in monetary return. Indeed, the prices for all the region's agricultural products rose, and in 1941, North Dakota farmers harvested their largest wheat crop (140 million bushels) and made more money than at any time since 1928. Such activity must have caused their memories of the misery of the early 1930s to recede somewhat.[34]

The second—and closely related development—was that the sugar beet industry once again required more laborers. For its Upper Midwest operations (Iowa, Minnesota, and North Dakota), American Crystal's field work needs increased from a little less than twenty-five thousand to twenty-seven thousand in one year (1939–40). An important element associated with this need for labor was, however, that even fewer local whites were willing to submit to the tough working conditions in the sugar beet fields now that more and better-paying industrial jobs, especially on the West Coast, were available. In fact, on the North Dakota side of the Red River, the pace of out-migration rose dramatically. Whereas local whites had composed about 30 percent of the sugar beet workforce in the valley in 1939, they declined to 24 percent by 1941; Mexican migrant workers amounted to three out of four field laborers. Moreover, all indications were that, by necessity, American Crystal would have to step up its efforts to lure betabeleros to the valley.[35]

The labor shortage problem began to manifest itself with the harvest in 1941. American Crystal reported sufficient labor available for field work cultivation from May into July, but as the harvest season approached for all crops in the region, a serious shortage of farm workers emerged. Cass County, North Dakota, one of the sugar beet counties, also needed 50 percent more workers for its wheat harvest that summer. By August the state's governor requested the use of Civilian Conservation Corps workers for the harvest of wheat and potatoes. Inclement weather delayed the sugar beet harvest that autumn, and many Mexican workers left early. Then, with the harvest in full swing, the area received a particularly heavy rain, followed immediately by a blizzard. As the temperature fell, the now soggy sugar beet fields froze. One American Crystal fieldman, watching workers struggle to get sugar beets out of the ground under such adverse conditions, wrote, "When watching them work, I really could not understand how the women and some of the men could stand it." Many apparently could not, as more Mexican workers abandoned the effort. The severe labor shortage led to a unique development. One evening, with the harvest running perilously late in the season, a delegation of about twenty workers appeared at the East Grand Forks sugar plant and threatened to organize a strike if harvest wages were not increased. American Crystal had no choice but to agree quickly; the company increased wages from $0.90 per ton to $1.10. Only by them doing so was the 1941 harvest completed.[36]

While this was the first indication of any union activity among betabeleros in the Red River Valley, other Mexican agricultural workers had engaged in union-building efforts during this era. Besides the pecan shellers' strike in San Antonio, other instances of unionizing occurred in Texas among Mexican workers. In 1930, the Catholic Workers Union of Crystal City formed and had some brief success with spinach growers before disappearing under duress from the spinach industry and its Texas political supporters. A similar effort to forge a labor union appeared briefly around the Laredo region five years later. In 1937, UCAPAWA (which unionized the pecan workers) launched an organizing campaign in South Texas, especially among vegetable and fruit packing-shed workers. By 1942, UCAPAWA had about five thousand members in the region. Outside of Texas, too, efforts were made to organize migrant workers, especially in the sugar beet areas of Michigan and Ohio and among midwestern onion workers. In Minnesota some union activity had occurred in American Crystal's Chaska district in 1937–38. Organizers there signed up about 50 percent of the sugar beet field workers, and the Minnesota State Federation of Labor chartered the group. Union representatives discussed working and housing conditions with American Crystal's management at Chaska but were rebuffed. The union fell apart at the end of the season when migrant workers departed, and organizers apparently did not renew their effort the following year. American Crystal's manager for the Chaska district reported that they had been able to thwart the union campaign, although he expected other attempts in the future. Unfortunately for betabeleros, neither the Minnesota Federation of Labor nor the CIO continued their activities with sugar beet field workers. American Crystal could not be certain, however, that a renewal of the union campaign might not occur. Thus, the problems with the 1941 harvest in the valley must have appeared ominous to American Crystal.[37]

And indeed, the labor situation became more precarious in 1942, the first full year of U.S. involvement in the war. American Crystal provided no employment numbers in that year's annual reports, as it had previously, probably because the labor situation was so chaotic. The manager's report from the Rocky Ford district is indicative, however, of the labor challenge that faced American Crystal and its growers. A severe lack of workers burdened that sugar beet region all year. People living in the area, including Mexicans who had worked in sugar beets, secured jobs in Colorado's rapidly expanding war industries. The company received a promise for a total of 3,500 workers from the Works Progress Administration, Farm Security Administration, and the U.S. Employment Service, but it received not a single betabelero. Only by hiring 400 local high school students and over 200 Native Americans, and by working out a sharing system with Great Western Sugar Company and the Holley Sugar Company for about 1,400 Mexican migrants, was American Crystal able to cultivate its sugar beets in Colorado. The Rocky Ford manager reported that "labor recruiting was acute with no holds barred." In addition, with only about 60 percent of the workers normally required on hand, the manager indicated that growers had a difficult time controlling these sugar beet workers.[38]

Though providing no employment statistics, East Grand Forks fieldmen reported securing labor to be an ongoing struggle because even fewer local whites turned out. Between those entering military service and those going to work in war industries, very few locals worked in the sugar beet fields. Company fieldmen turned to college students for field workers, recruiting among the student bodies of North Dakota Agricultural College, the University of North Dakota, and Moorhead State Teachers College (now Minnesota State University Moorhead). The college students did not work out, however, as one fieldman observed that bad weather "caused these workers to become discouraged." The labor problem became more severe for the harvest. American Crystal had a hard time competing with the other agricultural interests in the valley, especially potato growers who were paying premium wages for harvest workers. Near Grafton, an area of considerable potato cultivation, those sugar beet growers who did not produce potatoes had to hire Native American crews from nearby reservations.[39]

Betabeleros in the valley began to exploit this situation. The fieldman for the Grafton area noted that betabeleros were "hard to manage" because of the scarcity of workers and higher wages in other agricultural sectors. That the Mexican migrants had their own automobiles and trucks provided them leverage, too. Wheat shocking in

Polk County, Minnesota, paid 50 percent more in 1942 than it had the previous year, and while Mexican workers had not been used previously, they were able to take the opportunity to move over to wheat harvesting if they chose. One wheat farmer, revealing his prejudice against Mexicans, conceded, "I can't be to[o] fussy," as he hired twenty-six Mexicans to harvest his wheat. With these advantages, betabeleros insisted on better working conditions, particularly more days off and shorter work days. One fieldman reported, "Most of them quit work on Saturday noon and would not report back until Monday." Others limited their workday to only eight hours. Mexican sugar beet workers also wanted better housing: "There is no doubt that some of my growers will have to provide better living quarters for their labor next year. The worst offenders have been trying to get by with their old shacks." Now betabeleros expected better. Where American Crystal and its growers had generally held the advantage over their betabeleros, the situation, for the moment, had shifted.[40]

UNDER PRESSURE from virtually all agricultural sectors to address what they claimed was a labor shortage and motivated further by their migrant workers' ability to gain advantages, the federal government moved to address the labor situation in 1942. In one significant step, the government allowed draft deferments to laborers in what were considered crucial agricultural products, of which sugar was one. In North Dakota the measure led to deferments for over fifty thousand men; indeed, besides South Carolina, North Dakota had the lowest percentage of men in the military during the war. In addition, the United States Extension Service cooperated with local authorities to ensure that adequate agricultural labor would be available.[41]

But the most important labor measure, in regard to its long-lasting impact on Mexican migrant workers, was the U.S. agreement with Mexico, signed in August 1942, to allow Mexicans nationals to work temporarily in the United States in agriculture, popularly known as the *bracero* program. Precedents certainly existed for such an arrangement. In 1909, President Taft reached an agreement with the Mexican government for about one thousand laborers to work temporarily in the sugar beet fields of Colorado and Nebraska. During World War I over seventy thousand Mexican braceros came into the United States legally to work in agriculture and on railroads during the course of the conflict.[42]

The agreement reached in 1942 was, however, much more complex than the previous arrangements. First, numerous government agencies on both sides of the border would supervise the program; in the United States, principal oversight was from the U.S. Employment Service (Department of Labor) and the Immigration and Naturalization Service (Department of Justice), although the Department of Agriculture and the Department of State played a role, too. Workers from Mexico entered the United States with a written contract detailing where they would work, under what conditions, and how much they would be paid. In fact, the standards established in these contracts provided for better housing, medical attention, and food than the vast majority of American agricultural laborers enjoyed. A documented need for labor had to exist, and Mexican nationals were not to compete with American workers for jobs. The federal government paid the braceros' transportation costs both ways. And finally, the Mexican government insisted their workers should not suffer from any racial discrimination while in the United States. In this regard, Mexico had the power to prohibit the use of braceros in states that displayed overt discrimination against Mexican citizens. Indeed, Mexico refused to permit braceros to work in Texas during the course of the war, a measure that in and of itself had an enormous consequence for Texas betabeleros. Once the agreement was ratified, over four thousand braceros entered the United States during the autumn in 1942, primarily to toil in the sugar beet harvest, although apparently none in that year worked in the valley's sugar beet fields.[43]

Consequently, in response to the stated needs of the agricultural sector, prominent among them the sugar beet industry, an important advantage was given to American Crystal and its growers in their relationship with Mexican migrant workers—an enlarged labor pool reduced betabeleros' leverage to obtain better wages and working conditions. The real significance of the bracero program would not manifest itself, however, until after 1945.

THUS, THE PERIOD FROM 1930 TO 1942 was one of dramatic shifts within the sugar beet industry in the valley. American Crystal was forced to cut production during the economic downturn of the early 1930s. By 1942, however, sugar beets emerged as an even more important crop to the area than ever before. Mechanization and technological advances were changing the way sugar beets were grown. The organization of the farmers into the Red River Valley Sugarbeet Growers Association, in essence, provided individual producers with more influence than they previously enjoyed. Betabeleros gained more control over their lives as they purchased vehicles and received better wages and, for a time with the World War II–induced chaos within the agricultural labor pool, some strength to demand a better living and better working arrangements from their employers. By 1942, with at least 75 percent of field workers being Mexican, the racialization of the sugar beet workforce in the valley had been completed.

The dynamics among American Crystal, its growers, and the workers now included another player. The federal government essentially determined how much sugar American Crystal—and other sugar companies—could manufacture, provided monetary compensation to growers, instituted age restrictions on sugar beet workers, and certified the wages paid to these laborers. This was made even more manifest by the bracero agreement with Mexico.

Therefore, throughout these developments, the ebb and flow of advantage and necessity continued to govern the interactions of these actors. The remainder of World War II and the immediate postwar period would reveal that necessity yet determined who held the advantage in the sugar beet fields and how they would use it.

Mexican sugar beet worker, near Fisher, Minnesota, 1937

Young boy beet worker, near Fisher, Minnesota, 1937

Young Mexican girl topping a beet near East Grand Forks, Minnesota, 1937

Truck loaded with sugar beets, East Grand Forks, Minnesota, 1937

Field workers topping beets, 1944–1945

Mexican houses, Crystal City, Texas, 1939

Monument to Popeye,
Crystal City, Texas, 1939

Migrant housing, near East Grand Forks, Minnesota, 1937

Family of Mexican workers from Texas in East Grand Forks, Minnesota, 1937

Beet field cross-cultivation

Recruited bracero sugar beet workers, 1943

CHAPTER 3

War and Aftermath

DURING THE REMAINDER OF WORLD WAR II and through the immediate postwar period (to the start of the Korean conflict), the sugar beet industry and its participants in the Red River Valley made important adjustments in response to both domestic and international developments. A nationwide increase in sugar production, spurred by wartime demand and influenced by the continuing rise in world consumption, led American Crystal to expand production in the valley. A new sugar beet factory located in Moorhead, Minnesota, was the cornerstone of this growth. On the one hand, most of the region's growers profited by the rise in production, and technological advances improved the cultivation of sugar beets and made the work somewhat easier to perform. On the other hand, farmers grumbled about the ongoing oversight and limitations placed upon them—especially acreage limitations—by the federal government and, by extension, American Crystal. In addition, both the company and the growers remained dependent upon Mexican migrant workers; in that regard American Crystal constructed a dramatically new relationship with betabeleros when it opened a labor recruiting agency in Texas. Moreover, emerging social concerns about migrant living conditions in the valley prompted the first programs in the area designed to better the betabeleros' lives. The Mexican communities themselves, including migrant laborers, took a more active role in improving their situation in Texas and the valley. This activism was threatened, however, by a new wave of immigration from Mexico, the so-called wetback invasion, which eventually led to an unprecedented national examination into conditions migrant workers experienced through President Truman's Commission on Migratory Labor. By 1950, the three major participant groups in the sugar beet industry in the valley—growers, betabeleros, American Crystal—had realigned their relationships with one another to a marked degree.

THE MOST IMPORTANT DEVELOPMENT during this era evolved from American Crystal's response to the confused labor situation engendered by World War II: the creation of a company-controlled labor recruitment agency. Early in 1943, the company chartered the American Crystal Labor Agency and located it in San Antonio, Texas. In so doing, the company implicitly admitted that the old ways of enticing betabeleros to its fields no longer sufficed. With the other major sugar beet companies opening their own labor agencies in South Texas, American Crystal had to follow suit or jeopardize its future. In this heated competition for Mexican migrants, the betabeleros gained some important advantages.

After the Texas legislature passed the Emigrant Agency Law in 1929, which placed noteworthy restrictions and fees on companies recruiting labor in Texas for out-of-state work, American Crystal and other sugar companies generally withdrew from an active role in hiring migrant workers. In fact, the state of Texas issued only a handful of emigrant agency licenses during the 1930s. As competition increased for Mexican migrant workers as a result of the rapidly improving economy, spurred on by the war in Europe, Michigan-based sugar beet companies and grower associations in 1940 opened a labor recruitment agency in Texas. By the end of 1942, both the Great Western Sugar Company and Holley Sugar announced their intention to open their own labor agencies. After some hesitation, American Crystal did likewise.[1]

In February 1943, American Crystal hired Eduardo Aldrete, a man with prior experience as a sugar beet labor recruiter, to set up and run the labor recruitment agency. Shortly thereafter, he and two American Crystal managers set off from the Denver corporate office to assess the labor situation in Texas. Stopping in Dallas to meet with the local War Manpower Commission representative, Aldrete was at first discouraged when this official told him that the sugar companies would not receive many workers because of a perceived labor shortage in Texas. The War Manpower Commission, created to manage American labor resources during the war, had delegated coordination of farm labor needs the previous month to the U.S. Department of Agriculture. Though the USDA eventually turned farm worker employment matters over to each state's extension service, during the early months of 1943 confusion reigned in the nation's farm labor management structure. It was because of this uncertain environment that the War Manpower Commission representative initially blocked Aldrete's plans.[2]

Only in late March, with sugar beet field work less than two months away in the valley, did American Crystal (and other sugar beet companies) receive permission from the Texas Extension Service to apply for the state's emigrant agency license. The various fees and bonds necessary under the Texas Emigrant Agency Law cost American Crystal over $55,000 that first year. Aldrete and the others acquired office space in San Antonio (where the agency remained headquartered for the next thirty years) and began to hire recruiters to operate in eleven counties. In addition, American Crystal opened subrecruiting offices that spring in Laredo, San Marcos, Bridgeport, Dallas, Wichita Falls, Lubbock, and Crystal City. Aldrete employed eight recruiters; in Crystal City, W. A. Butler, an Anglo, was placed on a yearly salary. The other recruiters, all Mexicans, received a bounty ranging from two to three dollars for each worker they recruited. Aldrete later noted in his year-end report that the Mexican recruiters had very little experience with moving farm workers north but were selected primarily because of their Spanish fluency and their social influence among workers in their respective regions. Some American Crystal fieldmen from what was now being called the Eastern District (Red River Valley; Chaska, Minnesota; and Mason City, Iowa) were brought in to help coordinate the recruiting drive.[3]

One of the major headaches faced by the labor agency that first spring involved the expense and red tape of getting the workers to the sugar beet fields. With wartime rationing in effect, the recruiters had to arrange for migrant workers to be issued sufficient gas ration coupons to drive from Texas to their Eastern District job sites. Furthermore, because tires were also rationed and many betabeleros needed to replace theirs, the labor agency had to arrange for replacements through the Department of Transportation. In most cases, the company paid for the tires and then withheld that sum from the workers' checks. In addition, the labor agency had to provide liability insurance for its workers during their travel to and from the sugar beet areas, as mandated by the federal government in the 1935 Motor Carrier Act (something the agency continued to do thereafter). And finally, the recruiters advanced each contracted worker between fifteen and seventeen dollars to cover transportation expenses during the journey. American Crystal balked at doing this at first, but since all of their competitors offered the advance as a recruiting lure, necessity dictated that the company provide its laborers the same benefit. The cost of these advances during the initial year eventually amounted to over $62,000, and in total American Crystal spent over $120,000 that first spring recruiting in Texas. For its efforts the labor agency contracted with almost 3,300 betabeleros in Texas and dispatched 1,900 of them to the Red River Valley.[4]

During the remainder of the war, American Crystal depended heavily on its San Antonio labor agency to keep the Eastern District supplied with field workers, although it continued to procure labor from a number of other sources. The San Antonio office recruited 2,800 Mexican migrants in 1944 and over 3,200 the following year. The valley received the greatest numbers throughout the war, with over 1,900 in 1944 and 2,300 in 1945. Despite this high percentage obtained through the labor agency, valley growers needed more workers, and consequently the company also acquired field labor in other ways. Troqueros continued to bring crews to the valley, and some betabeleros, having established a work history with a particular grower, journeyed north on their own. A few growers had by now employed families or an individual betabelero for over ten years. For instance, a Grafton, North Dakota, family had a single Mexican migrant by this time who had worked for them almost fifteen years, and he would eventually cultivate sugar beets for them over forty years. Mexican braceros (four hundred in 1944), contracted workers from the British West Indies (mainly from Jamaica), Native Americans, and southern black migrants were employed as well. At various times, about eleven thousand German prisoners of war toiled in the valley, although how many specifically cultivated sugar beets is unknown. One sugar beet grower's family remembered Jamaican workers being housed in the city of Grafton's town hall and German prisoners being kept in another part of town while they cultivated sugar beets. Another grower employed three Japanese families from a Colorado relocation center in the summer of 1943. Moreover, the company continued its attempt to entice local college students, and some sugar beet farmers, desperate for harvest hands, scoured among "the bums on Front Street [in Fargo]" for workers. Ensuring an adequate supply of field workers plagued American Crystal and its growers in the valley throughout the war.[5]

Because of the widespread agricultural labor shortage in the valley, betabeleros gained other employment in the region, improving their overall situation. Farmers who grew potatoes, some being sugar beet growers as well, continued to turn to Mexican migrants for harvest help. Indeed, betabeleros became a regular component of the potato harvest in the valley and often used competition between sugar beet and potato growers as leverage to obtain better harvest wages. During the war, area wheat farmers depended increasingly on Mexican migrants brought up by American Crystal's labor agency. One wheat farmer at first rejected using Mexicans because the migrants wanted too much money and "weren't white"; however, a six-inch rainfall quickly forced his hand. The county extension agent arranged for twenty-six betabeleros to shock that farmer's 250 acres. Arriving just after lunch, the Mexican workers finished the task by dusk. The county agent reported that when it came to Mexican workers the reluctant farmer "was a changed man." Indeed, the excellent work Mexican farm laborers provided throughout the valley, the agent noted, reduced prejudicial sentiment among many valley farmers. This changing attitude and the region's ongoing dependency on Mexican migrant labor were partially responsible for the first organized social services offered to the betabeleros and their families.[6]

DURING WORLD WAR II, as Mexican migrant workers became ever more visible and vital, groups other than labor unions manifested concerns over their plight. Part of the interest sprang from health issues, as communities became increasingly aware that Mexican workers experienced high rates of tuberculosis and other illnesses. In San Antonio, a major recruiting site for migrants, the incidence of tuberculosis among Mexican residents was more than twice that among Anglos. In Crystal City the death rate from tuberculosis for Mexican residents was 2.9 deaths per thousand people, a figure deemed alarmingly high by Texas medical authorities. Epidemics of measles occurred more frequently among Mexicans, too. In addition, the miserable conditions of migrant life had received attention during the 1930s, especially in the photographs of Dorothea Lange and through John Steinbeck's *The Grapes of Wrath* (both book and movie). This interest sparked religious organizations and service groups around the nation to do something to improve the migrant workers' situation. Besides numerous health and education programs initiated mainly for betabeleros around the Great Lakes region during the war, the state of New York launched a migrant services program in 1942 that catered to various ethnic groups. Moreover, the Federal Security Administration camps in Texas and elsewhere began to address these concerns for migrant health, housing, and education.[7]

Concerned groups of citizens in the valley and service organizations based in the Midwest followed this national trend and launched several programs for betabeleros during the war. The first actually began in 1941 when local ministers and laymen, calling themselves the Polk County Migrant Committee, supported financially by the Home Missions Council of North America, opened a summer school for ninety migrant children in Fisher, Minnesota. The Home Missions Council, a Protestant social service organization based in Chicago, was already providing assistance to migrant families in the Great Lakes region. In this instance the Home Missions Council channeled its resources through an affiliated group, Church Women United in Minnesota, which was based in Minneapolis and was comprised mainly of members from Methodist, Presbyterian, and Episcopal congregations. The Polk County Migrant Committee noted that first year that the valley's "migrant problem" was comparable to that of Steinbeck's Joad family, with poor housing, widespread illness (especially tuberculosis), and lack of educational opportunity. The Fisher summer school attracted over one hundred children the following year, and the committee offered some evening social activities for adults, too. By 1944, the Polk County Migrant Committee provided educational programs or other social services to about six hundred Mexican migrants working near Fisher and Crookston.[8]

Similar efforts soon spread to Moorhead when a school for Mexican migrant children opened in 1943. Staffed by teachers sent from the Home Missions Council and assisted by education students from Moorhead State Teachers College, the school enrolled twenty-four children that year. Half of the funding for the school came from the Home Missions Council, but significantly, the other half was raised through contributions from "farmers, business concerns, and other interest groups." From mid-June to early August, volunteer drivers transported the migrant children to and from the school, Mondays through Fridays. The staff divided the children into three groups based on their English-speaking and reading skills. The teachers evaluated thirteen children as non-English speaking and designated them Group I; only four children were placed in Group III, having little "hesitancy" with English. Besides reading and writing, the students received instruction in citizenship, hygiene, and the arts.[9]

The teachers in the Moorhead school that first year drafted a comprehensive report detailing the program, which also offered other important insights into the condition of Mexican migrant children and their families in the valley during the war. All of the children were "American-born," hence their parents were Tejanos, naturalized citizens, or pre-1937 immigrants from Mexico. The children's attendance varied daily, sometimes significantly (barely half attended on June 28), as they suffered various ailments, including whooping cough and measles. Otherwise, teachers and staff noted children often being absent because of unexplained reasons. Therefore, it appears that the unhealthy living conditions that contributed to the sickness the betabeleros and their families endured in Texas was widespread in the valley as well. The report's "Individual Pupil Studies," compiled by the college students, revealed even more. Sophia L. was one of ten children who "is quite fortunate in that her parents speak English at home." Martina F. had come to the valley with her forty-five-year-old betabelera mother, while her father remained behind in Texas because of illness. Marcelina R., fourteen years old, started attending the school, was taken out by her father because "she was old enough to work in the field," but after a few days was allowed to return to school "every day." The teaching students must have asked themselves what circumstances would necessitate a mother leaving a sick spouse to bring her children on a journey of hundreds of miles to engage in such hard work: Could a family with ten children maintain a healthy lifestyle on migrant wages? How economically desperate must a family be to

require a fourteen-year-old girl to do stooped labor? As more individuals worked with the Mexican migrant families in the valley, the
answers and solutions to these questions became more obvious.[10]

Other social service programs aimed at the Mexican migrant population also appeared during the war. The same year the Moorhead
migrant school program started, St. Joseph's Catholic Church of Moorhead operated a day care center for thirty infants and preschool children whose migrant mothers otherwise might be "obliged to take
them to the fields." In a related effort in Clay County, American Legion
and Veterans of Foreign Wars auxiliaries helped prepare meals for the
children at the school and day care center. The Benedictine Sisters
took over operation of the migrant school in Moorhead the following
year—1944—but operated it as a boarding school partly in response to
the high absentee rate experienced the previous year among the children. Home Missions Council workers provided at-home visitation to
promote health, nutrition, and English lessons. They also operated a
family center in Moorhead for the migrants who came into town on
Saturdays. In 1944, the Home Missions Council hired a doctor to con-
duct tuberculosis tests on betabelero families; however, he died suddenly during the summer before examining many of them. By 1945,
between the churches and other interested groups, about five hundred Mexican migrant families were receiving some assistance, ranging
from education to health and hygiene instruction. Thus, the increased
presence and significance of Mexican workers to the valley's agriculture, especially sugar beets, prompted the start of social services for
them that continued to expand after the war.[11]

WHILE THE WAR SOMEWHAT IMPROVED THE SITUATION for Mexican migrant workers in the valley, it had a similar effect on American
Crystal and its growers. By and large, farmers in the region did well.
A large portion of them still produced grains, and wheat prices more
than doubled between the attack on Pearl Harbor and V-J Day. In the
northern end of the valley, those who grew potatoes also earned more.
And, of course, the demand for sugar rose. Consequently, Congress
extended the Sugar Act of 1937 (which was due to expire), and the
administration ordered price controls and rationing on domestic

sugar consumption. To encourage increased production, the government provided an additional support payment to sugar growers—separate from the AAA payments that continued, too—and allowed for an
expansion in sugar acreage. For American Crystal its total sugar beet
allotment in the East Grand Forks District climbed from 27,900 acres
to over 38,000 (a more than 25 percent spike). The average acreage
for each grower jumped from forty-six acres to sixty-one. When factored together, their income from American Crystal, the AAA subsidy,
and the wartime support payment resulted in earnings for the sugar
beet farmers leaping from $8.67 per ton of beets in 1942 to $13.12
in 1944.[12]

The war did create some disappointment within the valley's sugar
beet industry, however, because it delayed the planned construction of
a new factory. As the region grew in importance to American Crystal
and its growers wanted to produce more sugar, the limited capacity of
the nearly twenty-year-old East Grand Forks factory represented a
significant roadblock. The company had planned to break ground on
a new, modern facility in Moorhead, but the war-induced building restrictions and rationing of materials forced it to postpone that plan.
This created an additional difficulty in that, as the valley's production
soared, the only way most of the extra beets could be processed was to
ship them by truck or rail to Chaska.[13]

Despite the fact that the delay in construction of a new processing
plant limited their potential to increase production, the war years witnessed an important advancement for the sugar beet growers in the
region: the development of sugar beet–harvesting machines. Harvesting sugar beets had been an expensive proposition for the growers
from the beginning, and having enough labor available in the region
for the four- to six-week harvest frequently was difficult for American
Crystal to arrange, especially if the weather turned inclement. Inven-
tors and company scientists developed various mechanical prototypes
during the 1930s, but topping the beets remained a significant obstacle.
Between 1942 and 1945, John B. Powers, a California agricultural engineer, perfected a topping device. Coupled with other wartime developments that incorporated a mechanism to clean the dirt off the beets,
several viable harvester models had been designed by 1945. Over the

ensuing decade, these machines reshaped the sugar beet industry in the valley.[14]

Other technological advances in the sugar beet industry emerged during World War II. In 1941, engineers designed a more efficient mechanical cross-blocker. Using rotating knives set at right angles to a row of beets, the sugar beet plants could be uniformly blocked, thus making it faster for field workers to thin them. Scientists also created a segmented sugar beet seed that significantly reduced the number of plants grown from a single seed ball. This decreased the amount of seed required to plant a field from roughly twenty pounds per acre to about eight, an important cost-saving measure for growers, especially when the new seed also lessened the need for finger thinning. The segmented seed meant, too, that betabeleros spent less time on their knees. Indeed, in most cases segmented seeds shaved off about 50 percent of the hours needed to thin a field. Although these new devices and seeds were not available everywhere in 1945, by 1948 the industry calculated that the number of human work hours to cultivate an acre of sugar beets had dropped from about seventy-eight hours—in 1937— to about forty hours.[15]

While these events represented great potential, the end of the war in August 1945 also left the actors in the sugar beet industry in the valley with many questions. For the company the question of whether the federal government would continue to regulate the sugar industry and, if so, what that would mean was crucial. For both growers and American Crystal, much hinged on whether a new sugar facility could be constructed quickly. Moreover, how would they secure their supply of workers, especially if the bracero arrangement with Mexico was not renewed now that the wartime labor shortage had ended? For the betabeleros, would their improved circumstances, created by the federal government's policies and the competition for their services by agribusinesses, especially sugar beet companies, continue, and would it translate into better living conditions and economic well-being?

A CLIMATE OF OPTIMISM, albeit tempered by anxiety, permeated the valley in the early months of 1946. Soldiers returned home from overseas in greater numbers while the federal government slowly eased its grip on the economy. For one, the Office of Price Administration was beginning to phase out controls on agricultural commodities. For another, key industries such as steel and coal experienced labor conflicts resulting in long-lasting strikes. With the economy moving in fits and starts from a war to a peace mode, confusion was rampant. In Fargo a bread shortage developed, and beef prices surged upward. Many of Minnesota's breweries closed for a time, victims of the coal shortage created by a strike. Consequently, most bars in Fargo-Moorhead ran out of beer, and a run on hard liquor ensued. The local newspaper printed a series, surveying Fargo's infrastructure, ominously titled "Fargo's Problems Many." The reporters found that the community had not been able to maintain its sewer system and paved streets during the war and faced an enormous task with just catching up, a situation that threatened economic growth for the community.[16]

American Crystal confronted the same uncertain environment, especially in regard to the valley's sugar beet labor needs. Construction was to begin on the long-delayed new factory in Moorhead that summer if everything fell into place. The facility had the capacity to double sugar production in the area, but it also increased the demand for field labor. The German prisoners of war had returned home, and the bracero agreement with Mexico was to expire. Could the company secure enough laborers by returning to the old system of attracting field workers by relying on independent recruiters, troqueros, private employments firms, and word of mouth? Or should American Crystal maintain the expensive labor agency in Texas? These were the questions that M. C. Sullivan, head of the American Crystal Labor Agency in San Antonio, tried to answer early in 1946.[17]

M. C. Sullivan—"Sully" to his friends and associates—took over the agency from Aldrete at the end of 1944. Originally from a Minnesota farm family, he had become a labor recruiter for the Fairmount Canning Company, one of the largest such companies in Minnesota. Sullivan recruited heavily among South Texas Mexican workers for seasonal canning employees and became fluent in Spanish. Based on his experience, knowledge of the South Texas labor environment, and language skills, American Crystal offered Sullivan the position, which he held for the next twenty years. He made San Antonio his home and developed a cadre of recruiters in the region who, in most cases, worked for him year after year. Considered "easy-going" by coworkers, the soft-spoken Sully had an "uncanny ability" to recall names and faces, a trait that earned him significant respect from his Mexican recruiters and betabeleros.[18]

During the winter and early spring of 1946, Sullivan traveled throughout the Midwest evaluating the labor market. Everywhere he found bustle: more cars on the roads, hotels full of businessmen, and other clear signs of an incipient economic boom. Sullivan quickly ascertained that the labor market had dramatically changed from its prewar structure. The private labor agencies that American Crystal had previously depended on before the war were no longer in operation. Mexican residents of Omaha and Kansas City, who once worked as betabeleros, now told Sullivan that better-paying industrial jobs were available to them. He ventured as far as southern Oklahoma before encountering a Mexican family interested in returning as sugar beet field workers. Arriving in Texas, Sullivan discovered yet another agribusiness, the California Fruit Company, establishing a labor agency and that the other sugar companies had decided they would continue to rely on the agency system. Therefore, Sullivan recommended that American Crystal had no choice but to follow suit. By early February 1946, Sullivan reported that the San Antonio office was "ready to do business."[19]

The labor agency expanded its efforts that year in light of the "very keen competition" for betabeleros. The agency actively recruited in nineteen Texas counties (up from twelve the previous year), which meant increased costs for the company for the labor licenses, fees, and bonds. The number of recruiters hired by Sullivan also rose from eight to twelve. The labor agency printed more handbills and ran ads in *La Prensa*, the statewide Spanish-language newspaper based in San Antonio. Needing to fill the void created by the repatriation of German prisoners and the company's decision not to rely on braceros, the number of workers contracted jumped to over 5,100, with almost 3,500 of those sent to the Red River Valley. To help offset some of the costs for procuring their Mexican migrant laborers, American Crystal instituted a fee to growers of $2.50 per contracted acre. Thus, American Crystal institutionalized its procurement of betabeleros in Texas. The sugar beet companies and other agribusinesses now turned the state into a recruiting battlefield, especially the region from San Antonio southward through the Nueces Strip.[20]

THAT TEXAS—primarily the southern part of the state—became the focal point for agribusinesses' quest for seasonal labor occurred not just because they needed more workers; it was also a result of a new surge of immigration across the Rio Grande. Several factors sparked this so-called wetback invasion of Texas. In Mexico a relatively rapid increase in population, brought on by the combined factors of better government services in health and education and the ongoing high birthrate, meant that the country's economic growth failed to match the needs of its people. During the war Mexico also suffered from a rather high rate of inflation, which led to devaluations in the peso. Hence, earning American dollars represented an even greater gain for citizens of Mexico than before. In addition, the expansion of Mexico's own cotton production along the Rio Grande during World War II drew large numbers of Mexican seasonal workers to the border region. From there, South Texas agricultural employers found it rather easy to encourage them to work in Texas.[21]

Ironically, the nature of the bracero agreement between the United States and Mexico increased illegal immigration into Texas during the war. The agreement had allowed Mexico to bar any state that discriminated against Mexican people from hiring these temporary workers. The Mexican government designated Texas as a discriminatory state and stipulated braceros could not be employed in agriculture (some did work on railroads). The decision outraged Texas farmers, who believed they would experience a ruinous farm labor shortage. Though their cries of alarm were later found to be without substance, at the time the belief that a lack of workers would doom Texas farmers became an article of faith among them and Texas politicians. In an effort to get around the Mexican government's decision, Texas legislators managed to get an amendment to Public Law 45 (the act that authorized the bracero agreement) through Congress in early 1943, which removed all barriers to immigration into the United States for workers from any Latin American country, thus effectively overriding the bracero arrangement. Angered by this attempt to get around the terms of the bracero agreement, Mexican officials threatened to suspend the employment of temporary workers totally in the United States. The Roosevelt administration blocked the implementation of the amendment to Public Law 45 by instructing the Immigration and Naturalization Service to ignore it. Consequently, Texas farmers and political leaders proceeded to encourage Mexican nationals to enter the state illegally.[22]

In essence, Texas farmers, especially in the Nueces Strip, and their supporters engaged in a massive violation of the law. Thousands of Mexican farm workers crossed into Texas between 1943 and 1945 as enforcement officers on both sides of the border generally ignored the provisions of the Immigration Act of 1924 and Public Law 45. Pressured by the farmers and local officials, U.S. border agents most often turned a blind eye to the problem during the harvest period in South Texas. Mexico's border guards, too, were less than rigorous in their enforcement efforts. Indeed, by its lack of action to enforce immigration procedures, the Mexican government tacitly acknowledged that the country's economic shortcomings required allowing its border population access to this employment, whether Mexicans were discriminated against or not. These workers accepted low wages, therefore driving down wages for all agricultural workers living in South Texas. In addition, because of their illegal status, Texas growers found them easier to control and out of the grasp of out-of-state sugar companies and agribusinesses. Consequently, Mexicans, whether citizens or legal residents living in the region, needed sugar beet work as badly as the sugar industry needed them.[23]

The continued influx of Mexican farm laborers into the United States, whether legal braceros or illegal workers, contributed to the atmosphere of uncertainty in the Red River Valley and Nueces Strip in 1946. The two countries extended the bracero agreement year-to-year in 1946 and 1947, but it appeared likely to expire thereafter. Coupled with a growing demand for seasonal labor among agribusinesses nationwide, if the sugar companies lost access to these legal braceros, it would have a profound influence on the entire industry, including the participants in the valley's sugar beet economy. Even though Mexican agricultural workers in South Texas preferred mandated sugar beet wages to those available in their hometowns, American Crystal would be compelled to expand its recruiting efforts. Valley growers would have to pay higher fees for recruiting or seek labor from other sources. Through these developments, betabeleros might gain the leverage they needed to obtain better wages and working conditions, as they had in the early war years. In fact, in South Texas in the late 1940s, Mexican citizens were becoming more active in challenging the barriers that blocked their social and economic well-being.[24]

THROUGHOUT TEXAS, and especially in the Nueces Strip after the war, the Mexican population contested discrimination and the economic structure that kept the vast majority of them in poverty. While this civil rights struggle was undertaken mainly by the urban Mexican middle class at this time, its effect spilled over into rural areas and among the migrant workers. This social movement in South Texas had an important influence on the Red River Valley's sugar industry by the time the Korean War erupted.

A primary manifestation of the Mexicans' concerns about their legal rights and economic status was the emergence of two organizations: the League of United Latin American Citizens (LULAC) and the American GI Forum. The first of these, LULAC, had grown out of concerns by the Mexican middle class about their plight in the 1920s, especially the institutionalization of Jim Crow restrictions and the negative economic effects brought on by the influx of illegal immigrants from Mexico during that interval between World War I and the Great Depression. Several Mexican organizations had evolved during the 1920s, but it was LULAC, chartered in 1929, that became the most important. Based primarily in urban areas with large Mexican populations, such as Corpus Christi, San Antonio, and Brownsville, most LULAC members were from the Mexican merchant and professional groups. Well organized and increasingly visible to other Mexicans by the start of World War II, LULAC had spread into New Mexico and California and had over eighty affiliated chapters in the three states. The league focused its energies mainly on securing legal rights and equal opportunities for Mexican citizens while stressing the need for the Mexican population to become more "American." Relying on legal challenges to discrimination against Mexicans, LULAC won several court cases by World War II, especially regarding public education in Texas.[25]

Indeed, LULAC's emphasis on education as a means to social and economic betterment began to take root generally among the Mexican population in the post–World War II environment. More migrant families kept their children in school during the spring, and they endeavored to return home earlier in the autumn. A son of an American Crystal betabelero from Asherton, Texas (in the Nueces Strip), during this period remembered that his father kept all five of his children in school until it let out in May before they would pack up and go north. The family "would spend June and July and as much as August as we could, and then go back, make sure we were there for the first day of school." Each of those children eventually graduated from high school. In Crystal City more Mexican students graduated from high school in 1950 than in any previous year. In the consolidated school district of Pharr–San Juan–Alamo (near McAllen), a central area for migrant workers, Mexican youths became more prominent in high school. In 1945, less than 25 percent of the students were Mexican, and none of those were on the student council, in the band, or on the cheerleader squad. Five years later Mexican teenagers made up more than 40 percent of the student body, and the senior class president was Mexican. Moreover, that year the school had five Mexican teachers, where none had taught in 1945, and the first Mexican had been elected to the school board. As migrant families became more inclined to have their children in school near Labor Day, obtaining workers for the sugar beet harvest in the valley became ever more problematic for the growers and American Crystal.[26]

The other Mexican civil rights organization, the American GI Forum, developed out of the Félix Longoria episode in 1949. Longoria, a Mexican soldier during World War II, had been killed in action. His body was returned to the South Texas community of Three Rivers for interment in 1949, but the local funeral home refused his family's request for a wake. The resulting outpouring of anger by Mexicans in the region, especially among former soldiers, eventually led to Longoria's burial in Arlington National Cemetery. Mexican veterans, many attending colleges and universities under the GI Bill, organized themselves into the American GI Forum during the national attention paid to the Longoria family's plight, and this group became another voice for Mexican civil rights and economic opportunity.[27]

Besides these Mexican organizations, other groups focused attention on the status of the Mexican population in South Texas. In 1943, in an effort to promote better relations with Mexico and to encourage Mexico to lift its ban on braceros working in Texas, the governor of Texas created the Good Neighbor Commission. Though mostly a symbolic gesture and without enforcement power, the Good Neighbor Commission—by its very existence—promoted attention toward Mexican citizens and legal residents, especially during the tenure of its first director, Pauline Kibbe, and through her publication in 1946 of *Latin Americans in Texas*. In her book Kibbe offered a very candid description of the desperate conditions under which most Mexicans in the state lived and worked. She especially noted the adverse effect caused by the renewed surge of illegal immigrants into South Texas. Through the creation of the Catholic Bishops Committee for the Spanish-speaking, based in San Antonio, the Catholic Church also joined the chorus of those concerned with the Mexican people's status in Texas and the harmful effects to them from the unbridled immigration. By the end of the 1940s, public concern over the conditions of Mexican migrant workers and illegal immigration from Mexico increasingly influenced actions by the Truman administration. Even in the Red River Valley, these developments affected the sugar beet industry.[28]

ON THE ONE HAND, during the immediate postwar era the valley's sugar beet industry continued to grow and prosper, especially with the long-awaited construction of a new processing plant located in Moorhead. American Crystal began work on the four-million-dollar facility in the summer of 1946 with the intention of operating the factory the next year and expanding acreage by twelve to fourteen thousand. The processing plant was designed to eventually double sugar production in the region, and American Crystal planned to increase its contingent of contracted growers, especially in the southern valley counties of Cass, North Dakota, and Clay, Minnesota. Locating the new factory in Moorhead, a major rail junction in the Upper Midwest, placed these counties in the center of new operations. Officials in Moorhead and Fargo enthusiastically supported the venture and the three hundred new jobs it created. The Great Northern Railway designated the station serving the factory, about a mile north of Moorhead, as the town of Bingham, after J. B. Bingham, the manager of American Crystal's valley operations. Area newspapers regularly reported on the facility in front-page stories.[29]

All of these grand plans had to be suspended, however, in August. That month the company announced that, because of the numerous labor standoffs afflicting the nation, especially the coal and steel strikes, the plant would not be operational until 1948. Bingham also noted in the press release that farm implement dealers had not been able to secure the necessary sugar beet field machinery, including the newly developed harvesters, because of the strikes and the confusion created in the conversion to peacetime manufacturing. Thus, even had the plant opened, farmers could not have purchased the equipment necessary to meet American Crystal's expansion goals. Coupled with a widespread polio epidemic in the region that included a two-month ban on youth activities in Fargo and other nearby communities, 1946 ended on a very gloomy note.[30]

The new factory was finally dedicated in September 1948, in time for that year's harvest. Similar to the 1926 opening of the East Grand Forks factory, this event was an extravaganza for valley residents. The local school bands played; company officials and local politicians made speeches; and the affair was even broadcast nationwide on 162 radio stations as part of the popular NBC *Farm and Home Hour,* hosted by Everett Mitchell. The dedication coincided with the annual meeting of the Western Beet Growers Association, so industry bigwigs and growers from numerous western states attended the dedication ceremonies. American Crystal made good on its promised expansion, as valley farmers grew over ten thousand more acres of sugar beets than the previous year, an increase of about 30 percent. Coinciding with Congress's passage of the Sugar Act of 1948, increasing the allotments for sugar beet companies, the year was, indeed, a good one for the valley's sugar beet industry.[31]

In general, valley farmers also prospered materially during the period between the conclusion of World War II and the start of the Korean War. The vast majority of sugar beet growers still cultivated other crops, and these commodities overall did very well. Farm income in the region enjoyed what up until then were its three best years from 1947 through 1949. This helped push North Dakota's per capita income in 1949 to the sixth highest in the country, an increase of over 350 percent above the 1940 level. Sugar beet production jumped dramatically once the Moorhead plant was fully operational. In 1950, the company harvested 66,100 acres in the valley, up from 37,000 just three years earlier. Growers continued to receive federal government support payments in addition to their AAA subsidies. Hence, their earnings topped fourteen dollars per ton in 1949, the highest amount to that date. Sugar consumption soared during these years, too, with the USDA announcing in 1949 that per capita sugar intake in the United States had climbed to over one hundred pounds annually (it had been less than twenty in 1865).[32]

Sugar beet growers used their earnings to improve their living conditions. A study of North Dakota farms undertaken at the end of World War II by the state's Agricultural Advisory Council found that fewer than 50 percent of farm residences in the state had indoor plumbing, over 50 percent were in need of major repairs to roofs and floors, and 93 percent had no electricity and that, for most farm residences, insulation was "nonexistent." Just four years later, farm living conditions, at least in the valley, had changed significantly. About one-third of the region's farmhouses in 1948 had electricity, provided in a massive effort by the federal Rural Electrification Administration (REA); the REA planned to double the total number of farms throughout North Dakota with electricity by 1950. The number of farms in the state with indoor plumbing grew at a rate of over two thousand per year between 1947 and 1949. North Dakota rural families with telephone service doubled, too, during the period. Consequently, the Fargo-Moorhead newspaper in 1949 could report to its readers about one valley farm family that now had an electric refrigerator, range, deep freeze, and central heating system. Their milk house had been wired and a heater installed, making cows and workers more comfortable. The family members also enjoyed indoor plumbing, and "in five or ten minutes the electric dish washer erase[d] worry and work over cleaning the table for a meal for eight." Certainly, for valley farmers, more and more of whom grew sugar beets, life seemed to be improving rapidly.[33]

All was not completely harmonious, however, with the valley's sugar beet industry, especially with its migrant labor needs. The American Crystal Labor Agency in San Antonio generally took care of the summer field labor requirements, despite the rapid increase in acreage. The number of betabeleros recruited to work in the valley climbed from over 3,400 in 1946 to nearly 6,000 in 1950. The harvest proved, however, to be increasingly problematic. With the rising trend among Mexican migrant families to value their children's education and return them to school when it opened at the end of summer, fewer were available in October and November to harvest the sugar beets or, for that matter, potatoes. In 1947, American Crystal had to fly in about one thousand braceros to help harvest the sugar beet crop in the valley. This dependency on braceros was very expensive—about $153 per worker—as the agreement between Mexico and the United States obliged the company to pay for each worker's transportation. It was also difficult for American Crystal to plan ahead on braceros, as the agreement with Mexico was being renewed on only an annual basis. Not willing to pay such costs for braceros the following year, the company put out an urgent call throughout the region for five hundred workers to bring in the sugar beet crop. The potato growers, many of whom produced sugar beets, experienced similar shortages.[34]

Besides the sugar beet industry's dependence on Mexican migrant workers, their presence in the valley began to draw attention from other institutions. By 1949, local welfare agencies were concerned about the increase in the number of indigent Mexican families remaining in the region after the sugar beet season ended. Most betabeleros returned south when their contracts expired, but some wished to remain and others—for a variety of reasons—did not have the financial means to leave. Authorities also began to arrest illegal Mexican immigrants, lured to the region for jobs as betabeleros. Fourteen were apprehended in July 1949, although they continued to work in the sugar beet fields until a flight back to the Mexico border could be arranged. Twenty-three more were rounded up by authorities during the sugar beet harvest that same year.[35]

In another related development, the local media started to highlight violent crimes associated with Mexican migrants. During a fight in 1940, "a youthful Mexican" stabbed to death a farmer's twenty-two-year-old son near Grafton. Though the initial report suggested that the accused had been drinking excessively prior to the incident, a jury in Grafton two months later ruled that the Mexican worker had been acting in self-defense and set him free. The following year, "a Mexican family feud" resulted in the shooting of a betabelero in Clay County by his brother-in-law. Again in Grafton, two years later, "five Mexicans" were arrested after a tavern brawl left three white wheat harvesters with various knife wounds. "A Mexican sugar beet worker" was arrested in 1946 for killing his wife and beating to death a local Fisher, Minnesota, resident. The next year in Moorhead, a "Crystal City, Texas, migrant laborer" was stabbed to death by "a Mexican from Texas" during a fight over a woman. This story occupied the front page of the local newspaper for two days. A three-day front page story occurred in 1949 when a distraught Mexican migrant husband stabbed his estranged wife in front of Fargo's downtown J. C. Penney store in broad daylight. The wife survived, but her husband received a one- to three-year sentence in the North Dakota prison system. Three weeks after the Fargo incident, police apprehended "two Mexicans" for stabbing a Walsh County farmer. Although these cases hardly represented a crime wave, in a region that experienced less than a dozen murders per year, residents viewed these developments with alarm. In addition, the newspaper frequently used "Mexican" in the story's headline and always identified the accused as "Mexican" or "migrant." Over time this began to plant in the public's mind the association that betabeleros were prone to violence. Later, this notion had a more serious consequence.[36]

While these negative associations with Mexican migrant workers and their families began to pose some difficulties for American Crystal and its growers, a more immediate potential problem appeared in the late 1940s. As social service agencies, such as the Home Missions Council of Minnesota, worked more and more with migrants, they started to pressure both federal and state governments to redress the poor conditions in which many Mexicans lived. Therefore, toward the end of the decade, the Minnesota state government began to scrutinize the sugar beet industry and its treatment of migrant workers.

SOCIAL SERVICE AGENCIES had continued to expand their work with migrants in the valley after World War II. By 1945, the Minnesota Council of Religious Education and the Home Missions Council organized the Minnesota Migrant Committee. In 1946, their Polk County program had a staff of four regular workers plus volunteers running a nursery program and the summer school, and they were providing home visitations. At least two of the staff spoke Spanish fluently, enhancing their ability to work with Mexican families who might not speak English. In Clay County in 1947, the Migrant Committee conducted home visits aimed to assess the families' needs and to offer advice on health and nutrition matters to as many as one thousand Mexicans. The following year the Migrant Committee sponsored the Harvester, a vehicle that brought recreation equipment, films, and other entertainment to migrant workers. In Moorhead, St. Joseph's Catholic Church continued to operate and expand its summer boarding school. In addition, St. Joseph's provided a space for migrant musicians to perform, and eventually dances took place. The Migrant Committee staffers reported that sugar beet growers were generally supportive of their efforts, because these services encouraged betabeleros to remain on their farms, but the attitude of many growers later changed once state governments began to examine migrant living conditions.[37]

In Minnesota at this time, social agencies and church groups concerned about the plight of betabeleros and other migrants had a governor who was sympathetic to their cause. Luther W. Youngdahl, a Republican, was elected to the first of his three two-year terms in 1946. A devout Lutheran, Youngdahl was described by one historian as being "possessed of an impelling fervor for social betterment." During his three administrations he enacted legislation that provided for state-funded low-income housing, ended segregation in the Minnesota National Guard, and actively supported other measures for public health programs, welfare service, aid for the mentally ill, expanded education opportunities, and various other social issues. During his first term in office, exhibiting his concern about racism in the state, Youngdahl created the Governor's Interracial Commission (GIC) to "examine racial and religious problems which exist in Minnesota." The GIC drafted five reports between 1946 and 1949, with the fourth being *The Mexican in Minnesota,* which was submitted to Youngdahl in August 1948.[38]

Based on surveys and research from professors at Hamline University in St. Paul and the University of Minnesota, the report categorized the Mexican population into three groups: permanent residents,

"Mexicans born in Texas" working in Minnesota seasonally, and Mexican nationals (braceros). The researchers estimated four thousand permanent residents, of whom 80 percent lived in Minneapolis or St. Paul. The others lived in sugar beet–producing counties, especially Polk and Clay in the Red River Valley. The document claimed that as many as four thousand braceros came to the state during World War II, although the number of these workers had declined significantly since. In addition to working with sugar beets, the researchers noted that the braceros also had been used in canneries. *The Mexican in Minnesota* concluded, however, that more than any other industry sugar beets had brought all three groups of Mexicans to the state. Yet among the permanent population in St. Paul and Minneapolis, less than a dozen families still migrated to the sugar beet fields. Most had transitioned to work for the railroads or in packinghouses or had found other factory employment.[39]

The GIC report focused significant attention on Mexican migrants in the sugar beet fields, especially since the researchers viewed their living and working conditions as so problematic. The report acknowledged that betabeleros received a good wage for seasonal agricultural work. In 1947, the payment for field cultivation, based on the provisions set by the federal government, amounted to nineteen dollars per acre; harvest pay, converted from tonnage to acreage, came to twenty-two dollars per acre. The average betabelero received $383 if he stayed through the season, plus housing and transportation to and from the region. In addition, some growers paid a bonus to good workers who fulfilled their contracts. Based on computations of other seasonal work for the betabeleros, they made 60 percent of their annual income in sixty-five days working for American Crystal, "higher than in any form of agriculture in this state." Paychecks were disbursed on three occasions: on August 1, at the completion of the harvest, and in December, once the tonnage for that year's crop had been ascertained.[40]

It was not the pay that the GIC researchers criticized so much. Rather, they were concerned about the conditions under which the betabeleros lived. Some Mexican migrant families lived in quarters that were no more "than remodeled chicken or turkey houses." In the better migrant houses electricity was provided, but even these quarters invariably lacked indoor plumbing. To be fair, the report noted that American Crystal was pressuring growers to improve housing in order to attract and keep workers and that the condition of migrant housing "was not greatly inferior to those of some farm families." As to their health, investigators discovered that migrant workers and their family members tested for tuberculosis in the sugar beet area of Chaska reacted positively at a rate of almost 40 percent. The GIC study noted that the Minnesota public school system also failed the migrants' children. The report applauded the summer schools in Polk County and that of St. Joseph's in Moorhead but found throughout Clay County schools (rural and urban) only seven Mexican children enrolled at any time through the regular school year. And finally, the researchers concluded that, while Mexican migrant workers were "free from many discriminatory practices which they encounter[ed] in the Southwestern part of the United States," they endured some in the rural areas, especially in eating establishments.[41]

The GIC report closed with a list of recommendations regarding all Mexicans in Minnesota and some specific to migrant workers. Here it advocated that the state should play a greater role in supporting summer school programs in the sugar beet counties. Civic groups, industrial firms, and state officials should coordinate efforts to provide winter employment opportunities so that the betabeleros could remain in the state throughout the year. Migrant workers should be eligible for welfare assistance in between employment. The report flatly stated that Minnesota needed Mexican migrant workers; treating them better assured they would continue to come. Moreover, "when a Minnesotan treats a Mexican with reverence and fairness he may be making a contribution to a better world order." At least in Minnesota, it must have been obvious to American Crystal officials and its growers that the state government was likely to step up its oversight of their treatment of Mexican migrant workers.[42]

THE RECOMMENDATIONS IN THE GIC REPORT to Governor Youngdahl did not create an immediate change in the way migrant workers lived and worked in the Red River Valley, but it foreshadowed two developments that would have an enormous impact during the next decade. *The Mexican in Minnesota* clearly concluded that the sugar beet industry needed the betabeleros, and American Crystal agreed.

As the 1940s gave way to a new decade, the company began to pressure its growers to improve their interactions with their laborers and to upgrade migrant housing. In addition, the report represented a new trend in government policy, on both the state and the federal levels, to provide more regulation in the treatment of migrant workers. The 1950s would witness the inauguration of numerous social measures on behalf of the Mexican migrant workers and their families. Taken together with the Mexican population's aspirations for social, economic, and political betterment, the relationships among betabeleros, American Crystal, and the growers, by necessity, faced further alterations in the decade to come.

CHAPTER 4

Growers, Mexicans, and *Patronismo*

THE YEAR 1950 proved to be a pivotal one for American Crystal, migrant workers, and valley growers as the federal government launched an in-depth investigation into migrant labor working and living conditions, the Korean War broke out, and the sugar beet growers in the Red River Valley suffered an acute labor shortage. The onset of the conflict in Korea helped drive sugar production demands higher amid nationwide worries over severe agricultural labor shortages. For American Crystal and the growers, profits increased but so did oversight from the federal government. At the same time, the valley's growers tried to increase their sugar beet acreage allotments, by pressuring American Crystal to build more processing facilities and by encouraging other sugar beet companies to establish operations in the region. More sugar beet cultivation meant that even more betabeleros were needed, which forced American Crystal to offer additional benefits to its labor force. Despite increasing Mexican migrants' wages and improving their working conditions, the company and its growers continued to be plagued with harvest labor shortages. Ultimately, by necessity, the growers mechanized. Machines could not completely eliminate, however, the need for field workers. Hence, American Crystal and its growers fostered a more paternalistic relationship with the betabeleros, similar to the Hispanic traditional patronismo, in order to forge a loyal workforce. This northern version of patronismo brought some betterment in the working and living conditions of the Mexican migrant community, as did the rising scrutiny by federal and state governments and by social agencies into the nature of the migrants' lives. In fact, by the mid-1950s government's influence on the matrix of sugar beet production in the valley made it a more four-sided arrangement, rather than the previous triangle. Consequently, as the 1950s unfolded, the dynamics among American Crystal, its growers in the

Red River Valley, and the Mexican migrant workers they depended upon continued to evolve as advantage and necessity shaped their interactions.

SEVERAL FACTORS INDUCED PRESIDENT HARRY TRUMAN in 1950 to create the President's Commission on Migratory Labor. Truman had already established a pattern of promoting equal rights and better treatment for minority groups through his desegregation of the armed forces and federal facilities. Of course, these steps had been aimed primarily at African Americans and motivated by political concerns. Political considerations did provide some impetus to the 1950 migratory worker investigation in that organized labor, an important component of the Democratic Party, vociferously protested the continued importation of braceros to the United States, arguing that in some instances these Mexican workers had been used as strikebreakers and that their availability drove wages downward. In addition, the on-again, off-again bracero agreement with Mexico had generated considerable friction among various federal agencies, especially the INS and the USDA, because of their different missions. The ongoing flood of illegal immigrants had also stirred serious debate in the regions along the border. Growers wanted unlimited access to these workers while social service organizations and Mexican American groups, such as LULAC, demanded that these immigrants be turned back because they eroded wages, especially in places like the Nueces Strip. And finally, civil rights advocates, such as Roy Wilkins of the National Association for the Advancement of Colored People, linked migrant workers' living and working conditions with the emerging African American movement, which further influenced Truman's decision to launch a federal inquiry.[1]

On June 3, 1950, through Executive Order 10129, President Truman created a five-member Commission on Migratory Labor "to make a broad study of conditions among migratory workers in the United States and of problems created by the migration of workers into this country." While Truman received criticism from labor and civil rights groups for not appointing any Mexican Americans, African Americans, or union activists to the commission, the individuals he did choose were certainly not friends of agribusiness in America. Maurice T. Van

Hecke, selected to head the panel, was a labor law professor at the University of North Carolina and had served as labor mediator with the National War Labor Board during World War II. The other members were Noble Clark, who had experience with the United Nations' Food and Agricultural Organization; Peter Odegard, a political scientist from the University California at Berkeley; Archbishop Robert E. Lucey of San Antonio, known as an advocate for the Mexican population in South Texas; and William M. Leiserson, who had previously been on the National Labor Relations Board. Truman asked that the commission complete its work by the end of the year.[2]

Over the next five months, the commission worked at a frantic pace holding regional hearings, engaging in field trips, and organizing two conferences in Washington, D.C. The hearings, which formed the nucleus of the investigation, were conducted in Brownsville and El Paso, Texas; Phoenix, Arizona; Los Angeles, California; Portland, Oregon; Trenton, New Jersey; West Palm Beach, Florida; Washington, D.C.; Saginaw, Michigan; Memphis, Tennessee; and Fort Collins, Colorado. Over two hundred individuals—representing unions, social service organizations, state and federal agencies, growers, agribusinesses, and migrant laborers—testified before the commission, and hundreds of written reports and affidavits were also submitted by interested parties. Indeed, the commission amassed so much material that it was unable to finish its report until April 1951. The hearings in Brownsville, El Paso, and Fort Collins focused on the forces that connected the sugar beet industry to Mexican migrants from South Texas, especially the influx of illegal immigrants, which caused local Mexican residents to seek employment away from their homes. Thus, those proceedings were more directly revealing as to the nature of the sugar industry in the Red River Valley.[3]

No one disagreed that illegal Mexican immigrants were pouring into Texas. The Mexican government estimated that in 1947 about 120,000 of its citizens were working as illegal seasonal laborers in the United States, of whom 50,000 were in the Nueces Strip alone. In 1948, the INS office in El Paso reported more than 100,000 illegal immigrants in Texas, despite apprehending as many as 11,000 a month and returning them to Mexico. In his testimony during the migratory commission's hearings, the INS district enforcement officer for San Antonio—which included the Nueces Strip—estimated that 100,000 illegal Mexican nationals were employed in his region that year. In a separate survey completed in July 1950, investigators concluded that there were 100,000 illegal workers in just three Nueces Strip counties (Hidalgo, Cameron, and Willacy)—out of the sixteen counties that composed the region—a figure that represented one-third of those three counties' total population. Therefore, despite apprehending thousands of illegal Mexican immigrants each month, the authorities along the Rio Grande appeared to be helpless to block the massive numbers entering the United States from Mexico.[4]

The federal and state patrol agents were simply too few in ranks considering the miles of border they guarded and the number of Mexican nationals crossing the river. Essentially, the total number of INS agents along the southern border had remained constant since the early 1940s. For the entire 1,600-mile border with Mexico, the INS deployed fewer than nine hundred personnel. In one instance, the El Paso district had over nine hundred miles of border under its jurisdiction. The district director—when he factored in the days off, illnesses, court time, and vacation days for his agents—calculated that at any moment each on-duty border patrolman was responsible for over forty miles of boundary, often in rugged, remote terrain. In addition, when the INS brought charges against growers who arranged to bring in illegal workers, it could not get convictions. The El Paso district director complained, "Sometimes we have their [growers'] signed confessions and we take it before the grand jury and in most cases they will not indict." Some Texas residents charged the INS, however, with turning a blind eye to the problem during the Texas harvest season, as politicians pressured the agency to be more lenient when it came to apprehending illegal immigrant farm workers.[5]

Seasonal agricultural work drew these illegal immigrants into Texas, although the reasons why agricultural interests in the state needed them were in dispute. The agribusinesses and growers claimed that they required Mexican nationals, whether legal or illegal, for a variety of reasons. They maintained that they could not remain competitive if they paid the wages local residents demanded. In addition, growers and agribusinesses complained that American citizens, most notably those of Mexican descent, had grown less inclined to perform exhausting field work in a hot climate because "they had advanced." Workers from Mexico, however, a group of South Texas farmers testified, were "acclimated to our heat and can do the work well. In fact, we find Mexicans like to work in our hot weather." Growers also offered a racist explanation for this, claiming that, since many undocumented workers were Yaquis or Tarahumaras or were from other indigenous groups in Mexico, they better tolerated high-temperature conditions. The president of the Rio Grande Valley Farm Bureau Federation stated that South Texas growers hired "'raw' persons, almost one step away from the Indian living, [who] don't want floors in a house because they know how to sleep on the ground." And finally, Texas growers and their allies claimed that returning Mexican American military veterans were being spoiled by the one-year readjustment unemployment benefit that was then in effect—the returning soldiers could make more money from not working than by picking cotton or harvesting onions. What these Texas growers wanted, they repeatedly told the migratory commission, were no restrictions on hiring Mexican nationals.[6]

To union activists, social service groups, and Mexican civil rights organizations who opposed the employment of Mexican nationals, especially those crossing the border illegally, the issues boiled down to matters of wages and control. Field work and packinghouse wages in South Texas had climbed somewhat during the war, to as much as sixty cents per hour. By 1950, as a result of the so-called wetback invasion, pay had declined again to as little as twenty-five cents. At the same time, in the Nueces Strip wages for chopping cotton had been cut from nearly $2.50 per day to $1.25. Some witnesses before the commission testified that illegal workers were also being employed as carpenters, painters, and bricklayers and in other construction occupations, further reducing opportunities for legal Mexican inhabitants. Illegal seasonal workers hurt union-organizing efforts, too. Several American Federation of Labor organizers recalled some of their successes in the 1930s among packinghouse workers in South Texas but now lamented that those efforts had come to a halt because the growers preferred to hire undocumented Mexican workers, whom they could control. Any illegal seasonal laborer would be summarily dismissed or turned over to INS agents if he or she even glanced at union organizers. "Organization of workers is impossible, individual bargaining is futile. There are only two choices: work for what the wetback works for and live as he lives, or leave the area."[7]

Mexican citizens and legal residents of Texas, mainly from San Antonio and points southward, faced with declining wages and little opportunity to challenge the growers, joined the migrant stream. When commission member Archbishop Lucey asked a grower who paid his field labor twenty-five cents per hour if he and other producers thought that constituted "a living wage," the grower responded, "I would say we do not." The conditions in the Nueces Strip, according to a LULAC official, had never been so bad as they were "this very day, this very month, this very year." As a result, in 1949 nearly 55,000 Mexican residents left South Texas to seek out-of-state seasonal employment. In Hidalgo County, 50 percent of the Mexican population looked for employment out of Texas that year, most of them seeking seasonal agricultural jobs. When the commission held its hearings during the summer of 1950, a witness testifying about Crystal City claimed that "at this present time six or seven hundred little homes [were] all boarded up," their inhabitants in the migrant stream until autumn. Many of the migrants answered the siren's call from the sugar beet companies to leave their homes: "This spring our radio stations blared forth a rosy picture for San Antonio's unemployed with the annual appeal for beet workers in the northern states."[8]

The commission's hearings in Fort Collins centered significantly on migrant workers and the sugar beet industry, since at least three of the sugar giants—Great Western, Holley, and American Crystal—had extensive operations in Colorado and the state was home to their corporate offices. All who testified in Fort Collins stated that the sugar beet industry relied overwhelmingly on Mexican migrant laborers from Texas. In Colorado alone they estimated that between 10,000 and 18,000 out-of-state migrants performed most of the seasonal agricultural work; of these at least 50 percent cultivated sugar beets. For the fifteen states covered by Great Western, Holley, and American Crystal, 47,000 Mexican workers toiled in the fields that summer, according to industry officials. The companies maintained that it was the higher wages paid by the sugar beet industry that drew these migrants to their fields. In 1950, when piece rates were adjusted to hourly wages, a betabelero earned about seventy cents per hour, much more that the twenty-five cents being paid to South Texas seasonal workers.[9]

Despite the relatively better pay, others testified that the sugar beet industry's reliance on Mexican migrants resulted in personal harm. Migrants often journeyed in unsafe vehicles, crowded into trucks with up to fifty passengers, which drove without respite for periods of seventy to eighty hours. Betabeleros increasingly attempted to winter in nearby urban areas, such as Denver, usually becoming burdens to social agencies, medical facilities, and public health offices. One former betabelero, who had become a social worker for Denver area schools, testified that, while economic opportunities were improving for the area's longtime Mexican citizenry, the new migrants to Denver were not enjoying the same benefits.[10]

Along with the sugar company spokesmen, growers, social workers, and union organizers, the commission members heard the testimony of two Mexican migrant workers in Fort Collins who described the nature of their lives and sugar beet work. The first, a World War II veteran with six children, performed seasonal agricultural labor near Laredo, Texas, between November and April. He then drove north with his family to work in the beet fields in late April or early May (before school ended). He also worked in the potato and sugar beet harvests. The quality of the housing provided for his family varied, he testified, ranging from poor to what he called "a good house." He stated that, after five months of migrant work in the sugar beet and potato fields, he usually arrived back in Texas with only two to three hundred dollars when all of his accounts and expenses had been settled. The other testimony came from a female Mexican migrant who operated three trucks with other family members, transporting about seventy-five betabeleros from South Texas to Holley's beet fields in Wyoming. After finishing field cultivation, the outfit migrated to Colorado to pick beans and then to the Texas Panhandle to harvest cotton. She claimed that housing in the beet fields was "pretty good" and that the pay was better than other seasonal work.[11]

Since migrant housing was a point of complaint among many witnesses before the commission, the sugar beet industry countered that the domiciles provided by their growers were improving. Industry officials admitted that through World War II migrant accommodations had deteriorated, a development they blamed primarily on wartime shortages in building materials. Since 1947, however, when home improvement supplies were once more available, growers had tried to upgrade migrant housing. According to one Colorado witness, "80% of the farms have adequate housing." When asked by the commission to elaborate, the head of a sugar beet growers association stated that 10 percent of housing was "excellent," meaning it had indoor plumbing, electricity, and "attractive living conditions." Another 50 percent was deemed "good," having electricity and running water but outside privies. The housing on 30 percent of growers' farms was "fair," though that meant only that the structure had "other facilities." Only 10 percent of the housing was "poor," the grower claimed, because those structures belonged to "shiftless farmers."[12]

In addition, during the hearings in Fort Collins the commission members were keenly interested in why the sugar beet industry required migrant workers. Sugar beet officials argued that sugar beet cultivation was labor intensive but was usually conducted in thinly populated regions, such as the Upper Midwest or Rocky Mountain states. One grower stated that there was "no [social] stigma attached to thinning beets," but others disagreed. A farm placement supervisor testified that "urban people" would not do field work of this nature, and a university farm labor specialist (whose father grew sugar beets) agreed with a statement by a commission member that "a white man didn't do" sugar beet field labor.[13]

When the commission concluded its public hearings and gathered all of its related materials, the report issued in 1951 was both eloquent and wide ranging in its recommendations. The opening paragraphs described the migrant condition:

> One million migratory farm laborers move restlessly over the land. They neither belong to the land nor does the land belong to them.... As crops ripen, farmers anxiously await their coming; as the harvest closes, the community with equal anxiety, awaits their going.... They are the children of misfortune.... We depend upon misfortune to build our force of migratory workers.

To remedy this unhappy situation, the commission offered several proposals. The border with Mexico must be secured, and the INS should employ more agents to apprehend illegal aliens. Certification of labor shortages requiring the importation of braceros should be removed from the jurisdiction of the U.S. Employment Service because that agency had an obvious conflict of interest simply in making sure that agriculture had ample labor available. Instead, the bracero arrangement with Mexico should be turned over to the INS, which was responsible for immigration into the United States and, equally important, had fewer ties with agribusinesses and growers. Moreover, the INS should have "statutory authority" to prosecute those transporting or employing illegal alien workers. The commission also proposed the creation of a Federal Committee on Migratory Labor "to coordinate all federal activities relating to migratory labor" and advocated that states relying significantly on migrant workers create their own committees to "complement" the federal body. In short, what the commission wanted to see was more government oversight of seasonal agricultural labor that was less influenced by the private sector.[14]

In the short run, the work of the Commission on Migratory Labor had little political success in improving the working and living conditions for betabeleros and other seasonal workers. The federal government did not follow the commission's recommendations to create a Federal Committee on Migratory Labor or to have the INS take over management of foreign temporary workers. Congress did not enact laws providing penalties for those who employed illegal immigrants. In addition, before the ink had barely dried on the commission's report, Congress enacted Public Law 78, which continued the bracero program despite Truman's threatened veto. Truman dropped his opposition to Public Law 78 when it became clear Congress would override his veto. The importation of braceros into the United States from Mexico went on for fourteen more years. These political failures reflected the power of agribusiness interests and rural representatives in the legislative halls in Washington, D.C., during the early 1950s.[15]

In the long run the appointment, investigative work, and final report by the Commission on Migratory Labor indicated a growing public concern about the condition of migrant workers. This interest was reflected in the growth of other, non–federal government migrant programs. The Home Missions Council, which supported the migrant programs in the Red River Valley, had expanded to provide services to migrant workers and their families in twenty-three other states by the early 1950s. Several states, such as Colorado, New Jersey, Michigan, and New York, had already established committees to monitor migrant labor conditions within their boundaries. Wisconsin did likewise, initiating inspection of migrant housing and labor camps in 1951.[16]

In South Texas and in the Red River Valley, state governments and other social organizations strove to better the lives of betabeleros and their families. In South Texas several groups worked to improve migrant living and working conditions, including the Border Project, the Bishop's Committee on the Spanish Speaking, and the San Antonio-based Committee to Aid Migrant Workers. Minnesota established a governor's advisory committee on migrant workers in 1953, and North Dakota's government created a similar body five years later. Like Wisconsin, Minnesota's legislature enacted a Migratory Labor Camp Code in 1951 that authorized the state's health department to inspect migrant housing, albeit with no enforcement power. In the valley the Clay County Christmas Seal Organization sponsored a mobile field unit in 1950 and 1951 to test migrants and their families for tuberculosis. Moreover, the migrant summer schools in Moorhead and Crookston continued to operate and expand their programs, and another such school in East Grand Forks began to offer migrant educational opportunities and social services in 1951.[17]

While no dramatic change in the migrants' conditions occurred immediately from the work of the President's Commission on Migratory Labor, the existence of these social service organizations and state programs began to offer some solace in the lives of migrant laborers and their families. As these efforts started to have greater results, they began to influence the relationship among betabeleros, growers, and American Crystal in the Red River Valley. This became more important as sugar beet production expanded in the region and growers needed ever more betabeleros. In short, the industry found that improving the lives of Mexican migrant workers helped lure more of these indispensable laborers to the valley.

THOUGH THE INCREASE WAS NOT AS DRAMATIC as that in World War II, the war in Korea, along with international aid programs such as the Marshall Plan, helped spur sugar production in the United States during the early 1950s. American Crystal and its Red River Valley growers benefited enormously from the upsurge in sugar consumption. The company contracted a total of 119,500 acres in 1949, with about 62,000 allotted to the Red River Valley. In 1950, however, contracted acres leaped to 170,000, with 76,000 for those in the valley. Contracted acreage declined slightly in 1951 and 1952, but in 1954 American Crystal entered into agreements with growers for almost 177,000 acres—over 90,000 acres of which went to Red River growers. Thus, within five years the company expanded its operation over 30 percent both nationally and locally.[18]

During this rapid expansion in production, American Crystal's valley operation gained more acreage than did its other districts. In the Missoula, Rocky Ford, and Clarksburg districts, because of their aging facilities, American Crystal actually reduced its contracted acres between 1949 and 1954. The other districts—Grand Island, Mason City, Chaska, Oxnard—registered only miniscule increases during the period. Hence, by 1954 the valley grew more than 50 percent of all of American Crystal's sugar beets. Moreover, the company added numerous new growers to its ranks. In 1949, American Crystal contracted with 780 growers in the region, but by 1954 there were over 1,100 growers. The amount of acreage growers received in their contracts rose sharply—from an average of around seventy-five acres to almost ninety acres per grower. Indeed, American Crystal did not have to pressure farmers in the valley to increase their production or to add their names to the company's roster as growers clamored to become sugar beet producers.[19]

More valley farmers wanted to become sugar beet producers in the early 1950s out of economic necessity. In general, farm income—throughout the nation—began to decline. World War II and its immediate aftermath had been good years for growers in the valley. In fact, 1947 represented the pinnacle of that era of agricultural prosperity. Farm income began a noticeable decline in 1949, however, and continued to sag throughout the 1950s. Several factors contributed to this phenomenon. Certainly, overproduction continued to plague the countryside as mechanization, technology, and science all helped to boost output. Between the conclusion of World War II and the end of the 1950s, a time when cultivated acres actually declined in the United States, farm production still rose about 20 percent. With farmland yields outstripping consumption, market and grocery store prices for these commodities dropped. Of course, falling prices meant less income for farmers; by 1955 the average farm family enjoyed an income of less than 50 percent of that earned by the rest of the population. Only through rising government subsidies were many farmers able to continue. Moreover, while income overall was at best stagnant, farm debt was increasing. Mechanization and technology made farming more costly, while land values were on the rise. Farmers wishing to expand their operations had to borrow more money to pay for those acres, and their property taxes increased. Thus, farmers found themselves caught between the need to expand their operations and employ the new technologies precisely at the time the price they received for their efforts declined. This imbalance created precarious conditions that brought economic hardship to many rural families during the 1950s. Many growers were simply forced out; one-third of all American farmers and their families left agriculture between 1945 and 1960.[20]

This downward spiral for growers was mirrored in the Red River Valley, especially among those who produced wheat, as most did. Wheat farmers had two main problems. First, per capita consumption of flour in the United States declined from 158 pounds at the end of World War II to less than 120 pounds fifteen years later as Americans favored more preprepared and processed foods, such as television dinners. Second, between 1945 and 1955 new strains of wheat rust appeared in the Midwest, requiring expensive fungicides, increasing wheat growers' costs still further. As elsewhere, land values climbed rapidly in the valley, more than doubling in the postwar decade, creating more debt and potential bankruptcy for growers attempting to expand their holdings. In North Dakota the total number of farms declined by more than 20 percent in the fifteen years after World War II.[21]

Consequently, sugar beets represented once again an attractive alternative crop in the early 1950s as the price of sugar increased, at least modestly, and demand rose. Between 1950 and 1954, the earnings from sugar beets ranged between $13.29 per ton of sugar to $13.81. With an average during those years of $13.55 per ton and yields of about eight hundred tons, a sugar beet grower grossed well over $10,000, or roughly the average rural per capita income in the region. As one sugar beet grower remembered this era, "The beet return per acre was superior to anything else."[22]

Hence, valley sugar beet growers, and those who wanted to be, saw sugar as a key to financial betterment and pushed to expand production, even to the point of encouraging other companies to set up operations in the region. American Crystal was amenable to expanding its Red River Valley operation and to that end announced two major projects in May 1952: the building of a large four-hundred-thousand-bag warehouse and construction of a new nine-million-dollar sugar-processing plant, both situated in Crookston, Minnesota. The Crookston facility was completed in time for the 1954 harvest and represented an important determinant in the growth of American Crystal's operation in the region during the early 1950s; however, local growers wanted an even greater opportunity to partake of sugar beets' earning potential. This was especially true of farmers in the far upper and lower ends of the valley. During the winter of 1952–53, American Crystal learned that growers in the valley's northern counties had approached Great Western about establishing a sugar plant in their area. The following summer Walter Ross, a beet grower for American Crystal near Fisher, and Hugh Trowbridge, president of the Red River Valley Sugarbeet Growers Association, enticed representatives of Holley Sugar Corporation to tour both the northern and southern extremities of the valley in order to assess potential for their company. Chamber of commerce leaders, Great Northern Railway officials, county agents, and others helped with the Holley promotional visit. Nothing substantial came from these efforts to lure American Crystal's competitors to the area. That the farmers were taking a more active role in promoting sugar beet production did signal to American Crystal, however, that it would need to continue to enlarge its operation in the valley or risk a competitor entering the region.[23]

In a related development, the communities in the valley acknowledged the importance of sugar beets to their economic well-being. This was certainly reflected in increased newspaper coverage of sugar beet developments. They reported on virtually any political or economic activity that might have an effect on the sugar industry. When J. B. Bingham died suddenly of a heart attack in 1950, it was front-page news for the region's newspapers. The announcement of the start of the yearly beet harvest also moved to the front page by 1954. Other manifestations abounded of the importance of sugar beets to the area. One of the most visible of these began in 1954. That year, Clay County held its inaugural Sugar Beet Festival. The two-day celebration included a downtown parade, a block party and dance, and a coronation ball in which a masked King Sugar Beet (also known as Rex Beta Vulgaris) crowned Miss Moorhead as that year's Sugar Beet Queen. The Sugar Beet Festival became an annual autumn event. Clearly, the sugar beet industry had gained significant status in the region. As it did so, however, the industry became ever more dependent on securing enough migrant workers each year to sustain this growth.[24]

AS SUGAR BEET ACREAGE EXPANDED IN THE EARLY 1950S, it was matched by a corresponding increase in the number of betabeleros needed in the valley. Consequently, the labor agency in Texas continued to play a pivotal role in securing field laborers. In 1949, M. C. Sullivan and his recruiters signed up 6,600 betabeleros, of which almost 4,800 were sent to the valley. From there, however, the number of migrants needed grew rapidly. By 1954, the labor agency contracted with over 9,600 migrant workers, dispatching 6,700 of those to the Red River area; the valley received almost 70 percent of all the workers recruited in Texas.[25]

Paradoxically, obtaining such a large number of migrant laborers became an ever more difficult proposition in the early 1950s as American Crystal and other agribusinesses scoured Texas for Mexican seasonal workers. On the one hand, there was a surplus of potential farm workers created from the waves of illegal immigrants crossing the Rio Grande from Mexico. The sugar companies may have recruited easily among those desperate workers. On the other hand, American Crystal and the other companies clearly were reluctant to recruit among the illegal population for a variety of reasons. First, the federal government, through the sugar act regulations, monitored betabeleros more closely than farm workers in other agricultural commodity production. The sugar companies were not anxious to draw more federal attention to their labor operations. Second, sugar beet field laborers needed to be experienced and dependable. True, illegal immigrants could be trained fairly quickly; however, insuring they were there when needed and gone when not presented more problems than the companies thought worthwhile. As noted previously, illegal Mexican immigrants were apprehended on occasion in the valley, so obviously some were hired. Nonetheless, American Crystal preferred to rely on legal residents, whom they could train and then depend on returning year after year.

In 1950, the Red River Valley district alone needed one thousand more field workers than they did the previous year because of the increase in acreage, and Sullivan reported that the competition for workers was "as keen as ever." Contracting migrant laborers that year was further complicated because another sugar company—the Utah-Idaho Sugar Company—entered the recruiting fray in South Texas for the first time. Because of such pressures, Sullivan found he had to begin recruiting earlier each season. For the 1951 season he established his operation in San Antonio the second week in January; for the following year's recruitment campaign he started staffing his office as early as November 1951. Moreover, Sullivan expended more funds to secure these workers. By 1951, the labor agency employed as many as twenty recruiters in Texas. In addition, most American Crystal recruiters now received three dollars for each worker placed under contract (up from $2.50 per worker), and the recruiter for the Dallas–Fort Worth region was paid fifty cents more than the others. Sullivan also had to increase the monetary advances to betabeleros for travel to their job locations in order to match competing sugar beet companies. These cash advances grew from about thirty dollars per worker in 1950 to almost thirty-seven dollars three years later. In all, the total operating costs for the labor agency climbed from $225,000 in 1951 to over $325,000 in 1954. The labor agency had to dispatch workers to the valley earlier, too, to counter the region's climate disadvantage. Otherwise, sugar beet companies operating in climates with an earlier growing season might secure the best betabeleros before the valley's sugar beet cultivation began. The labor agency sent several hundred Mexican migrants

to the valley as early as mid-April, about a month before they could re-
alistically begin cultivation. Sullivan asked growers to give these early
arrivals other employment until the fields were ready to be worked.[26]

Despite these efforts, Sullivan and his recruiters, a group he described as "reliable and dependable as can be found in the business
in Texas," came up short each year. Therefore, during the early 1950s
American Crystal, along with other sugar beet companies, often turned
to braceros. In 1951, the company contracted with 1,498 braceros and
sent 1,053 of them to the valley. The number dropped somewhat the
next year—1,174 total with 670 to the valley—before spiking upward
in 1953 to 1,637 braceros total and 924 to the Red River area. Most of
these traveled by air, flown into the region by the Flying Tiger Line in
large C-46 transport planes, at a cost of over $150 per worker. With
these difficulties and financial costs mushrooming, American Crystal
began to pressure growers to mechanize their operations in order to
reduce labor requirements, the expense of recruiting betabeleros, and
the costs to the growers themselves.[27]

Certainly, the growers' labor costs climbed noticeably in the early
1950s. The company still assessed each grower $2.50 per contracted
acre to help cover the costs of the labor agency operation in Texas. In
addition, as stipulated by the Sugar Act of 1948, the federal government continued to establish the minimum wages for sugar beet field
labor, and these rates increased. By 1954, if the sugar beet plants had
to be hand thinned and hoed twice (which was normal in the valley),
a betabelero received over twenty-one dollars per acre. If it was a wet
year, as it often was in some location in the valley, fields had to be hoed
a third time, which brought the betabelero's earnings up to nearly
twenty-five dollars per acre. Conversely, if the field had been mechanically blocked or cross-cultivated, the pay was significantly less—by as
much as one-half if it was mechanically thinned. Thus, relying on machines and requiring fewer Texas betabeleros could save a grower a
considerable sum of money.[28]

During the early 1950s American Crystal initiated a campaign to promote mechanization to reduce its own and its growers' labor expenses.
Since the initial outlay would be costly for growers, fieldmen found they
had to harangue farmers to convert to machines. American Crystal

hammered home the mechanization message in the quarterly publication mailed to its growers, *Crystal-ized Facts*, which the company launched in 1947. In articles such as "Sugar Beet Cultivation Is Changing," "A History Making Event," "Cross Blocking and Cross Cultivating as an Aid to Hand Labor," and "The Dawn of a New Era in Sugar Beet Production," the company repeatedly told its growers that labor recruitment and field labor costs were enormously expensive for all concerned but were unnecessary if they mechanized. Nonetheless, American Crystal had only limited success with mechanizing field cultivation during this time since the expense was simply more than many growers could bear in the difficult agricultural economy. In addition, those sugar beet growers who also produced potatoes continued to be fearful that reducing the numbers of workers for sugar beets might lead to labor shortfalls at potato harvest time. Consequently, the 15 percent of valley growers who used the new mechanical thinners in 1950 increased to only 23 percent by 1954.[29]

The company did have considerable success, however, in getting growers to mechanize the harvest, especially after near disaster in 1950. The year started with several major blizzards in the region, resulting in large snowfall accumulations. Consequently, the Red River and its tributaries flooded the valley with snowmelt throughout April. With fields inundated, growers had to delay planting, which meant that betabeleros being sent to the valley had little to do. Some growers created work to keep their migrant workers available, but many could not afford to do so, and their field workers in many instances moved on to look for other jobs. Growing conditions improved through the summer, and the sugar beet plants eventually matured well. The beet harvest began on schedule on September 18 but was slowed by a shortage of workers in the fields and at the company facilities, partly from enlistments and drafts associated with the Korean War and partly by those betabeleros who opted to return to Texas in order to enroll their children in school on time. Sullivan and other labor agency personnel roamed throughout Wisconsin, where many migrants harvested cherries in the late summer, and into the Texas Panhandle cotton fields trying to entice migrants to return to work the sugar beet harvest. Then on October 2, the region received an early snowfall, but more important, temperatures plummeted to highs of only twenty degrees Fahrenheit over the next five days. By the time the weather improved, many migrants had fled the region, and valley growers were short an estimated 1,500 harvest workers. Indeed, conditions became so dire that area high schools dismissed classes so students could at least help with the potato harvest. Most of them could not legally harvest beets, as the Sugar Act of 1948 had continued earlier limitations on youths participating in sugar beet work during school hours.[30]

While growers eventually harvested successfully all but a few acres of sugar beets, it had been a close call. Moreover, it had been expensive since, as American Crystal acknowledged, it had been able to keep those betabeleros it had only by offering them "special inducements"—higher wages. Thus, the migrant workers had clearly gained at least a temporary advantage over the company and its growers during the harvest. Beginning that winter the company launched a drive to persuade farmers to mechanize the harvest, especially in the Red River Valley. *Crystal-ized Facts* published article after article trumpeting the benefits of the mechanical harvesters. One article in particular addressed the cost factor of investing in a mechanical harvester and concluded that any grower with forty acres of beets—less than half of the average acreage in the valley—would realize a profit on the machine in the third year of its use. With area banks offering special equipment-loan rates, these efforts rapidly brought results. Whereas only 45 percent of growers used mechanical harvesters in 1950, over 75 percent did the following year. By the time the Korean War had ended, 96 percent of the valley's sugar beet crop was machine harvested. Thus, sugar beet growers virtually eliminated the need for Mexican migrants at harvest time, although those farmers producing potatoes still wanted Mexican migrant workers. The other growers limited their migrant harvest needs to only a few workers—those who owned trucks or drove the growers' vehicles—in order to help transport the beets from the fields to the processing plants. Moreover, the mechanical harvester slashed the time needed to bring in the crop from six weeks to less than four, allowing an additional margin of safety for the sugar beets if adverse weather conditions occurred. Consequently, a major component in the relationship among growers, American Crystal, and Mexican workers disappeared. Nonetheless, the valley's sugar industry still required a growing army of Mexican seasonal workers in the spring, and to keep those laborers returning year after year, American Crystal and its growers increasingly relied on forging a closer, paternalistic bond with the betabeleros.[31]

WHILE THE TRADITION OF PATRONISMO had been seriously undermined by the demise of the cattle industry in South Texas and its replacement with the more impersonal capitalistic agribusiness employer-employee relationship, paternalistic ties between bosses and the bossed in the Nueces Strip had not been totally eradicated. Indeed, numerous studies from the mid-1900s found patronismo still relatively common in South Texas, in both rural and urban settings. A study of a small South Texas town undertaken by anthropologist Octavio Ignacio Romano v found that the role of patrón was fulfilled by the owner of the local brick factory, which in the 1950s was that community's main source of employment. While the brick factory owner did not serve as a godfather to children, because he was a Protestant, he donated land for a Catholic church, a community baseball field, and festival grounds. He also provided free housing and utilities for workers, homes for aged former employees, and numerous other services associated with a patrón, including "small loans, assistance with alien registration, income tax, social security applications, and the like." In another South Texas town, social scientist Ozzie G. Simmons discovered that the patrón system was common in both rural agricultural and urban commercial settings. Employers provided free use of land, vehicles, financial loans, medical care, burial expenses, and other gestures of caring in return for their employees' "loyalty and obligation." Simmons further found that "if the employer subsequently acts in accord with the Mexican's expectations, that is, paternalistically, the latter's [employee's] obligation deepens." In addition, the worker was likely to remain in the job for a longer period of time when the employer acted like a patrón. Simmons also concluded that the larger the town or city, the less one found these paternalistic ties, and this form of social interaction was less prominent than in the pre-1930 patronismo structure. Researcher Douglas E. Foley (and others) estimated, however, that, as late as the early 1960s, 25 percent of Mexicans in South Texas were in patronismo relationships. Indeed, another researcher, Arthur J. Rubel, found in the community he studied—which he called Mexiquito—that among some Mexican workers the inability to forge a relationship with a patrón was a source of frustration to the employee. Considering Sullivan's knowledge of Mexican people and his ongoing relationships with his Mexican recruiters, some lasting more than a decade, that he would encourage American Crystal to promote a more familiar, paternalistic relationship between growers and betabeleros was not surprising.[32]

American Crystal's *Crystal-ized Facts* was a primary venue to encourage a more paternalistic tie between growers and Mexican migrant workers. In the late 1940s and early 1950s, the articles advised growers to spend more time in their fields getting to know their workers. The writers concluded that this would not only eliminate misunderstandings but also provide the grower with knowledge of the way betabeleros thought. Some migrants had been treated badly and defrauded—even by sugar beet growers, the magazine admitted. If growers spent more time with their field workers, there would be more trust and fewer problems. While in the field, *Crystal-ized Facts* recommended, the grower should refrain from berating workers if they were sloppy or lazy. Instead, migrants responded better to good-natured kidding. American Crystal further urged growers to have other work available for the betabeleros in case bad weather delayed sugar beet field labor. Growers were urged to make sure their migrants had credit available in local stores, and if the betabeleros did not have a car or truck, the grower should drive them to town at least once each week. As to monetary credit, the grower needed to monitor how much the migrant workers charged so as to insure they did not get too deep into debt. In the matter of financial responsibility, the grower should "determine whether [the betabelero] has reached an adult stage of maturity," the criteria of which, according to the publication, depended upon whether migrants spent money to provide clothes for their children or ornaments for their cars. If the latter, the grower should watch more closely how the betabeleros spent their wages.[33]

The company's magazine advised that maintaining a relationship with a proven betabelero during the winter further promoted the creation of a loyal worker. Growers should write letters to their workers over the winter and send them Christmas cards. The letters should deal with business matters, such as making sure the migrants had received their last paycheck, but should also include personal details. The growers were instructed to tell the Mexican migrant how things were going on the farm that winter and to inquire about the betabelero's family. Sullivan noted in one article that "the workers are proud of such letters, [it] proves that their employer is concerned about them." Sullivan reminded the growers of how difficult it was to recruit betabeleros, and therefore "a personal letter from you to your labor at their Texas home, is the best assurance we have of securing good labor."[34]

As the government and the public grew more attentive to migrant living conditions, American Crystal folded this concern into the matter of encouraging a paternalistic relationship between growers and betabeleros. What brings a migrant back to the sugar beet fields, *Crystal-ized Facts* asked. An important factor, the magazine answered, was good housing that was ready when the migrants and their families arrived. "In many cases, the labor comes non-stop from Texas and they are tired and cold when they arrive. They want to hear their house is ready." Therefore, in the early spring, growers should inspect their migrant housing and make any necessary repairs. In addition, growers should continually update the quality of the betabeleros' living quarters. The company reminded the growers that housing standards had changed over the years and that betabeleros expected more amenities, a fact that was "not often appreciated by growers." The houses should have screens on the windows and electricity, water, and gas installed. Growers might also think about including a refrigerator in the migrant's house, and a radio or an electric iron would be a nice touch. A *Crystal-ized Facts* article admonished growers to view betabeleros as "human beings like the rest of us."[35]

Whether inspired by *Crystal-ized Facts*, advised by American Crystal fieldmen, or discovered through their own experiences with Mexican migrant workers, many growers appeared to have developed a more personal, paternalistic relationship with the betabeleros and their families. Growers did establish credit for migrant workers in area stores and vouched for those advances. Of course, that meant growers took a paternalistic interest in how much their migrant families charged on the accounts. As one grower recalled, "Some of them [migrants] would get carried away. They'd be buying cigarettes and they'd go out and buy beer. So you had to watch. That was one thing you had to watch pretty close." Some growers loaned their migrant families money directly. To help with transportation to and from the fields, growers provided migrants with free gasoline for their automobiles and in many instances made down payments or cosigned loans for cars so workers could gain that mobility. One grower freely allowed his betabeleros to use his shop and tools to make repairs on their cars. If betabeleros did not have cars, growers often took them into town on their days off. In addition, some growers hired migrant women and teenage girls as domestic help during the summer, thereby augmenting the betabelero's family income. If migrant workers or their families required medical attention, growers sometimes made those arrangements. One grower remembered being awakened at two o'clock in the morning by a migrant worker whose wife had gone into labor. "We got her in the back seat of the car and she was back there groaning and moaning and every time she groaned I hit it a little harder. I swear, I was doing about 90 miles an hour by the time we got to St. Ansgar's [hospital in Moorhead]." At least one grower provided burial plots in the family cemetery for a longtime Mexican migrant laborer and his wife.[36]

Children often played a significant role in cementing paternalistic ties between growers and the Mexican migrant families who worked for them. Sometimes growers gave betabelero children small jobs on the farm, such as mowing the lawn, gathering eggs, or chopping weeds in the farmer's garden, which helped the migrant family's finances. In some cases migrant children spoke better English than their parents and served as communicators between the migrant family and the grower. Growers gave migrant children presents or food treats while they were in the valley, and a few growers were known to send Christmas presents to them in South Texas. One sugar beet grower's daughter noted that her father "would buy boxes of cracker jacks and things, and take it over for the children." The growers' and betabeleros' children often played together during the summer months, and in the process Anglo and Mexican families drew closer and created bonds that were maintained later when a grower's child became a sugar beet farmer. One betabelero came to regard the grower his family worked for as "more to me than a father." In later years that same grower financed the home they bought when that migrant family decided to remain in the valley. In another instance, a grower recalled that he "grew up with a family of migrants, and we [children] looked forward to their arrival every spring, and cried when they left, because I basically grew up with them. They were on our farm for sixteen or eighteen years."[37]

The growers who formed paternal ties with betabeleros and their families tended to improve their migrant housing. One family of growers admitted that early migrant housing on their land was poor, but later they moved their migrants into houses that previously had been the homes of neighbors who gave up on farming. These were later enlarged; plumbing was installed; and a laundry was put in for the migrant families' use. In essence, "we [the grower's family] got the houses fixed up better in the fifties." Another sugar beet grower bought a house in town and transported it out to his farm for the migrant family he employed; he later provided them with individual mobile homes. Others built small houses or remodeled others for their migrant families, with indoor plumbing and electricity, as *Crystal-ized Facts* advised.[38]

Growers who created or unconsciously formed a paternalistic relationship were likely to be more successful in securing a stable, loyal workforce. As a grower noted, "You acquire a mutual trust." One grower had three longtime Mexican migrant families that worked for him, including one that spanned two generations of betabeleros and another that returned to work for that grower annually for forty years. Another sugar beet grower employed two families for a long period of time—one for over thirty years. Sometimes betabeleros found themselves with a year-round job on a beet grower's farm because of the bonds created between them and the farmer. These long-term relationships allowed American Crystal Labor Agency to boast in the early 1950s that it had many betabeleros who had already worked each season continuously for fifteen years and that 80 percent of its Mexican migrant workforce returned to the valley from one year to the next.[39]

How much Mexican migrant workers appreciated this paternal tie was unclear. Most likely, any betabelero who could secure a better-paying job did so whenever the opportunity arose. The evidence suggests, however, that if the Mexican migrant workers thought they were being treated well, they reciprocated with their loyalty to that grower and usually benefited from the relationship. One betabelero remembered that his father worked first with a grower for two years and then three with another. Afterward, his father developed "a pretty good relation" with the next grower, for whom he worked for the following twenty-seven years. Furthermore, during his father's time with that grower, the farmer made significant improvements in his migrant housing. Indeed, this individual's seasonal sugar beet job evolved into year-round employment. Another betabelero's family worked for four growers over a thirty-year period, and one grower contracted with them for sixteen consecutive years. Yet another betabelero toiled in a grower's field for several years, did a hitch in the military, and then returned to work for that same farmer for several more years. In the autobiography of her migrant youth, Elva Treviño Hart related that her father received a loan for a car from a sugar beet grower in the valley when he promised to come back and work for that grower the following year, which her family did for several more seasons. Moreover, she spent those summers in the valley sometimes riding horses with the grower's daughter.[40]

As American Crystal and its valley growers came to understand their need for a steady source of seasonal labor, treatment of Mexican migrants gradually improved. While not an exact replica of the older form of South Texas patronismo, a quasi-paternal pattern emerged in many instances. Most growers had only two or three families working for them, perhaps eight to twelve people, a rather small number of individuals to come to know. Moreover, both grower and betabelero lived in a rural environment, and their interactions frequently continued after the working day was done. Of course, in every instance the relationships were not harmonious or even paternalistic. One grower admitted that there were farmers who "wouldn't let their kids play with the migrant [kids]." An American Crystal fieldman acknowledged that there were growers who "thought of a Mexican the same as early Southerners thought of a black man, you know, as trash." Another former fieldman recollected that interactions were "blemished by a few"; however, for many growers and betabeleros there existed "a warm friendship between them," and they more often than not regarded each other with "goodwill and respect." Though they certainly did not work in an idyllic environment, many Mexican migrant workers gained benefits and better living arrangements from the paternal relations that they had with the growers who employed them. This would not have occurred had not the betabeleros become indispensable to the sugar beet industry of the valley.[41]

BY THE MID-1950s several patterns were well established in the valley's sugar beet industry. First, sugar beets provided a stable, even growing, income for farmers—an important consideration for growers in an agricultural economy locked in a downward trend. Consequently, in a region where agriculture had long dominated, sugar beets were becoming more vital to the prosperity of the valley. Second, to American Crystal the region assumed an ever more prominent place in the company's profitability since about half of its sugar was processed along the Red River. In short, the company and its valley growers became more deeply wedded. Third, as the sugar beet operation expanded, it required more field workers. True, their dependency on betabeleros for the harvest had been cut, but each year they seemed to need more migrant help in the spring. And finally, the Mexican migrants benefited by improving wages and living conditions, albeit slowly, from this circumstance. In fact, more Mexican migrants came to appreciate that life in the valley could be better than life in South Texas. Each year more migrants remained in Moorhead, Crookston, or another valley town at the end of the season. As this pattern of growth continued—in sugar beets, in growers, in migrants, in a Mexican resident population—new manifestations of advantage and necessity emerged.

CHAPTER 5

Anxieties and Reassessments

BY THE MIDDLE OF THE 1950s, American Crystal, its growers in the Red River Valley, and the Mexican migrant workers upon whom they relied to cultivate the sugar beets had interacted with one another for about thirty years. The federal government had established considerable oversight in the manner in which these groups engaged with each other now for over twenty years. In addition, the company's labor agency in Texas had linked growers with migrant workers for over a dozen years. In short, the relationship among these groups that composed the valley's sugar industry had reached a period of maturity and familiarity in which certain rhythms and patterns directed them through each year.

Though the company, the Mexican migrants, and the growers had established norms of behavior by the mid-1950s, nothing remains the same forever, and in the latter half of the decade things began to shift. A fundamental change that became more pronounced during this era involved Mexican laborers dropping out of the migrant stream and settling in the valley. As this emerging resident Hispanic population grew and became more visible, other groups in the region, besides American Crystal and its growers, reacted with alarm to the newcomers' presence. Coupled with other anxieties, especially concern over crime and juvenile delinquency, political officials, civic organizations, and American Crystal launched an effort to replace betabeleros with local workers. Other groups continued the effort, however, to improve the working and living conditions for Mexican migrant workers. And finally, the nature of the sugar industry further evolved through mechanization and agricultural technology, while growers discovered they would need to expand their production capabilities if they were to survive in the rapidly changing agricultural environment of the 1950s.

FOR MEXICAN MIGRANT SUGAR BEET WORKERS in South Texas during the 1950s, the rhythm of their lives—dictated by their low economic circumstance—revolved around the seasons. The beginning of each year, January through March, found them at home performing whatever temporary work might be available. In the Lower Rio Grande Valley, there was a variety of seasonal jobs, mostly in winter vegetables, citrus, and cotton. The citrus industry had been hurt by several severe frosts during the early 1950s and was only beginning to rebound to its previous levels of output. The wages for picking the fruit and/or packing it in the shed, when adjusted from piece rates to hourly pay, ranged from thirty-five to fifty cents per hour. In addition, these poorly paid jobs usually did not provide continuous, regular employment. The Mexican agricultural workers might toil fourteen hours per day one week and then be idle throughout the next. If the migrants lived further up river, say, near Laredo, the largest number of winter jobs involved onions, tomatoes, cauliflower, and broccoli, which paid a wage scale similar to that in the lower Rio Grande area. Around Crystal City, which supplied more Red River Valley betabeleros than any other town in Texas besides San Antonio, most seasonal agricultural jobs involved field cultivation of spinach and onions for very low pay. Moreover, Crystal City's largest single employer—Del Monte—relied mostly on braceros to package its products, which forced even more residents to become migrant workers. Throughout the Nueces Strip, winter wages paid to Mexican agricultural workers averaged only about $500 per year, and the annual median income throughout South Texas for Mexican workers ranged between a low of about $1,600 in Laredo to $3,200 in Corpus Christi. No wonder then that many South Texas Mexicans were ready to hit the road to somewhere else by spring.[1]

Those Mexicans who had worked for American Crystal received their last paychecks from the preceding season in late December or early January. American Crystal typically disbursed earnings to betabeleros in three installments. The migrant workers were paid some money in the summer, another portion at the conclusion of their contract, and the remaining third after American Crystal evaluated the sugar beet crop and processed it into sugar, several months after the harvest. In addition, if migrant workers received a bonus—both American Crystal and many individual growers offered bonus incentive programs, usually for exceeding the number of acres allotted or for higher sugar content in the beets—those funds were included with their last check. Assuming a betabelero and his spouse were average workers and cultivated about thirty acres between them (individual averages, according to company records, ranged between thirteen and seventeen acres in the mid-1950s) at $23 per acre, the couple earned almost $700. That meant that their final payment would be around $230, plus any bonus. The final American Crystal paycheck, therefore, significantly augmented the meager earnings Mexican migrants received during the winter in Texas.[2]

The living conditions of betabeleros during those winters in South Texas were changing, however, in the mid-1950s. An important factor contributing to this development originated from the federal government's decision to finally address what they called the wetback problem. Starting first in California in June 1954, the INS, in cooperation with local law enforcement agencies, launched the ill-named Operation Wetback. During this two-year campaign, over 800,000 illegal Mexican workers were apprehended and returned to Mexico. In addition, the INS sent a strong signal to employers who hired illegal Mexican workers that their businesses would be disrupted by raids. While Operation Wetback also mistakenly arrested and deported some Mexican citizens and was further criticized by LULAC and GI Forum leaders for targeting Mexican labor union organizers, the campaign did noticeably curtail illegal immigration from Mexico throughout the remainder of the 1950s. For that reason some large agricultural employers in Texas, such as Del Monte in Crystal City, turned to braceros. In other instances, however, many Mexicans in South Texas found other employment opportunities, such as in the construction industry, opening to them as they were hired to replace the disappearing pool of illegal immigrants. Whereas in 1940 over one-third of all Mexicans in Texas were labeled as agricultural workers, by the end of the 1950s less than one-quarter were so categorized, although the general decline statewide in the agricultural sector accounted for some of that lower percentage.[3]

Betabeleros experienced other adjustments in the way they lived in South Texas. In Crystal City, for example, city officials applied for urban renewal funds in the mid-1950s and used some of that money to begin paving streets and improving sanitation in the Mexican portions of town. Ironically, some local Mexican businesses actually benefited by the braceros hired at Del Monte and other agribusinesses in South Texas. These Mexican proprietors were more willing than Anglo merchants to extend credit to braceros who shopped in their stores and to stock items that the braceros desired. The Mexican business owners advertised in Spanish and spoke the braceros' language, an important advantage over those Anglo store owners who might not. Consequently, in the communities with significant numbers of bracero workers, such as Crystal City, the Mexican part of town experienced some commercial prosperity from their presence. These commercial successes caused a ripple effect into other ventures, such as the opening of movie theaters that catered to Spanish-speaking audiences. Equally important, in some communities Mexican proprietors organized themselves into Mexican American chambers of commerce (MACC), which also lobbied on social issues such as the hiring of more Mexican public school teachers and encouraging Mexicans to run in local school board elections. The MACC in Crystal City fought to gain access to the public swimming pool for Mexican children. Even some betabeleros who operated small businesses on the side during the winter months found their circumstances changing for the better in such an economic climate. Throughout South Texas during the latter years of the 1950s, more Mexican residents became homeowners and bought appliances at Sears or Montgomery Ward. These national chain stores actively sought Mexican customers, even hiring local Mexican salesclerks to make their customers more at ease.[4]

Educational opportunities were also developing for the children of betabeleros. With increasing frequency, Mexican migrant workers kept their children in school between September and May. A study of Red River Valley betabeleros during the early 1950s found that about half of Mexican migrant workers remained in Texas until school let out in late May. Moreover, a new education law adopted in Texas during the decade changed the funding formula for public schools from one based on a school's total census to that of a school's "average daily attendance." Public school administrators now found it in their interest to encourage Mexican migrants to keep their children enrolled throughout as much of the school year as possible.[5]

As Mexican school attendance rose, the sons and daughters of betabeleros found more school activities opening to them. In Crystal City, for example, more Mexican youths played high school sports, became cheerleaders and band members, and participated in such school clubs as the Future Farmers of America. The principal of the Crystal City high school noted that, when he started in the 1930s, the school had 120 Anglo students and 1 Mexican student. When he retired in the mid-1950s, the high school still had about 120 Anglos but had grown to include over 300 Mexican youths. In 1954, the Pharr–San Juan–Alamo high school elected its first Mexican homecoming queen, and over 50 percent of the players on the varsity football team were Mexican. To be sure, many public schools instituted quota systems to keep Mexican youths from getting too much control over school activities or gaining more recognition than white children. For instance, in Crystal City teachers took over selection of cheerleaders and band majorettes, limiting the number of Mexican females in these very public positions. Nonetheless, as Mexican high school attendance grew in South Texas between 1950 and 1960, their graduation rate almost doubled. Thus, on many levels, betabeleros witnessed improvements in their families' lives during these years. Yet many Mexicans in South Texas were compelled to answer American Crystal's call for betabeleros each spring.[6]

If migrant workers had previously performed well as betabeleros in the valley, then American Crystal's labor agency and its recruiters wanted them back. The company and the grower had already sent letters and cards during the winter. In early March the labor agency usually began to approach them, either through the mail or by personal visits from recruiters, about signing a contract for the coming season. The vast majority of the recruiters employed by American Crystal were Mexican residents of South Texas who, according to M. C. Sullivan, either were previously troqueros or had been labor recruiters for other agribusinesses. Thus, these agents were individuals with some previously established connection to the migrant worker communities. Not much else is known of these recruiters, however, other than the fact that most worked for the labor agency for many years. Between 1943 and 1974, the labor agency hired a total of forty-four recruiters, all but three of whom were Mexicans. Twelve of these Mexican agents worked more than fifteen years for American Crystal, and 50 percent worked at least five continuous years. The majority of those who were employed by the labor agency fewer years lived in areas in Texas where American Crystal did not recruit annually, such as Bridgeport, Lubbock, and Wichita Falls. During the 1950s recruiters usually received three dollars per contracted worker, except in San Antonio; the two recruiters assigned there were paid hourly. In Crystal City the recruiters were paid only one-half the amount of the others—presumably because the town was comprised of mainly migrant workers and recruiting was therefore easier. In 1960, a recruiter could earn, for about four months' work, as much as $4,605 in Laredo and $4,356 in San Antonio to as little as $318 in Austin. In general the recruiters contracted with families, or at least a husband and wife. Gender among the Mexican field workers was relatively balanced. For example, in 1956 the labor agency contracted with 4,077 males and 3,183 females; in 1959 the breakdown was 3,539 betabeleros and 3,045 betabeleras.[7]

The contracts made between the labor agency and the betabeleros primarily stipulated the date by which the laborers should report for work, the grower for whom they would work, the wage scale (depending, for example, on the number of hoeings and whether the fields were machine thinned), and whether they were to work the harvest season (less a factor after mechanization). The labor agency also provided vehicle liability insurance and a food allowance—fifteen dollars per worker traveling from a point north of San Antonio and seventeen dollars for those from San Antonio and points southward. The company provided the same food allowance for the return trip home to betabeleros who had completely fulfilled their contract. In addition, betabeleros could receive monetary advances for automobile repairs and tires and for the annual Texas state vehicle inspection. Of course, these types of advances were monies that were later deducted from the migrants' checks. All together, liability insurance, food allowances, and monetary advances during the 1950s averaged around thirty-three dollars per migrant worker and represented a significant portion of the labor agency's costs. In a typical year in the mid-1950s, American Crystal spent about $350,000 on its Texas recruitment campaign.[8]

Though some migrants made the journey through the nation's heartland to the Red River Valley in late April, most betabeleros departed at the end of May. Two main national highways—U.S. 75 and U.S. 81—carried them north from South Texas. Both conduits in the 1950s were two-lane roads with few bypasses around towns and cities. Migrants crossed into Oklahoma on U.S. 81 just east of Wichita Falls; traveled through the red dirt region west of Oklahoma City to El Reno and Enid; navigated through the streets of Wichita and Salina, Kansas; traversed eastern Nebraska and South Dakota; and entered the Red River Valley on the North Dakota side. Those betabeleros taking U.S. 75 went through Dallas; up to Tulsa, Oklahoma; on to Topeka, Kansas, and Omaha, Nebraska; into southern Minnesota; and onward to the east side of the valley. Via either route, it was a 1,200- to 1,500-mile journey.

Migrants usually traveled to the valley as quickly as they could in order to save as much of their food allowance as possible. Those traveling by truck made the journey faster than those traveling by car or pickup truck because there were more people to share the driving and because the space in the back of the truck was frequently overcrowded. No one wanted to endure those conditions, which often included standing for prolonged periods, any longer than absolutely necessary. Elva Treviño Hart remembered that, on her first trip to the valley, her family traveled with another extended family in such a truck without stopping for anything other than refueling. They traversed the distance from South Texas to the valley in less than forty hours. The driving time for Mexican migrants bound for the Upper Midwest from Texas in the 1950s—whether by car or truck—typically averaged about thirty-five hours. That was true of one migrant family, as their son later recalled, who made the trip from South Texas to the Minnesota side of the valley in thirty to thirty-five hours each year. The family packed food with them and would "keep on going until we [ran] out of gas."

Another migrant remembered how he and his siblings rode in the camper on the back of the family's pickup truck while his father and mother took turns driving. "We would always just be sleeping or reading or fighting. And that's all we did. We [ride] in the back and our parents drive and eat and sleep." Betabeleros traveling in their own automobiles might move at a more leisurely pace, however, if they chose to do so. One betabelero related how his family came to the valley in their pickup truck, stopping at roadside parks along the way to eat and sleep. It took them almost a week to make the trip from South Texas.[9]

Migrant workers and their families increasingly made the journey in their own cars and pickup trucks, again because it gave them more flexibility and greater control over their lives. In fact, a manifestation of patronismo in the valley was growers' lending money or cosigning on notes for automobiles. Indeed, one betabelero's son went to work for a used car dealership in East Grand Forks during the 1950s, first as an interpreter between prospective migrant buyers and used car salesmen and later as a salesman himself. Mexican migrant customers had become a major portion of that dealership's business. In 1950, according to the labor agency's records, Sullivan and his recruiters dispatched 620 trucks and 551 cars and pickups belonging to migrant workers from South Texas; by 1959 only 218 trucks made the trip, compared with 1,010 cars or pickup trucks. The automobiles still must have been very crowded as 4,425 workers (those over fourteen years of age) traveled in that manner—almost 4.5 workers in each one, plus, most likely, some younger children, too.[10]

The labor agency offered other forms of support to the migrants during their journeys north. Sullivan and his recruiters provided route maps for those making the trip for the first time. If the labor agency knew of potential problems, such as a town noted as a speed trap or areas with lengthy road construction delays, betabeleros received that information before setting off. The migrants carried emergency contact phone numbers to use if they ran into trouble along the way. The company would wire money—again, as an advance—to betabeleros stranded somewhere by mechanical problems or illness.[11]

Once in the valley, and depending upon the weather conditions, the betabeleros spent most of the next six to eight weeks cultivating the sugar beet plants. Segmented seeds, machine thinners, and cross-cultivators made the task less taxing than in previous decades. The short-handled hoe had all but disappeared from the valley's sugar beet fields by the mid-1950s. Two former betabeleros' fathers had used the short-handled hoes, but by the time the sons started working in the late 1950s, they used only the long handle. Elva Treviño Hart's parents in 1953 "worked standing up, touching only the hoe." The days of crawling from beet plant to beet plant were generally over.[12]

The federal government–mandated wages were adjusted downward, however, for fields mechanically thinned or cross-cultivated, because the hours required to cultivate such fields were fewer. Since these fields required no finger thinning, betabeleros were paid only for hoeing: $12.50 per acre for two hoeings compared with $23.00 per acre if finger thinned and hoed twice. Of course, workers could cultivate more acres if the fields were machine thinned, which actually more than offset the lower piece rate. American Crystal calculated that a betabelero could handle twenty acres if the fields had been mechanically thinned, but each worker could cultivate only ten acres if the field had not been prepared mechanically. Thus, a betabelero made a little bit more money and had an easier time with the machine-thinned acres. As this became more obvious to betabeleros, they actively preferred growers who mechanically thinned fields and sometimes refused to work for growers who did not. The company later used this trend as leverage to encourage growers to purchase mechanical thinners. By 1959, most of the growers used mechanical thinners or cross-cultivators in the valley's sugar beet fields.[13]

The betabeleros and their families toiled long hours in often difficult conditions during the six to eight weeks they were in the valley. Usually, they started early—around 6:00 AM—took occasional water breaks, ate lunch and rested a short time, and then continued to work until about 6:00 PM. A betabelera recalled that "[my] dad would wake us up at five in the morning to be there at the field by six. That was the worst part, waking up in the morning, helping my mother do tortillas, do tacos for the morning, and then sandwiches or something for the afternoon eat." Although laborers were less likely to work stooped over, field working conditions remained unpleasant. The valley's weather could fluctuate drastically from day to day; it might be cold with a snow shower one day but sunny and over ninety degrees the next. Worse, the valley's wet landscape was (and remains) one of the best breeding grounds for mosquitoes in the United States, and these insects tormented those working outdoors. Some Mexican migrants found the weather more pleasant, however, than the very hot, humid conditions that prevailed in South Texas during the summer. For the betabeleros, evenings were mainly a time to visit with fellow workers and to rest. Most Mexican migrants worked only a partial day on Saturday and took Sundays off. By the 1950s the Crookston Catholic diocese offered a Spanish-language mass on Sundays. Also on the weekends, betabeleros and their families enjoyed some recreational opportunities, usually in the form of dances and festivals sponsored by valley churches, social service organizations, and in the Fargo-Moorhead area by the Latin Club, a community organization founded in the 1950s by Mexican residents. At least one valley radio station, KROX in Crookston, offered a daily Spanish-language broadcast early in the mornings and played the Mexican music popular among the betabeleros from South Texas.[14]

In mid-July most betabeleros departed the valley for other seasonal work. For a large number of them, the next job had been arranged prior to leaving the region through a process that came to be referred to as the Annual Plan. The Annual Plan was an effort by the U.S. Employment Service (USES), the Farm Placement Service, state employment agencies, and agribusinesses to bring some order in the utilization of migrant labor. The system began to evolve during the chaotic labor situation immediately after World War II but did not become very effective until the early 1950s. Representatives from states relying heavily on migrant labor, USES and Farm Placement Service personnel, and agribusiness officials would hold a conference during the winter to estimate each state's agricultural labor needs for the coming year and develop plans to manipulate the migrant stream so that a sufficient number of workers would be available where and when they were needed.[15]

Within this broad plan smaller groups attempted to coordinate their needs. In the case of the valley's betabeleros, American Crystal, Great Western Sugar Company, Holley Sugar Company, regional potato growers, Minnesota canning companies, and other parties formed the Joint Labor Committee. This group met during the early spring to decide how to implement the national Annual Plan. One early example of this involved American Crystal and the Fairmont Canning Company of Minnesota recruiting together in South Texas during the early 1950s (Sullivan had once recruited for Fairmont Canning before being hired by American Crystal). They would sign up betabeleros and then offer them additional contracts to work in the cannery after they fulfilled the terms of their sugar beet agreements. Thus, a Mexican migrant family left Texas knowing they had at least two seasonal jobs: in the valley sugar beet fields until mid-July and then to southern Minnesota to work at the Fairmont cannery for four to five weeks. During the early 1950s when migrant laborers were needed for the sugar beet harvest, they could proceed from Fairmont back to the valley. The cannery hired only a few hundred workers, so the Annual Plan helped just a small group of betabeleros in this arrangement.[16]

By the mid-1950s, however, the Annual Plan had become more extensive and better coordinated, especially on the Minnesota side of the valley. The Governor's Committee on Migratory Labor and other migrant social service agencies attempted to offer migrant workers a steadier employment environment through what they called the Farm Placement Program. The Farm Placement Program staff contacted Mexican migrants when these workers arrived in Minnesota to toil in the sugar beet fields in order to contract them to other jobs once sugar beet cultivation was completed. In fact, sometimes they contracted them for their next two jobs. In 1957, for example, 5,449 betabeleros in the valley and at Chaska—more than 50 percent of those working in Minnesota—contracted for other jobs while still cultivating sugar beets. The majority received seasonal jobs in either Minnesota (e.g., detasseling corn, harvesting green beans, canning) or Wisconsin (mainly harvesting cherries and cucumbers). Others went to seasonal jobs in Illinois, Michigan, or other Midwest states. Over 250 betabeleros that year contracted to work the cotton harvest in the Texas Panhandle while they were in Minnesota. Though this arrangement obviously benefited growers and agribusinesses, the Annual Plan and Minnesota's Farm Placement Program—in which North Dakota participated by the end of the decade—provided thousands of Mexican migrant workers with more continuous employment opportunities than had previously existed for them.[17]

Once the Mexican migrants finished harvesting cucumbers or canning corn, as noted earlier, those with school-age children returned to their homes in South Texas by Labor Day with increasing frequency. Others might journey back to the valley to harvest potatoes or hire

Sites of American Crystal and betabelero interactions in Texas, 1920s–1970s

themselves out as truck drivers for the sugar beet harvest before jour-
neying south to Texas. There they would seek the seasonal jobs that
they hoped would carry them through the winter until American Crystal called for them again. A few more opted to remain in the valley
each year, however, and forgo the return trek to Texas. This emerging Mexican community came to be associated with other anxieties
plaguing the region. Along the Red River the communities' response
to this fear helped spawn an effort to wean the sugar beet industry
from its need for betabeleros.

LIKE THE REST OF THE UNITED STATES, the Red River Valley's
inhabitants experienced their share of the anxiety often associated
with American society in the 1950s. The American public worried
about the spread of communism, both at home and abroad; they
feared the potential destruction of humanity by nuclear weapons; they
fretted over social issues such as civil rights, women working outside
the home, juvenile delinquency, and organized crime. A casual examination of the valley's main newspaper finds all of these concerns
prominently reported, from the lynching of Emmett Till in Mississippi in 1955 to growing alarm over events in Vietnam and Cuba at the
end of the decade. Although avoiding the appearance of overt racism
toward Mexican migrant workers, the region's media headlined any
violent crime associated with betabeleros and their families. Likewise,
the newspapers applauded approved teenage behavior but missed no
opportunity to inform their audience about juvenile crime locally and
nationally. In response to these local social fears in the mid-1950s,
public officials, civic groups, businesses, and others in the valley began
to address these issues. The plan they ultimately developed involved
replacing migrant workers in the sugar beet fields with local teenagers.
They reasoned that this would halt the area's growing Mexican settlement, while local youth would be deterred from delinquent behavior
through hard work.[18]

The Mexican population in the valley expanded at a greater rate
during the 1950s as many betabeleros decided to stay after the migrant
work season ended. Improved social services in the valley for migrants,
educational opportunities for their children, and a desire to escape

discrimination and institutional Jim Crow in South Texas encouraged more betabeleros to settle permanently in the region. Moreover, where some Mexicans stayed and formed communities, chain migration began. One former betabelero who remained in Crookston after the 1953 sugar beet season remembered that his decision was made easier because his wife's family earlier chose to reside there. Later, when he had trouble getting a permanent job, he and his wife moved to Grand Forks, where other Mexicans resided, and he was hired to fill cylinders at a gas factory. The 1960 Fargo-Moorhead city directory contained thirty-five Spanish-surnamed domiciles, up from only eight in 1950. Furthermore, city directories often underreported the Mexican population. Many Mexican seasonal field laborers resided in rural areas at the time when the information for the directories was compiled, and those betabeleros who obtained year-round work with housing on a grower's farm likewise were not counted. The 1960 U.S. census clearly supported the notion of an expanding Mexican population when it tabulated 230 inhabitants whose country of origin was Mexico in the counties on the North Dakota side of the valley and another 52 on the Minnesota side. Factoring in a significant number of Mexican residents who were born in the United States and not counted separately by census takers, the total number of Mexican residents in the valley had become much more substantial during the 1950s. Their rapidly growing numbers made them much more visible throughout the region.[19]

One aspect of an increasing focus on the Mexican presence in the valley revolved around social services. The Truman Commission on Migratory Labor, the Minnesota Governor's Interracial Commission, and the growing civil rights movement among African Americans caused more public examination of migrant housing conditions, migrant health issues, education for migrant children, and other related migrant social problems. On the one hand, the valley community took pride in the various summer school programs offered to migrant children. The local newspapers often carried human interest stories about the children and the people who taught them. On the other hand, many valley inhabitants, especially sugar beet and potato growers, resented this public scrutiny and the expense they associated with improving migrant housing and sanitation facilities. As one American Crystal official complained for his growers, "We don't need clubs over the heads of growers to make them comply with [housing] regulations."[20]

An apparent spike in violent crime associated with migrant workers in the mid-1950s produced further unease toward Mexicans in valley communities. In this regard, 1955 seems to have been a watershed year. In early May, a "22 year-old Grand Forks [North Dakota] Negro and a 30-year-old transient" were arrested in Fargo for the beating death of another transient after "a drinking party" at an apartment rented to one Pedro Flores and his brother. A photo of the Floreses' apartment on the newspaper's front page showed a run-down, trash-strewn residence. In June, police arrested Jesus S. Robledo, a betabelero who had been working on a farm near Hillsboro, North Dakota, for beating and attempting to rob a woman in Moorhead.[21]

Only three weeks later, a more sensational—and to valley residents more threatening—incident took place when police arrested "five migratory farm laborers" and charged them with assault, robbery, and rape. This event drew considerable attention from the local news media for several weeks. According to the Fargo-Moorhead newspaper, the five Mexican migrant workers (ages sixteen to twenty-six) approached two local teenage couples parked in a car one night, beat one of the males, held a knife on another, sexually assaulted both girls (ages seventeen and fifteen) in a nearby cornfield, and then robbed the two couples. The newspaper published an extensive, lurid description of the crime scene, including how the girls' clothing and shoes were scattered in the muddy field. Eventually, the three adult migrants received prison sentences for these crimes, while the two juveniles were sent to the facility of the Minnesota Youth Conservation Commission. Nonetheless, parents of teenagers in the valley were probably frightened by the crime.[22]

In October, "a street battle" among Mexican migrant workers in Grand Forks resulted in the shooting death of one migrant, a bullet wound to another, and one being stabbed with a knife. The "fracas" occurred at a harvest dance attended by about "350 migratory workers . . . one of a series [of dances] held during the summer [for betabeleros and their families]." The front-page article accompanying this story included photos of disheveled, bloodstained Mexican youths and captions naming all of the participants, including those who were minors (something rarely done with local white youths).[23]

The valley's concern about violence and Mexicans was inflamed further by articles carried in the local newspaper about a so-called terrorist society called Pachucos, composed of Mexican servicemen, being investigated by the U.S. armed forces in the 1950s. Pachucos had first appeared among Mexican youths in border communities during the 1930s. Noted for a rebellious stance toward "the world of their parents and that of the American mainstream," Pachucos had been linked to the Zoot Suit Riots during World War II. Now in the mid-1950s they again caught the attention of the nation's media, and the valley's newspapers tagged along. The Fargo-Moorhead newspaper in an editorial worried "whether it [Pachuco society] has spread elsewhere."[24]

Even a tragic accident in 1955 seemed to point to a proclivity for violence among Mexican migrant families. In mid-July Paul Martinez, a Mexican migrant worker's eight-year-old son, shot and killed the eight-year-old son of a Clay County, Minnesota, farmer. The betabelero's child, who spoke no English, told authorities through an interpreter that he fired his father's rifle at two boys with a large dog who approached his siblings and him while his parents worked in a field of sugar beets about a half mile away from their temporary house. The young Martinez had been allowed to fire his father's weapon the previous day "as a reward for doing chores around the house." Police charged the father with second-degree manslaughter for keeping a loaded gun within reach of his son and for failure to provide adequate supervision for his children. The judge hearing the case had the boy taken from his parents and placed in a nearby Catholic boarding home while delinquency charges were being considered against him as well. Eventually, authorities dropped all charges against the father and son, partly on the request of the victim's father, who believed the legal proceedings only compounded the tragedy, and the Martinez family soon departed the valley for their home in Texas. The fact remained, however, that a region which rarely had more than a half-dozen murders per year witnessed in a single year three deaths involving Mexican migrant workers, plus the other violent crimes. To many valley inhabitants, Mexicans and mayhem went hand in hand.[25]

Just how far this concern for Mexican violence extended outside of the valley's urban environment is unclear. Among sugar beet growers, long familiar with betabeleros and their families, there appears to have been little reason to fear Mexican people. Of the growers interviewed for the Red River Valley Sugar Beet Oral History Project, none could recall any significant criminal or violent episodes with their migrant families. One grower who employed Mexican sugar beet workers for thirty years could not remember anything more dire than some alcohol-related fights, but nothing serious: "I never did have one of my crew end up in jail." An American Crystal fieldman queried about migrant violence and crime avowed that it occurred "very seldom." American Crystal did, though, provide local law enforcement agencies in the valley with betabeleros vehicle license plate numbers when they arrived in the region, information that was used by at least one county sheriff to call on migrant workers when they appeared in his jurisdiction and order them to turn in any weapons they possessed. Most likely, American Crystal found itself caught between community fears and its own need for field labor and attempted to placate local authorities.[26]

Like other areas in the United States, the valley region succumbed to the worry about teenagers and their delinquency that proliferated in the 1950s and 1960s. Concern about juvenile behavior was cyclical in post–World War II America, and public apprehension spiked between 1954 and 1956 and again in 1962 and 1963. The initial period, what historian James Gilbert in *A Cycle of Outrage* (1986) called "The Great Fear," grew out of an apparent teenage crime wave, the emergence of rock and roll, and Hollywood's portrayal of youth out of control in such movies as *The Wild One* and *The Blackboard Jungle*. Indeed, over sixty Hollywood films in the 1950s focused to some degree on juvenile delinquency. That teenager violence and deviant activity was increasing from previous levels received further credence from actions by government agencies and public officials, especially the U.S. Justice Department and J. Edgar Hoover's Federal Bureau of Investigation. By 1961, a President's Committee on Juvenile Delinquency

and Youth Crime existed, and Congress enacted the Juvenile Delinquency and Youth Offenses Control Act. Indeed, John F. Kennedy's
much-heralded physical fitness programs were partly motivated by
concern about inappropriate youth behavior.[27]

While the American people discussed a variety of causes and solutions to this so-called crisis, public opinion polls consistently ranked
lack of control and supervision, idleness, too much leisure time, and
teenage unemployment as significant factors in the deterioration of
youth behavior. To be sure, these polls usually rated the breakdown
within the home of parental control as the number one problem, but
if parents were unable to keep their children out of trouble, then other
methods were deemed necessary. Some communities, such as Buffalo,
New York, attempted to find local solutions to promote teenage social
control through programs such as *Hi-Teen* (a radio music program)
and Dress Right (a school-mandated dress code). Another resolution
prescribed by some sociologists involved finding employment for
these young adults. They argued that working addressed many of the
causes presumed to explain the increase in delinquency: control and
supervision, excessive leisure time, and, another factor often cited in
poor youth behavior, low self-esteem. Community leaders in the valley eventually tried all of these measures to deal with juvenile delinquency during the 1950s.[28]

It certainly appeared—at least from the local media—that valley
youth were prone to criminal and delinquent acts, although apparently
not of the violent type. The Fargo-Moorhead newspaper routinely
reported youths arrested for theft or burglary. For example, the newspaper published an account of a group of boys in Barnesville, Minnesota, a rural community southeast of Moorhead, whom authorities
placed in a juvenile home for running a rod club, an extortion ring in
which kids paid the club members small sums of money to escape
being beaten up or having their bicycles vandalized. These same youths,
ages twelve to seventeen, broke into service stations and stores to steal
cash and cigarettes. In another case, police charged nine Fargo boys
in a series of car prowls (breaking into automobiles) and burglaries of
small businesses. While these episodes may seem somewhat benign by
today's standards, valley community leaders reacted with alarm.[29]

Numerous measures to address this juvenile misbehavior were undertaken. Mayors from Fargo, Moorhead, and other communities in Cass and Clay counties convened to discuss the issue. Mayor Herschel Lashkowitz of Fargo told his fellow mayors that, while juvenile delinquency might not be severe in their communities, finding brass knuckles among area youths indicated to him that a problem existed. Many area communities adopted curfews aimed at teenagers. Fargo Central High School—mimicking the Buffalo, New York, program—adopted a behavior code that intended to reduce "drinking among teen-agers, non-chaperoned parties, late hours, careless motoring, and so on." The North Dakota Welfare Department launched a study of juvenile crime in fifteen rural counties (three in the valley). The results, published under the ominous title of "Imperiled Youth," reported that the number of delinquents was proportionally less than in urban areas but significant enough to "explode some previous 'sacred cow' idea" that rural communities were immune from the problem.[30]

That putting young people to work might be part of the solution to juvenile delinquency seemed obvious to local authorities. Noting that inappropriate behavior stemmed from the "misfits of society," the Fargo-Moorhead newspaper informed its readers that "juvenile jobs are the answer" and that school dropouts, cited as primary instigators of youth crime, "could gain self-respect through a job." Unfortunately, the teenage job market in the region was very poor during the latter part of the 1950s. Therefore, putting youths to work in the valley's sugar beet fields seemed a good solution; it would decrease the number of Mexican migrants being drawn to the region and curtail juvenile delinquency. To American Crystal officials such a plan offered an immediate additional benefit: the elimination of their need for the more expensive bracero workers.[31]

State officials and those involved in the valley's sugar beet industry exuded confidence that such a program would succeed. For one thing, sugar growers had just eliminated migrant workers from the harvest in a very short time. By 1955, the sugar beet harvest in the valley achieved a 97 percent mechanized rating. Encouraged by this success, growers and industry officials waxed confident that new beet seed drills, mechanical thinners and cultivators, improved seed varieties, and chemical herbicides would soon further slash field labor needs. As the North Dakota State Employment Service trumpeted in 1960, the "need for large numbers of migrant workers . . . is expected to become a thing of the past."[32]

In 1956, American Crystal, sugar beet growers, state employment officials, and other interested parties initiated the first effort to procure youth for field labor. That year followed the spike in violence associated with Mexican migrants in the valley and was at the peak of the first nationwide crisis over juvenile delinquency, although poor weather conditions likely contributed to their decision, as well. The spring of 1956 was particularly wet, and field work was significantly delayed. Some Mexican migrant workers left the area to seek work elsewhere, eventually resulting in a labor shortage. Thus, American Crystal again had to fly in about seventy braceros to work in the valley at a considerable expense. On the North Dakota side of the river, American Crystal and state employment officials urged the recruitment of "commuter youth groups." Arguing that sugar beet field work "no longer need to be stoop-labor jobs," they declared that there existed no reason why local youth could not perform the tasks. About 170 locals worked on the North Dakota side that year, although how many of those were teenagers is impossible to ascertain because the term "local" was previously used by American Crystal officials to describe resident white adults, resident Mexican betabeleros, and Native American field labor crews.[33]

North Dakota state officials emphasized recruitment of youth beet workers the following year, but the implementation of that drive was poorly organized. About 800 "locals" worked in the fields that year, of which at least 110 were Native Americans. In the Grand Forks–Grafton region, 85 teenagers worked the whole season, "although the number starting out was considerably higher." In Fargo, 20 teenagers signed up to work, but when rain delayed the first thinning and hoeing, these youths never made it into the fields. The growers to which the teenagers had been assigned did not wish to rely on unproven workers when their crops were already late.[34]

According to state employment officials, one of the major problems obtaining youth workers centered on the method of payment for sugar beet field work. Federal officials determined the acreage piece rate for sugar beet workers, as stipulated by the federal sugar act currently in force. Of course, this would have meant low wages for inexperienced workers, laborers unable to thin beets and hoe weeds rapidly. In 1957, according to North Dakota statistics, the pay for all locals employed in the sugar beet fields ranged between $0.75 and $1.25 per hour when converted from the piece rate. One can assume that betabeleros and other experienced locals achieved the higher range; the unskilled teenagers probably garnered less than $1.00 per hour for very hard work.[35]

Over the next three years, the effort to recruit youth workers received more attention, and growers, state officials, and community leaders became more optimistic about their potential. In 1958, North Dakota hired an individual to coordinate youth recruitment for areas near Fargo, Grand Forks, and Grafton. The following year, that became a regular staff position in the state's farm labor supervisor's office, with duties to oversee youth recruitment on the entire North Dakota side of the valley. North Dakota also hired two additional seasonal employees to assist further with the program. That same year, the Minnesota Farm Placement Service in its annual report first published data on local youth working in sugar beet fields in the Red River Valley.[36]

Local organizations helped, too. In 1958, the Fargo-Moorhead newspaper ran a lengthy Sunday-edition piece devoted to youth beet workers. Referring to the program as the "Youth Job Club," the story centered on a crew of twenty teenagers, ages fourteen (the minimum age for agricultural workers) to eighteen, supervised by "Mrs. Betty Rodriguez of West Fargo," working on a farm in Cass County. The club served several functions, according to the newspaper, including employment for local teenagers, reducing the number of out-of-state workers, and "keeping more money in the state." The article quoted an industry official as stating that the quality of the kids' work was "excellent," although they performed "a little slower" than Mexican migrant laborers. The accompanying photos showed the youths working with hoes in an upright position and one fourteen-year-old who had just completed an acre earning the "$18 in the pockets of his dust-saturated jeans." The newspaper reporter predicted that the boy would "be back in the fields next year." Interestingly, the news item went on to report that the teenagers could not sharpen their own hoes but

came to Mrs. Rodriguez, likely an experienced betabelera, for that part
of the job. In a follow-up letter to the editor, the superintendent of the
Children's Village in Fargo wrote of his appreciation for the opportunity beet field work provided for his charges. Eleven orphaned or
abandoned youths from that agency learned from beet work "that
physical labor is satisfying, that money can be earned and saved, and
that work is not a dirty word." Besides the newspaper and Children's
Village endorsements, the drive to hire youth beet workers in Fargo
was sponsored by the local chapter of the Sertoma Club, which continued to support the youth beet campaign well into the 1960s.[37]

By the end of the 1950s, the plan to substitute teenagers for betabeleros had yielded mixed results. True, more youths cultivated a
greater number of sugar beet acres by 1960. That year about eight
hundred local teens took care of over three thousand acres. State government reports were optimistic that the "need for large numbers of
migrants in thinning and hoeing [was] expected to become a thing
of the past." Creating a capable workforce proved difficult, however,
partly because the youths were expected to work only a few years any-
way, but also because getting the teenagers to complete even one season was a challenge. For example, in 1958, 471 youths were recruited
on the North Dakota side, but at any one time, fewer than 300 worked.
Officials acknowledged that year that "a relatively small percentage
continued through the season." The following year the turnover rate
was at least 30 percent, and in 1960, nearly 45 percent. While inclement
weather, family vacations, and other employment opportunities received most of the blame for the teenagers' quitting early, certainly
wages must have been a factor. According to North Dakota state reports, for very hard work the youths were paid an average of about
eighty cents per hour (adjusted from piece rates), less than the minimum wage for nonagricultural workers in 1960.[38]

Nonetheless, the attempt to use local teenagers in the beet fields
continued, primarily for three reasons. First, communities along the
Red River remained concerned about juvenile delinquency well into
the 1960s. Second, by 1960, government oversight of migrants' working and living conditions had become more vigilant. On both sides of
the river, state governments had created at least voluntary housing
standards, a harbinger of closer state supervision in the future. In

Minnesota, inspections of migrant housing became more frequent in the latter part of the decade, and North Dakota officials launched migrant housing inspections in 1959. In addition, in 1960 both states began to examine migrant health issues. Consequently, some growers, resentful of government regulations or not willing to invest in the better migrant living standards, viewed youth labor as a way to avoid what they saw as government interference. And third, while the numbers of betabeleros coming to the valley remained relatively high, employing local teenagers allowed American Crystal to cease importing braceros. Although the company continued to use braceros in some of its sugar beet districts, by 1959 it no longer required braceros in the valley. The recruitment of teenage labor and the elimination of braceros were, however, only some of the changes occurring with sugar beet growers during the latter years of the 1950s. Indeed, sugar beet growers continued to adapt themselves to the changing nature of agricultural production.[39]

IN THE LATE 1950s an important development for all growers—including sugar beet producers—throughout the Red River Valley involved their search for profitable crops. Since farm earnings in general continued their downward trend throughout the decade, especially from wheat, regional growers looked to other products. In North Dakota, wheat acreage declined by more than 25 percent between 1950 and 1960; Minnesota's wheat production suffered a similar decline. These changes were mirrored in the valley, where overall barley acreage edged out wheat by the latter part of the decade. Traditional crops such as oats and corn held relatively steady in the region, especially the latter, since over 50 percent of valley farmers maintained cattle, primarily dairy cows. More salient was the increase in acreage of crops with greater cash value. Potatoes, whose price slumped in the late 1940s, rebounded in the 1950s with the popularity of chips and french fries. Thus, potato acreage climbed about 15 percent by the end of the 1950s in the northern valley counties. In the southern counties growers turned to cultivating soybeans, and production of that crop soared because an acre of soybeans earned almost ten dollars more than an acre of wheat. Soybean acreage more than quadrupled in the valley between 1950 and 1960. In Cass County alone during the 1950s, soybean acres expanded more than 500 percent. An important factor influencing the surge in soybean cultivation in the area was that the federal government placed no restrictions on its production, unlike sugar beets. Hence, growers readily planted soybeans and other more profitable crops in the counties where they could.[40]

After years of often incredible growth, sugar beet production in the valley nearly stagnated during the latter half of the decade. Growth mainly slowed because the nation's sugar supply began to reach a saturation point. Therefore, amid howls of protest by sugar beet and sugar cane growers throughout the country, the federal government in 1955 suddenly cut the production quotas by 11 percent. The price growers received per ton remained stable, thanks to the government's support payments, now averaging about $1,200 per grower in the valley, but growers had to make do with fewer acres and, thus, fewer dollars in net income. Reflecting how important sugar beets had become to the region, the Fargo-Moorhead newspaper covered these developments on its front page and in an editorial lamented that the cutbacks placed area growers in "economically impossible positions." The federal government restored most of the lost quota acreage the following year, but for the remainder of the decade, sugar beet production grew relatively slowly in the valley, and only because American Crystal reduced production in some of its other districts. Total acreage climbed less than 10 percent during those years and, despite valley farmers' clamoring to contract with American Crystal, the company added only about eighty new growers.[41]

Whether searching for more profitable crops or striving to receive a contract from American Crystal, many area farmers found it difficult to stay in agriculture as the decade waned. Besides the decline in earnings from traditional crops such as wheat, land values continued to grow, and the Red River Valley counties had some of the most expensive land in the region. Clay County rural land values virtually doubled between 1954 and 1959; at the same time, Cass County farmland values grew over 30 percent. The emphasis on technology and mechanization meant higher operating costs as well. In Cass County, for example, farmers' fertilizing expenses doubled. Caught between higher operating costs brought on by mechanization and declining earnings, growers either got bigger or got out. The number of growers in Cass County declined by 10 percent during the second half of the 1950s. On the one hand, statewide, Minnesota lost over twenty thousand farms during the same period. On the other hand, the average size of farms in the valley expanded from 472 acres in 1954 to 530 acres in 1959, which meant that farmers were taking on more debt to acquire the additional land and paying higher property taxes.[42]

Despite the expense, those valley sugar beet growers who survived relied even more on mechanization during the late 1950s, especially mechanical thinners. These had been improved significantly since World War II, and the uniform stands of sugar beets resulting from segmented seeds made the machines more efficient. The rapid mechanization of the harvest had fueled an increased interest in what technology might do for the growers, and as more growers employed the thinners, the machines became a mark of the forward-thinking, modern farmer. Concerning the mechanical thinners, an American Crystal official reported that those who used them "are doing a lot of talking and boasting [among] themselves over their results and, naturally, this will encourage others to do the same." Moreover, field labor wages were inching upward, and the growers who needed to employ betabeleros only to hoe their acres two or three times could cut their field labor rates by almost 50 percent. In addition, the campaign to entice local youths would be helped if stooped toil was completely eliminated. And finally, in 1956 and 1957, American Crystal offered attractive deals on several hundred mechanical thinners with financing at 4.5 percent, and the company sold every one. By 1959, over two-thirds of the valley's growers relied on mechanical thinners, up from barely one-fifth only five years earlier. With more thinners in use, the company calculated that the average field worker could now cultivate over eighteen acres. Besides the mechanical thinners, beet seed drills (now called planters) were becoming larger, including a twelve-row planter deployed by the end of the 1950s, which further reduced grower operating costs.[43]

By 1959, the increased use of machines and local youth finally began to erode the numbers of betabeleros needed from Texas. Almost 5,900 had been contracted in 1955, and that figure held relatively steady over the next two years. In 1958, however, the number of migrant workers required from South Texas dropped suddenly to barely 4,800 and then declined further to 4,400 the following year. This was also partly a result of more Mexicans settling permanently in the area; however, the boast that migrant workers would soon be eliminated from the valley seemed to be coming true. Furthermore, the labor agency found it could reduce the number of counties in which it recruited—thus cutting those labor contracting fees and licenses required by Texas—and they closed a recruiting office in Dallas. Overall, the labor agency lowered its operating expenses by about 20 percent between 1955 and 1959.[44]

Certainly, these technological efficiencies and cost-cutting matters were important to American Crystal, too. By the end of the 1950s, with the growth of sugar beet production slowing in the nation, American Crystal seemed to be losing steam as a dynamic corporation. True, it remained the third-largest beet sugar producer in the country, but just barely, as Amalgamated Sugar, based in Utah, challenged American Crystal's overall rank in the industry. The company had not opened any new districts since the 1930s, and while it had constructed new facilities in Moorhead in 1948 and Crookston six years later, there were no immediate plans to significantly expand its operation in the valley. Hence, sugar beet growers in the region must have been somewhat wary of their futures as the 1950s ended. If American Crystal did not increase production in the valley, how prosperous could the growers remain?[45]

THE LATTER YEARS OF THE 1950S, on the surface, appeared to be a time of overall stability in the sugar beet industry in the Red River Valley. Certainly, American Crystal did not expand its operation to any significant degree, as it had in the decade after World War II, and what growth did take place occurred only because it reduced its operation in other areas. Though relying more on technology, as far as their economic circumstances were concerned the company's growers were treading water. Some of them failed and some expanded, but mainly, growers were fortunate if they simply maintained what they had. Though it had weaned itself from braceros by using local youths, the industry in the valley remained dependent on Mexican migrant workers, albeit not quite so many of them.

This period of stability or stasis came to an end suddenly in 1960 for two reasons. First, that year American Crystal introduced to valley growers a technological breakthrough for the sugar beet industry: the monogerm seed. From that moment on, the monogerm seed would dramatically alter the way in which sugar beet plants were cultivated. Second, in response to the increasing tension between the United States and Fidel Castro's Cuba, in the summer of 1960 the Eisenhower administration barred the importation of Cuban sugar into the United States. In essence, the sugar beet industry took over Cuba's contribution to America's sugar supply. That meant, of course, that sugar beet production in the valley would grow rapidly in the 1960s, requiring more acres, more growers, and more sugar beet field workers.

CHAPTER 6

Cuba, Texas, and the Red River Valley

THE EISENHOWER ADMINISTRATION's move to block Cuban sugar from coming into the United States had important consequences for the industry throughout the nation, including the Red River Valley. On the one hand, the ban created an enormous void in the country's sugar supply; the Cuba quota for the U.S. market had been nearly two million tons a year. When the Kennedy administration decided to maintain the embargo, it meant that the domestic sugar industry had an opportunity to expand its share of the U.S. market. In fact, to foster domestic output, the federal government suspended virtually all production quotas for the next four years. American Crystal and the other sugar companies responded to this situation by rapidly expanding their output. American Crystal increased contracted acreage between 1959 and 1962 by over 80,000 acres, a leap of about 33 percent. The valley's sugar beet acreage climbed from 94,000 acres to over 143,000, which meant the region garnered the lion's share of the company's increase. On the other hand, American Crystal and the other major sugar companies were stymied by the fact that their sugar-processing facilities quickly reached maximum capacity. The period of spectacular growth, in other words, soon hit a ceiling. Between 1962 and 1964, American Crystal could add only 3,000 more acres and even had to reduce some growers' acreage in the valley simply because the factories in East Grand Forks, Moorhead, and Crookston could not keep up with the huge tonnage of beets being harvested. Indeed, since American sugar processors could not expand their capacity quickly enough, much of the early 1960s shortfall in the sugar supply created by the ban on Cuban sugar was filled by foreign suppliers.[1]

This volatility within the sugar beet industry created tensions and anxieties among those involved as they adjusted to these developments. In the valley the company, its growers, and the betabeleros were forced to make alterations within their relationships with each other. Technological advancements by the sugar beet industry, federal and state government policies, and the growing Mexican American civil rights movement further influenced how these groups interacted. In addition, in order to expand its sugar output, American Crystal had to add more growers and field workers quickly. The result was that the relative stability which had reigned in the valley's sugar industry since the end of the Korean War disappeared. In this new and rather chaotic climate, the company and its growers began to reassess their relationship with one another to the point that the growers came to view American Crystal's management decisions as a hindrance. The Mexican migrant workers they depended upon searched for new ways to find a more advantageous position within the valley's sugar industry.

AMERICAN CRYSTAL boosted its production in the early 1960s in three ways. First, it simply increased acreage allotments to its cadre of growers. In 1959, the average acreage contract in the valley was about seventy-one acres. Three years later, each grower received, on average, about ninety-three acres. The growers had difficulty expanding their capacity much more quickly than that. One reason was that American Crystal still required sugar beet acreage to lie fallow the year before it was sown. Growers had established patterns of yearly crop rotations that would have to be drastically altered unless they purchased more acreage. Many did seek to enlarge their land holdings, but land prices had risen even further since the 1950s, which made buying land an expensive proposition. The growers would likely need to buy more farm implements if they increased their operations. And more sugar beet acreage meant hiring additional workers and providing more housing for the migrants. All of these measures were expensive, and no one could be certain how long the federal government would allow this unlimited domestic sugar production to continue. What would happen to a grower who invested in more land, more housing, and more machines if sugar controls were put back in place at pre-1960 levels? In fact, once American Crystal had reached maximum output at its factories in 1962, it had to impose its own ceiling to expansion and actually reduced acreage allotments slightly. The average acreage allotment fell to about eighty-eight acres.[2]

A second strategy followed by American Crystal to increase production involved adding more growers. Certainly, the company had no lack of eager applicants during the 1950s, as valley farmers searched for profitable crops. In 1962, the company entered into contracts with 1,345 growers, about 75 more than in 1959. As with the increase in acreage allotments, American Crystal reduced its growers' roster by ten in 1963 because of overproduction, although most of that decrease came from grower retirement or death. Nonetheless, that no new growers were added that year was a disappointment to many valley farmers. J. C. Tanner, American Crystal's district manager for the valley (Tanner was appointed after Bingham died), reported "a terrific demand" from farmers in the region seeking contracts in 1963.[3]

The third route taken by American Crystal to increase production involved technology. The company encouraged its sugar beet growers in the valley to use chemical herbicides and pesticides at an even greater rate in the early 1960s. A newly developed chemical, Avadex, was effective against wild oats, a common problem throughout the valley and especially burdensome to sugar beet growers. Farmers liberally applied older chemicals such as Carbyne, TCA, and Dowpon to other weeds that plagued the region. Against the common sugar beet pests, such as wireworms, cutworms, and maggots, the company recommended Lindane, Toxaphene, and Endrin. By 1963, American Crystal reported that chemicals were used on over two-thirds of the sugar beet acreage in the valley. These chemicals helped growers produce 13.5 tons of sugar beets per acre in 1963, up from around 12 tons just five years earlier.[4]

In 1960, the application of chemicals was made much easier by the introduction of another major innovation: the monogerm seed. Segmented seeds—in use since their development in the 1940s—had helped to reduce the number of plants that emerged from the seed ball, thereby decreasing the number of seeds required for each acre and, therefore, growers' costs. The segmented seeds proved easier to modify in order to combat some sugar beet diseases. Segmented seeds still required some thinning, however, and growers found it difficult to apply chemicals among the thick stands of plants. The monogerm seed, which was first tested in western states in the late 1950s, yielded only a single sugar beet plant that was virtually uniform in size with the next. Moreover, using machine planters and the new monogerm seed, growers could create a field with uniform plant spacing. Therefore, the seed virtually eliminated the need to thin fields, and it made applying herbicides and pesticides much less difficult because nozzles could be adjusted precisely to the even spacing of plants. By 1962, American Crystal made the monogerm seed widely available in the valley, although some growers, aware that the seed had been developed earlier, were irritated that the company had taken so much time to introduce it into the valley. Grower unhappiness over the company's seemingly tardy adoption of the monogerm seed, coupled with the wild gyrations in the sugar industry in the early 1960s, began to fray the relationship between American Crystal and its Red River Valley growers.[5]

THE MAIN AREA OF CONTENTION that emerged between the growers and the company involved the growers' (and other neighboring farmers') desire to see the valley increase sugar beet output. The fact that sugar beets continued to be a viable, profitable crop in an era of depressed grain prices caused valley farmers to chafe at what they perceived to be foot dragging by American Crystal. The growers wanted the company to contract for more acres and to either construct new sugar beet–processing plants or expand existing facilities in order to process a greater output of sugar beets. American Crystal had opened the Moorhead facility in 1948, followed six years later by the factory in Crookston. Now, in the early 1960s, with the government's lifting of domestic sugar quotas and the industry limited only by the capacity of its processing plants, almost a decade had passed since American Crystal had invested in a new factory for the valley. The only move the company made in the early 1960s was to add three new piling stations (storage points for beets before being sent to the factory), some warehouse space in Moorhead, and palletizing machinery, which was designed to improve the process of turning leftover pulp from beets into livestock feed. This three-million-dollar investment by the company did not add one pound of sugar-processing capacity in the valley, however, and left valley farmers frustrated and even more critical of American Crystal's management.[6]

Various groups of farmers became strong advocates for expanded sugar beet production in the region. The RRVSBGA had continued to increase its membership throughout the 1950s, becoming an ever more prominent voice for the growers. The RRVSBGA helped finance a publication called, appropriately enough, the *Sugarbeet Grower*, a periodical dedicated solely to the interest of those farmers. By the early 1960s the organization had also established a main office in Fargo, thus gaining significant visibility in the region, and had hired its own lawyer. In addition, other groups of farmers, business interests, and commercial proponents established organizations up and down the valley to promote the sugar beet industry, such as the Southern Red River Valley Sugarbeet Development Corporation, the Tri-County Sugarbeet Development Association, and the Drayton Economic Development Council.[7]

The main barrier to American Crystal's willingness to invest further in the valley, the growers and local commercial interests believed, centered on the company's board of directors. A wealthy Denver family, the Boettchers, held enough stock in the company by 1960 to exert primary control over board meetings. The Boettchers' primary investments in hotels, a cement company, and a railroad were mainly located in Colorado. The family was also very visible in Colorado from its philanthropy—through the Boettcher Foundation—and much of that foundation's funds were generated from American Crystal stock dividends. In the early 1960s the company's dividends jumped dramatically as the agribusiness giant Archer Daniels Midland attempted to gain control of American Crystal. The intended takeover failed, but to many of the sugar beet interest groups in the valley, American Crystal appeared to exist only to benefit the Boettchers and Colorado, not the people of North Dakota and Minnesota.[8]

Therefore, impatient and frustrated, the various sugar beet associations in the valley attempted as they had done ten years earlier to entice other companies to set up operations in the valley. The Drayton Economic Development Council, representing that community (about forty-five miles north of Grand Forks) and nearby farmers, took the lead in this campaign. It focused on luring Holley Sugar, one of the largest firms in the sugar beet industry and a company that previously had considered opening a facility in the valley during the early 1950s. Holley also seemed very promising to the farmers because the company had recently started a new sugar beet operation in the region along the North Dakota–Montana border. The Drayton Economic Development Council's flirtation with Holley apparently paid off because American Crystal soon promised to construct a new processing plant just north of that town and to add more growers. The facility, which processed beets for the first time in the autumn of 1965, had a capacity of 600,000 tons of sugar beets and allowed for a substantial extension of sugar beet acreage into the northern part of the valley. Consequently, in the mid-1960s the valley's sugar beet industry underwent another period of expansion that, at least temporarily, satisfied many farmers and commercial entities. By 1967, American Crystal had added about three hundred new growers and contracted for over 40,000 more acres in the region than it had had prior to the opening of the Drayton factory.[9]

Nonetheless, sources of friction between the growers and American Crystal remained, and these issues began to fester as the decade unfolded. Growers did not like some contractual restrictions placed on their operations, such as buying only company-supplied seed. Many growers claimed that with chemical herbicides it was no longer necessary to leave land fallow the year before it was planted. Land not producing, the growers argued, only lowered their earning potential. While the company had added more piling stations, to some growers there were never enough. Thus, the distance they had to travel to unload harvested beets consumed too much of the growers' time and money. They also complained that the company did not do enough to insure an adequate supply of railroad cars being available in the region during the harvest. The longer it took for beets to arrive at the factory, the more likely they were to lose some sugar content. In addition, some growers resented the cost of procuring betabeleros—the per-acre fee assessed for the operation of the labor agency. And finally, American Crystal officials had become some of the most visible members of the state government committees working to improve migrant living conditions, a source of irritation and expense to many growers. This latter issue became more relevant as the valley now needed more field workers to take care of the surge in sugar beet acres.[10]

THE NUMBER OF FIELD WORKERS HAD DECLINED somewhat at the end of the 1950s because of technological advances, but that trend was rapidly reversed with the sudden increase in domestic production brought on by the ban on Cuban sugar. From requiring about 4,400 betabeleros for the valley in 1960, the following year American Crystal directed its labor agency to send 5,800 (out of 9,250 needed for all of the company's districts). Of course, all of the other sugar beet companies recruiting in Texas were striving to secure more Mexican workers, and Sullivan had to expand his network to encompass nineteen counties (up from fifteen the year before). The company also sent him two additional fieldmen to help the other recruiters. Nonetheless, the labor agency fell a little short of its goal, supplying about 5,600 betabeleros from Texas. Luckily for the company and the growers, a number of "unsolicited workers" (sometimes called freelancers), drawn to the area by word of mouth, appeared. The net result was actually a surplus of workers that year.[11]

The labor situation experienced severe turbulence over the next four years. In 1962, the labor agency in San Antonio failed to meet its goal for the valley by almost five hundred betabeleros. Wet weather in some areas of the region allowed migrant crews, however, to be moved from those areas to the dry fields. In other cases, betabeleros just worked longer hours in order to cultivate up to thirty-five acres per individual. Of course, that did translate into bigger paychecks for what must have been very exhausted workers. The next year, though, American Crystal slightly reduced its contracted acres, and the valley needed only about four thousand migrant workers. In addition, introduction of the monogerm seed and chemical herbicides caused the company to raise the number of acres it calculated that each betabelero should cultivate to twenty-three; hence, worker productivity had jumped 25 percent in less than five years. This led the labor agency to project downward the number of workers it needed to recruit each year. Two years later, however, with the opening of the Drayton plant and the addition of 40,000 more acres, the valley quickly needed more workers. In 1965, the labor agency dispatched over 9,900 Mexican migrants from Texas; 5,500 were directed to the valley, or 25 percent more than in 1963. Therefore, labor recruitment varied widely in the 1960s and added to the general uncertainty within the valley's sugar industry.[12]

The labor agency in Texas encountered other changes during this period. At the end of the 1962 season, Sullivan retired after almost twenty years as the agency's manager. William Knoll, who had previously worked seasonally for the agency, took over for the 1963 campaign. For unknown reasons, though, Knoll lasted only that single year. The company replaced him in January 1964 with Joseph W. Axelson, who directed the labor agency until it eventually ceased operation. Axelson had worked for American Crystal since 1945 when he was hired as a language interpreter for the Chaska district and then promoted to fieldman. Because of his fluency in Spanish, he was frequently in Texas during the 1950s as one of the liaisons between the labor agency recruiters and the fieldmen in Minnesota and North Dakota. In 1962, Axelson was promoted to manager of the Chaska factory. Thus, he was familiar with virtually all aspects of the production and processing of sugar beets. By all accounts he got along well with Mexican migrants, although he apparently was less relaxed in his demeanor than Sullivan. As one American Crystal official recalled, "Joe was a different type. Very structured, very precise, [he] tended to tell you everything there was to do."[13]

Another factor that influenced recruiting in Texas during the mid-1960s was the termination of the bracero program. By the early 1960s numerous developments signaled that the days were becoming numbered for the legal importation of workers from Mexico. In 1959, Eisenhower's secretary of labor, James Mitchell, released the results of a study that demonstrated the "adverse effects on domestic workers [U.S. citizens]" caused by the bracero program and called for the drafting of new regulations requiring that migrant workers who were American citizens receive identical benefits to those provided to braceros. Mitchell's actions helped spur the creation of a Senate subcommittee to investigate the condition of migrant workers in the United States. That subcommittee's report, "The Migrant Farm Worker in America (1960)," was also harshly critical of the bracero program, especially in its conclusion that braceros had a very negative effect on wages paid to other seasonal agricultural workers throughout the United States. That same year, the nationally televised documentary *Harvest of Shame* mortified many urban Americans with its graphic depiction of the abject conditions in which migrant workers lived and toiled. The plight of these workers increasingly drew the attention of groups comprising the liberal coalition that helped elect Kennedy in 1960, and the new president likewise signaled his opposition to the bracero program. In addition, by 1960 the numbers of rural congressmen had declined noticeably from the previous decade, thereby reducing the farm sector's political strength. While the Kennedy administration was unable to muster the votes to end the program in 1962, Secretary of Labor Willard Wirtz did establish relatively high minimum wages for braceros. These higher wages made braceros less cost-effective for agribusinesses and were met by vociferous protests from many agricultural interests. In 1964, Wirtz raised the minimum wage for braceros even higher and in the fall announced that the Johnson administration would not certify the importation of braceros for 1965. After more than two decades, the legal importation of foreign agricultural workers from Mexico into the United States ended.[14]

As the handwriting appeared on the wall that the bracero program was on its way out and that agribusinesses throughout the nation would have to find an extra 200,000 workers per year from within the United States, agricultural labor agencies turned even more to Texas to find seasonal workers. The American Crystal Labor Agency reported more companies competing with them for workers between 1961 and 1965. The total number of migrant workers from Texas rose almost 3 percent annually in the early 1960s, and in 1965, the first year without the bracero program, out-of-state agribusinesses hired about 22,000 additional Mexican migrants who were Texas residents. American Crystal's labor agency recruited in a greater number of counties than before 1961, and the agency's expenses remained high. In 1965, Axelson reported he had increased monetary advances for "a number of our old workers" in order to keep them from going with labor agents from other companies. Therefore, Mexican migrant workers obtained some economic advantages from having various companies compete for their labor. In response to such an environment, the valley's sugar industry stepped up its promotion of local teenage sugar beet field workers to reduce its dependency on betabeleros.[15]

CONSIDERING THE ACUTE NEED FOR SUGAR BEET FIELD WORKERS in 1961, it was no accident that the state of North Dakota formally launched the Youth Beet Program (YBP) that year. True, valley civic leaders and the public were still concerned about the juvenile misbehavior that summer employment was supposed to curb. In addition, the Mexican population continued to grow in the region, although it appeared that the violence associated with the migrants from the mid-1950s was declining. Moreover, the effort to use local teenage beet laborers had yielded some positive benefits—eliminating the need for braceros. That sugar beet acreage expanded suddenly in 1961 and that American Crystal added many new growers in Richland County, North Dakota, who had not used migrant labor before—and who were very unlikely to have even minimum housing in place—helped spark the creation of the YBP in North Dakota. Minnesota encouraged local youths to work in sugar beets, too, but never developed a separate sugar beet program. In border cities such as Moorhead, East Grand Forks, and Breckinridge, Minnesota teenagers were incorporated into North Dakota's YBP organization, and young people were deployed in sugar beet fields on both sides of the river.[16]

The first three years (1961–63) of the newly launched YBP were encouraging to local officials. The number of youth willing to become sugar beet field workers climbed from 700 that initial year to over 1,000 in 1963, and the acreage they cultivated likewise increased from about 2,700 acres in North Dakota to almost 4,300. The number of growers willing to hire the teens almost doubled from thirty to fifty-eight. Both states added extra staff to oversee the YBP in the valley, and in North Dakota, offices were opened in Grafton, Grand Forks, Fargo, and Wahpeton to coordinate the program. Community groups up and down the valley came on board, too. The Sertoma Club remained the primary sponsor in Cass and Clay counties, and in other locales the chambers of commerce, veterans' organizations, and city police and fire departments served as advocates for the YBP.[17]

While state officials and local public supporters were officially optimistic about the potential of the YBP to fulfill the sugar beet industry's need for more workers and to ultimately reduce the need for betabeleros, statistics told a less optimistic story. True, the youth added about 1,600 acres in North Dakota between 1961 and 1963, but sugar beet acreage in the state grew overall by more than 17,000. Alarmingly, the youths' productivity hardly improved during those first three years.

In 1961, each teenage worker averaged 3.9 acres, and in 1963 their average output had risen to only 4.1 acres. Conversely, in 1963 betabeleros averaged 23 acres per worker. If the local youths were to ever replace Mexican migrants, the teenagers either were going to have to work faster or a lot more were going to be required.[18]

Of course, spurring youth productivity required developing an experienced cadre of workers, and this proved nearly impossible to do. Three related factors conspired to retard the teenagers' output: weather, wages, and turnover. Each year it seemed a weather calamity struck somewhere in the region. In 1962, it was heavy rains and flooding in the southern end of the valley. The following year, a late freeze struck the central valley, resulting in the replanting of three thousand acres of beets on the North Dakota side. These unfortunate weather events forced field workers to be idle and left fields so infested with weeds that herbicides were less effective. Weed-choked sugar beet fields were exhausting to cultivate and led one YBP official to lament that "this discouraged the youth." In addition, until the teenagers could increase their productivity, individual remuneration remained low. In 1961, the average youth worker earned the equivalent in wages of about seventy cents per hour; by 1963, that figure increased to only eighty-three cents. Low pay, idleness, and difficult work, therefore, contributed to a high rate of turnover each summer. In 1962 and 1963, about 50 percent of all YBP participants left the sugar beet fields before the season ended.[19]

While the performance of the YBP teenagers fell far short of expectations throughout the valley, the Grafton region, which encompassed Pembina and Walsh counties, seemed to hold promise. These counties, where the Drayton plant opened in 1965, were the most rural in the valley. With fewer summer job opportunities than in urban regions, Pembina and Walsh county youths likely viewed sugar beet field work more positively. Moreover, they were probably more familiar with farm toil in general. The communities in these counties also provided significant support to the teenagers. The *Walsh County Record* ran numerous articles trumpeting the benefits of the YBP. In Walhalla, Pembina County, beet growers staged an evening dance and buffet for the youth workers, and farmers in Walsh held a picnic for them. A Grafton bank offered a twenty-five-dollar U.S. Savings Bond for the boy and girl with the most acres cultivated each summer. By 1967, the youths in the Grafton YBP worked an average of 13.3 acres of sugar beets each, and they earned the equivalent of over one dollar per hour. The other districts—Grand Forks and Fargo—attempted to emulate the Grafton model, but their results were less positive. Grand Forks' best year occurred in 1966 when youth there cultivated an average of 5.4 acres. In the Fargo region the results were even more dismal: 3.8 acres in 1967. Apparently, urban youths' field labor capabilities fell short of their country cousins'.[20]

The real culprit was the local teens' finding field work simply too unpleasant. For them there was never enough drinking water, field toilet facilities, and other "youth conveniences," as one Fargo YBP supervisor bemoaned. The Youth Beet Program and American Crystal officials admonished the growers to "praise [the youth]" and "make [the youth] feel they belong." Growers were urged to make "acreage for the youth selective [less weed infested] so as not to discourage them." To provide for more immediate financial rewards, American Crystal developed a method of payment just for the teens in which they received two-thirds of their wages each week; meanwhile betabeleros continued to be paid only twice during the summer. Some growers reduced the youths' work day from eight hours to six. Despite these measures, growers could not make field conditions much better. Bad weather happened; fields became overrun with weeds; and workers sometimes fell behind schedule. One grower remembered he had to fire his entire contingent of YBP workers and replace them with betabeleros because the teens decided to take off over a long Fourth of July weekend, despite the fact the youth crew had fallen behind in its work. The teenagers complained in the newspapers about blisters, heat, mosquitoes, sunburn, and the monotony of hoeing. With pay scales hardly rising to more than $1.00 per hour, at a time when the federal minimum wage was rising to $1.40 per hour, the youth voted with their feet; the turnover rate for the Fargo district remained at least 50 percent each summer between 1963 and 1967, and the other districts did not do much better.[21]

Despite the teenagers' shortcomings in productivity, the sugar beet industry and civic groups in the valley doggedly continued to support the YBP through this period. For one thing, summer jobs for teenagers remained scarce throughout the valley during the mid-1960s. This poor employment situation coincided with another spike in juvenile-delinquency fears. The local media warned the community of Fargo-Moorhead about two thousand youth who spent their summers literally "sitting around," waiting for something to happen, and, more ominous, "drinking." Parents were further advised about the growing problem of teenagers "cruising" city streets at night looking for some "action." That the YBP kept youths employed, at least for a part of the summer, seemed worthwhile. As one local resident attested, "At the present time in the face of so much delinquency it is rewarding that a community of area farmers are concerned and creating job opportunities for youth. The community that builds young people, builds itself." And finally, obviously, with the need for sugar beet field workers on the rise and public scrutiny of migrant living conditions becoming more acute, the YBP young people filled a void for many growers. After all, *Harvest of Shame* and congressional investigations focused national attention and debate not just on braceros but on seasonal agricultural workers in general. In fact, the world of Mexicans in Texas, including that of the betabeleros and other migrant laborers, was experiencing dramatic events in the early 1960s.[22]

WHILE *Harvest of Shame* helped rally support to those groups opposing the bracero program, the film also represented to a degree the broader forces that were changing the conditions of life for Mexicans throughout the United States. An important element in this new direction came from Mexican community leaders' decision to become more active in the political arena. Emulating, to a degree, the African American civil rights strategy against de jure discriminatory practices, Mexicans created new organizations, such as the Mexican American Political Association (MAPA) and the Political Association of Spanish Speaking Organizations (PASO), intended to promote political activism, especially convincing more Mexicans to vote. These groups launched campaigns to register Mexican voters, to raise funds to pay poll taxes for them in Texas, and to assist Mexicans who had never gone through the naturalization process to obtain their citizenship. The emergence of these new political-oriented groups seemed to energize LULAC as well. In Texas it started the popular program the Little School of 400, a campaign to provide Mexican preschool children with a vocabulary of four hundred key English words, thereby easing the children's transition into public school. In 1960, these efforts bore fruit, especially in Texas, where PASO joined with the Democratic Party to spark the Viva Kennedy campaign that helped the Democrats carry Texas and regain the White House. Indeed, it was partly Kennedy's debt to the Viva Kennedy activists that led the administration to begin the process that ended the bracero program.[23]

These new strategies during the early 1960s also influenced local politics in South Texas, such as in Crystal City. The small Mexican commercial community in Crystal City had prospered somewhat in the late 1950s from the customers drawn from Del Monte's bracero employees. These Mexican businesspeople had formed their own chamber of commerce and began to pressure the local school board for change, especially to end segregation in the elementary schools. In 1960, a Mexican insurance salesman ran for election to the local school board. He did not win, but he garnered a surprising number of votes. Under pressure from these commercial leaders and others in the Mexican community, the Crystal City school board began to desegregate the elementary schools. The emerging Mexican political assertiveness in Crystal City had other manifestations, too. When an unprecedented freeze during the winter of 1962 wiped out much of the vegetable crop along with those seasonal jobs, a large contingent of Mexicans confronted the Zavala County government (whose seat was Crystal City) demanding assistance. The county capitulated and provided over three thousand Mexican residents with support through a "surplus-commodities program." That same year, another Mexican ran an unsuccessful campaign for a position on the county commission.[24]

In 1963, however, this upsurge in Mexican political activism in Crystal City paid off. In the early 1960s the local Del Monte factory had begun phasing out its reliance on bracero employees, and many Mexican residents of Crystal City had finally gained employment in the town's largest business. Subsequently, a San Antonio–based local of the International Brotherhood of Teamsters had organized among some of these workers. In 1963, the All Latin Party, formed by PASO members, union organizers, and some local Mexican groups, started a drive to pay the $1.75 poll tax for all eligible Mexican voters in Crystal City. A slate of five Mexican candidates, drawn primarily from the Mexican commercial class and referred to as Los Cinco, campaigned for election to the city's governing council. Despite intimidation from the Anglo community and the Texas Rangers, Los Cinco handily won the election; incredibly, Mexicans now controlled Crystal City's government. In the short run, their victory proved hollow, as the Anglo community eventually was able to co-opt most of Los Cinco. For many Mexicans in South Texas, however, the triumph at the polls in Crystal City was enormously encouraging, demonstrating what they might achieve.[25]

Along with their rising political activism in South Texas, Mexican residents in the region also began to organize to improve their working conditions. To a significant degree, the events in California in the early 1960s inspired Mexican agricultural workers in the Nueces Strip. César Chávez and others had been organizing California farm workers throughout the early 1960s into what ultimately became the United Farm Workers (UFW). During the summer of 1965, the UFW went on strike against grape growers around Delano, California. While less than successful at first, the strike and subsequent consumer boycott drew tremendous attention from the nation's news media. Chávez himself became an immensely motivational figure for Mexicans throughout the United States who wished to follow his lead, to work to organize seasonal agricultural workers, and to improve the socioeconomic status of migrant and temporary farm workers.[26]

In South Texas one immediate result of the farm workers' strike in California was an impromptu work stoppage in Starr County. What began as a wildcat strike against a few melon growers in 1966 eventually grew to become a major strike and boycott against La Casita, one of the largest agribusiness conglomerates in the Lower Rio Grande Valley. While the La Casita strike ultimately failed, it did galvanize other Mexicans to take up the farm workers' cause. Sympathy walkouts occurred, in particular among Mexican students in numerous high schools in South Texas, such as Del Rio, Laredo, and Kingsville. In addition, Mexican packing-shed workers in Crystal City went out on strike. As worker militancy grew in the Nueces Strip, it was inevitable that it would be carried outside the region by migrant workers.[27]

Between 1965 and 1967, labor organizers, many of whom were Mexicans, began to organize migrant workers coming out of South Texas to work in the Upper Midwest. One group that emerged, Obreros Unidos (Workers United), centered its efforts in Wisconsin and for a while was especially promising because of kinship ties among migrant workers from Crystal City. Obreros Unidos organized significantly among cannery workers and, by 1967, had received some support from the AFL-CIO. Obreros Unidos collapsed soon thereafter, however, because of financial problems. Another group of union activists, the Farm Labor Organizing Committee (FLOC), appeared in 1967 in Ohio. It also had close ties with South Texas migrants and garnered assistance from other union affiliates in Ohio, such as the Teamsters and United Auto Workers. In the late 1960s FLOC focused its energies on Mexican migrant workers from South Texas employed by Ohio tomato growers and, following Chávez's example, on community organizing throughout the Great Lakes region.[28]

The sugar beet industry and American Crystal kept careful watch on these union efforts, too. Axelson reported to American Crystal that at the federal governmental wage hearings in San Antonio in 1965 to establish the pay for sugar beet field workers that coming year union representatives were also in attendance. The following year Axelson advised American Crystal that "unions and the 'Do Gooder' faction tried to make a case for their existence and failed" at the wage hearings held in McAllen and San Antonio. In 1967, Axelson again noted the presence of union organizers at wage hearings. While there is no evidence that labor organizers were in the valley during the mid-1960s, certainly many betabeleros must have been approached while in South Texas or at least felt some of the growing activism stirring in Mexican communities. Quite likely, a factor in American Crystal's ongoing support of the YBP could have been its awareness of the changed mood among Mexican migrant workers. More likely, the increased number of social programs and activities available to betabeleros and their families—supported by American Crystal—sprang from the attention that migrant workers were receiving from their own leaders, the news media, and political factions throughout the nation. Clearly, the conditions of life for Mexican migrant workers in the valley were improving by the mid-1960s.[29]

THROUGHOUT THE VALLEY REGION, more attention was given to and more services made available for Mexican migrants between 1960 and 1967. One symbol of the importance of betabeleros to the Red River region appeared in Crookston in 1962. The city, which had long supported migrant social services provided through the Catholic Church's diocese headquartered in Crookston, wanted to accommodate Mexican workers' accessibility to downtown by putting up parking signs in Spanish. The signs that initially appeared read "Parquiador para trocas, camienetes ye caros." Unfortunately, the signs were riddled with misspellings, as they should have been spelled, "Parqueadero para trocas, camionetas y carros" (parking space for trucks, station wagons, and cars). Nonetheless, the city's attempt indicated both the growing importance of Mexican workers to the valley and a willingness on the part of many of the region's inhabitants to make life better for these vital laborers (as well as encouraging them to shop in Crookston).[30]

The federal and state governments provided the impetus for many of these efforts. First, the Kennedy administration initiated a new era in regard to the socioeconomic needs of many disadvantaged groups in the country. Besides scaling back the bracero program, the other key measure for migrant workers passed during Kennedy's term was the 1962 Migrant Health Act. This measure provided grant funds to public or private organizations willing to use the money to establish health clinics for migrant workers and their families. In 1964, employing funds secured under the Migrant Health Act, the state of Minnesota opened a clinic in Moorhead to provide "health counseling, nursing care and rehabilitation" for betabeleros and their families. Starting with a staff of only two nurses, by 1966 the program had eleven nurses and three sanitation experts, and the clinic made referrals to physicians for migrants when necessary.[31]

During the Johnson administration, the federal government launched more social and economic measures benefiting migrant workers, beginning with the termination of the bracero program altogether. Other changes were tied to Johnson's Great Society program. Under the Elementary and Secondary Education Act of 1965, North Dakota and Minnesota applied for joint grants to provide more educational facilities for Mexican migrant children in the valley. By 1966, five schools provided education services to almost 300 migrant elementary-age children, and another 140 were enrolled in a Head Start program. In addition, these schools served as day care centers for over 160 children and provided employment for about 40 migrant family members. Clay and Wilkin counties, in Minnesota, joined together to receive a Head Start grant in 1967 for rural children, over 50 of whom were the children of betabeleros. That same year, the Johnson administration's Department of Labor issued new regulations designed to improve migrant housing structures and sanitary conditions.[32]

Besides these programs implemented in Minnesota and North Dakota with the infusion of federal aid dollars, the two state governments continued their own operations to assist Mexican migrant workers in the valley. Both states extended their participation in the Annual Plan and contracted betabeleros in the valley for other seasonal jobs once they finished their work in the sugar beet fields. In 1963, for example, 80 percent of the betabeleros in the area had their next jobs arranged for them by North Dakota and Minnesota state employment service agents. The two state governments continued to provide inspectors for migrant housing. By 1963, Minnesota inspected 100 percent of the migrant housing in the state; North Dakota officials inspected 180 migrant domiciles representing over 50 percent of the migrant housing in the valley. According to the North Dakota inspectors, improvements in migrant residences had occurred especially in regard to "water supply, garbage disposal, and toilet facilities." At least 82 percent of the houses had refrigerators, and over 90 percent had access to laundry facilities. North Dakota inspectors noted, however, that some migrant housing continued to fall in the "poor" category. But by 1966, North Dakota officials noted that at least 85 percent of migrant residences in the valley met the "prescribed standards."[33]

Nongovernment entities also provided services to better social conditions for betabeleros in the valley. The summer school operated by St. Joseph's Catholic Church in Moorhead continued to grow. In 1962, it offered educational courses, recreational activities, health services, and meals for about 150 Mexican children. Indeed, St. Joseph's summer school still drew considerable attention from the local media. Virtually every year during the 1960s, at least one lengthy human-interest article appeared in the local newspaper about migrant children at the school. The long-running summer school program in Crookston also maintained its activities through the 1960s. In addition, the Minnesota Council of Churches continued to provide home visitations to migrant families in the valley, and the Minnesota Tuberculosis and Health Association provided free chest X-rays for betabeleros and their families. Churches near Comstock, Minnesota, raised money in 1963 to purchase an automobile for a "migrant missionary" from Laredo who needed the transportation to deliver food donated by local churches to migrant families in the valley. Many of the various groups and organizations providing social services to Mexican migrants in the region came together to form Migrants Inc. in 1965, in order to channel their programs through a single entity.[34]

One of the newer and more enterprising social programs for Mexican migrant workers in the valley emerged in the small community of Manvel, North Dakota, about twelve miles north of Grand Forks. In 1964, Manvel opened the first public summer school for migrant children in North Dakota. The town of about 350 residents had organized a Community Improvement Council in 1960 that launched several drives during the decade. In addition to the migrant shool, the council also promoted efforts such as building a new public elementary school, opening a city park, and operating a local Teen Club. The Manvel migrant school in 1964 included a day care center for eight infants, educational programs for forty children, and free health services for the youths. The Women's Club of Manvel arranged the operating funds and solicited supplies from area businesses and sugar beet growers. In 1966, the Manvel Women's Club received a national award in recognition of its efforts in starting the migrant summer school program. Other communities also acknowledged the importance of betabeleros in the region. The Catholic Daughters of America group in Minnesota provided an annual picnic with live music and dancing for migrant workers and their families during the 1960s.[35]

The existence of these initiatives to promote better Mexican migrant housing and living conditions was not universally supported in the valley. When American Crystal expanded acreage in the early 1960s, it moved to establish operations in Richland County, North Dakota. The county had virtually no history of using Mexican migrant workers, and therefore the farms had either no migrant housing at all or housing that would not meet government standards. Believing that most of these new sugar beet growers would not be willing to suddenly invest in regulation migrant housing, American Crystal encouraged them to use YBP crews instead of betabeleros to cultivate sugar beets.[36]

In the main, however, these programs and other opportunities for Mexican migrants in the valley encouraged more to take up permanent residence. North Dakota seasonal labor statistics included a category of seasonal sugar beet field labor that was separate from those hired from outside of the state (a migrant worker) or those enrolled by the YBP. In 1963, 368 seasonal workers were counted in this "local" designation; by 1967 that number had grown to 570. The vast majority of this increase likely were former Mexican migrant workers who had taken up year-round residence in the valley. Moreover, many betabeleros at this time became full-time farm workers in the region. In 1967, Migrants Inc. started a program to place Mexican migrant workers into permanent agricultural jobs in the valley, especially with sugar beet growers. American Crystal promoted this effort as well because it would lower the yearly expense of recruiting and transporting temporary workers. As farm mechanization in general became more widespread, sugar beet growers with large farms recognized the value of having trained, permanent employees for all of their farm's activities. Many Mexican migrants dropped out of the migrant stream when such opportunities were offered to them. In fact, some betabeleros were becoming farm owners themselves. One such family, which had first come to Marshall County, Minnesota, as betabeleros in the early 1950s, made the transition to local landowners when they purchased a one-hundred-acre farm in the early 1960s. For betabeleros, whether in South Texas or in the Red River Valley, the changes in their circumstances paralleled other noteworthy developments influencing the sugar beet industry by the middle of the decade.[37]

THE MOST IMPORTANT ALTERATION continued to be the expansion of the number of sugar beet growers and the acreage throughout the region. Although the federal government reinstituted quotas on the sugar industry in 1965, the domestic share of that quota had increased, primarily as a result of the ongoing enmity between the United States and its former major supplier—Cuba. American Crystal received its portion of the increase and channeled more of its operations into the valley. In fact, by the mid-1960s American Crystal had closed the older, inefficient plants at Oxnard, California; Missoula, Montana; and Grand Island, Nebraska. The company's Clarksburg, California, district recorded a slight decrease in acreage between 1965 and 1967, but the Mason City, Iowa, factory saw its acreage slashed by more than 50 percent. Therefore, the Red River Valley district, Chaska, and the Colorado operation at Rocky Ford became the real core of American Crystal's sugar beet industry. The valley enjoyed the greatest gain as its acreage rose from 122,500 in 1964 (the year before the Drayton plant opened) to over 167,000 acres in 1967, which represented almost two-thirds of American Crystal's total of 249,000 acres that year.[38]

The company directed most of its expansion efforts in the valley at this time to the addition of new growers. Average acreage in the region edged upward about ten acres per grower between 1964 and 1967. American Crystal enlisted significantly more growers, however, during the same period. Two factors primarily contributed to the company's decision to add more growers instead of increasing each grower's contracted acreage. First, the company needed more growers in the northern end of the valley to fill the Drayton plant's processing capacity. Second, the company recruited more growers in the southern end, in Richland and Wilkin counties, to pacify the farmers there and to discourage their courtship of Holley Sugar.[39]

Indeed, farmers throughout the region anxiously desired to get in on the mid-1960s sugar boom. One sugar beet grower remembered, "Farmers were just wild to get beet acres. Every farmer in the valley wanted beet acres." One reason for this sugar beet mania derived from the ongoing deterioration in agricultural earnings from some of the more traditional crops grown in the valley. On the North Dakota side of the valley, corn acreage declined by about 60,000 acres between 1960 and 1964; likewise, many farmers reduced their wheat output. Problems in the dairy industry led to widespread milk dumping in the valley in the spring of 1967. More farmers gave up completely on agriculture in the region, too. A three-county study in 1966 (Cass and Barnes in North Dakota, Clay in Minnesota) revealed that over seven hundred "farm operators" had quit during the preceding five years.[40]

That American Crystal chose to add more growers while only modestly increasing each grower's number of acres fuelled more animosity on the part of the members of the RRVSBGA toward the company. One valley sugar industry official recalled that "the growers began a lot of meetings to figure out what they could do to improve their situation of being able to grow more beets in the Valley." In 1965, disputes concerning acreage spilled over into grower complaints about labor costs (wages had increased slightly each year between 1963 and 1965), the company's requirement that growers purchase only its seed and chemical agents, and even allegations that the company cheated growers financially by underreporting sugar yields. That year marked the first time in the valley that a contract between the company and the growers' association was not ratified until May, after cultivation had already began. During the harvest that year, H. A. Tvedten, American Crystal's new valley manager, reported a "strained grower-company relationship." As a result, contracting with individual growers in the valley was delayed again the following year.[41]

The strain between the company and its growers was exacerbated by American Crystal's very public role in promoting better treatment of migrant workers. A company official served on each of the state committees in North Dakota and Minnesota overseeing migrant worker matters. On the one hand, to some degree this must have been because the company wanted to retain influence over any matters dealing with migrant workers and because taking a visible part in improving migrant conditions was good public relations for American Crystal. On the other hand, the company, more than the growers, was acutely aware of the increasing need for betabeleros, of how stiff the competition for them in Texas had become, and of the labor agency's operating expenses. In addition, American Crystal agents knew of the increased presence of union organizers among migrant workers throughout South Texas and the Upper Midwest. Having betabeleros somewhat satisfied with their working conditions, the wages they earned, and their living environment was much more important to American Crystal, especially the labor agency, than to the RRVSBGA.[42]

Through its fieldmen's interaction with growers and in virtually every edition of *Crystal-ized Facts*, American Crystal encouraged farmers to treat their labor well and to provide good housing and living conditions for their betabeleros. In a 1963 article, for example, the company advised growers that migrant workers were more inclined to come to regions that had growers who related well to the laborers, better "living accommodations, and community acceptance." Growers were advised they should provide one house for every fifty acres of beets they planted and insure that it was properly equipped with "decent beds and mattresses, bottle gas stove, refrigerator, adequate cooking utensils and electric lighting." The betabeleros and their families should have access to sufficient laundry facilities, and everything should be clean when the workers arrived. Another article two years later bluntly noted "good will is the biggest advertising asset on the labor market." In fact, the company on occasion weeded out growers who created too many problems with migrant workers. One grower recalled that, when a fellow sugar beet farmer refused to pay his workers a bonus he had promised them, American Crystal did not renew that grower's contract the following year. That the company would take sides with betabeleros, in some instances, probably angered at least a few growers and contributed to the developing rift between the RRVSBGA and American Crystal.[43]

BY THE MIDDLE OF THE 1960s, important new currents began to affect how the traditional triad responsible for the sugar industry in the valley reacted to each other. American Crystal had pulled out of unprofitable regions in order to concentrate its processing capacity in the valley. Moreover, the increased domestic production quotas established by the federal government provided for an increase in what American Crystal could process and offer for sale. The growers, pressed by economic woes partially created by lower agricultural prices, wanted an even bigger slice of the sugar beet pie to be located in the valley. To them, American Crystal was not growing fast enough, and other company policies only vexed them more. These two entities clearly were becoming estranged. Both the growers and the company still badly needed workers, whether they were Mexican migrants, local Mexican residents, or Anglo teenagers. The Mexican laborers benefited from the increased attention—locally and nationally—as well as from their own activism to gain more social services and economic opportunities. This relative improvement in the quality of their lives encouraged even more betabeleros to settle in the valley. More than anything, the sugar industry in the region had entered a new period of flux, and all the participants sought to gain advantages from these circumstances. As a result, in less than a decade, the traditional composition of the sugar beet industry in the valley would be completely reconfigured.

Grower examining his sugar beets

A sugar beets piling station

Trucks unloading sugar beets

American Crystal Sugar beet-processing plant, Moorhead, Minnesota

Field workers hoeing, near Moorhead, Minnesota

Sugar beets on conveyor belt

Stacked bags of processed sugar

Close up of hoe preparation

Migrant housing near Moorhead, Minnesota, circa 1970

Home life, eating at table

Family practice center

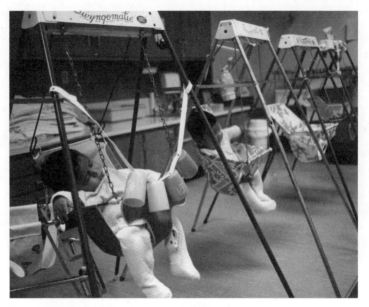

Day care facility at migrant summer school

Migrant summer school classroom

CHAPTER 7

The Growers Take Control

BY THE LATE 1960s the interdependency among American Crystal, the betabeleros, and the growers had endured in the valley for about four decades. Certainly, important changes had occurred through these years, but the basic structure remained unchanged: American Crystal controlled the distribution of a significant share of the nation's sugar market, created in the sugar-processing factories it built, operated, and maintained; the company contracted with rural landowners to grow the sugar beets to be processed into sugar; and both of these entities depended upon Mexican migrant workers—recruited by the company for the growers—to journey great distances to cultivate the sugar beet plants for a relatively short time each year. Though the benefits from this industry were certainly not parceled out equitably, most participants gained some reward. For nearly five decades American Crystal made vast sums of money from the "white gold"; farmers in the valley—increasingly cash-strapped through much of the half century between 1920 and 1970—often found sugar beet earnings a lifesaver; and most Mexican migrant workers from South Texas received their best seasonal wages from the valley's sugar beet industry.

During the late 1960s, however, the growers began to question much of this long-running arrangement. Pressured by economic problems in the nation's agricultural sector and driven by a desire to increase production in a commodity that earned more money for them than most other crops available, growers in the valley moved to gain control of American Crystal's sugar-processing facilities. In 1973, the growers turned this desire into reality when the RRVSBGA formed a cooperative and bought American Crystal. In addition, the growers found government regulations regarding recruitment and employment of migrant labor expensive and irksome. When they took control of American Crystal, the RRVSBGA concluded that the labor agency in Texas was a financial burden. In 1974, the American Crystal Labor

Agency ceased operation after more than thirty years of recruiting betabeleros for the valley. From that point on, each betabelero and grower would negotiate their own contract within federal guidelines. Therefore, in a remarkably brief period of time—seven years—the triangular relationship of the sugar industry in the region, long shaped by necessity, disappeared.

VOLATILITY WITHIN THE DOMESTIC SUGAR INDUSTRY during the late 1960s spurred many growers in the valley to reexamine their relationship with American Crystal. Unable to reach political agreement on domestic quotas for 1968, Congress placed no limitations on that year's production. The American economy in the late 1960s suffered significantly from an inflationary spiral, and rising sugar prices were a very visible manifestation of the higher costs plaguing consumers. An increase in sugar production would lead to lower prices, hopefully, in many food items. Therefore, the federal government, after restoring production quotas only three years earlier, again removed all limitations on sugar output. The nation's sugar companies, thrust into unfettered competition, rushed to increase production. In order to placate its growers in the valley—the company's most important district—American Crystal contracted for about 194,000 acres in the region, an increase of almost 20 percent from the 1967 acreage. Moreover, most of that extra acreage went to growers already with the company. For valley growers and American Crystal, 1968 proved to be one of the best years ever financially.[1]

The following year, however, the federal government reinstituted the domestic sugar quotas. For 1969, these turned out to be above those previously in existence, and American Crystal decided to retain most of the increase in its quota in the valley. Unfortunately for the sugar industry, the government ordered a reduction in sugar production for 1970. The federal government's motivation this time was partly to decrease government support payments to sugar beet and sugar cane growers but also to gain control over an industry that seemed to American consumers to be too powerful. What the new lower quotas meant for the valley's growers was, though, that sugar beet acreage was nearly reduced to the 1967 level. Acreage allotments for growers were cut—generally across the board—and the opportunity dried up for other regional farmers to become American Crystal growers. Burdened with the national inflationary crunch and seeing their income likely to stagnate from the lower production quotas, the sugar beet growers believed their well-being jeopardized. Throughout the valley, farmers focused much of their unhappiness on American Crystal's management.[2]

Farmers who were not part of American Crystal's operation looked for some other way into the sugar business. Over five hundred growers and allied commercial interests in the southern part of the valley organized into the Southern Red River Valley Sugarbeet Development Corporation and courted various sugar companies in 1967 at an industry convention in San Francisco. Farmers near Harwood, North Dakota (about ten miles north of Fargo), encouraged Holley Sugar Company to open a processing plant in that community. Holley initially agreed to do so but later, in 1968, announced postponement of construction on the facility until after 1970. In the end, that factory was never built, as Holley decided to concentrate its expansion on the other side of North Dakota, along the Montana border. Corn growers in western Cass County, organized into the Lake Agassiz Sugar Corporation, did convince Northland Research Company to operate a facility in Mapleton to process sugar from corn. In 1968, Great Western Sugar Company purchased Northland Research, but it cut back production at the Mapleton plant in favor of a similar operation that Great Western owned in southern Minnesota. All of these schemes hatched in the late 1960s were indicative of what might be described as a sugar mania that had grabbed farmers in the valley.[3]

Of course, much of this sugar beet interest was driven by the shaky agricultural markets for other crops. For example, two of the valley's traditional grain crops—wheat and barley—recorded price declines in 1967; wheat prices dropped from $1.65 per bushel to $1.50, and barley, from $1.07 to $1.00. Moreover, oats barely gained, going from $0.56 cents to $0.65 per bushel. It was no wonder that farmers in the region searched for more profitable crops. In North Dakota, sunflower acreage leaped 150 percent in 1967, and soybeans moved ahead 40 percent.[4]

Sugar produced from beets climbed steadily in value during the late 1960s, in 1967 reaching $16.50 per ton. With an average yield of 1,008 tons, a valley grower lucky enough to have a contract with American Crystal grossed over $16,500 from sugar beets. He further received, on average, almost three dollars per ton from government support payments. Some sugar beet growers were doing so well financially that American Crystal fieldmen began to experience delays during the long, cold winters getting contracts signed because they were waiting for "vacationing growers to return from the south." Valley sugar beet farmers had joined the ranks of the snowbirds, those people who fled the cold northern winters for the warmth of the southern states. The federal government decided how much sugar could be processed nationally, however, and American Crystal determined the valley's share; growers could not just simply expand, as they might with soybeans or sunflowers. They had to either convince the government to allow more production or get American Crystal to allocate a greater percentage of their quotas in the valley. Growers tried both approaches.[5]

The RRVSBGA members stepped up their activities in the late 1960s. In the summer of 1968, the group hosted a conference in Fargo for most of the other sugar beet grower associations in the country. A major result from that meeting was the decision by six of the associations, including the RRVSBGA, to open a national office in Washington, D.C., in order to further the political influence of sugar beet growers. To help pay lobbying costs and to have funds to support other valley sugar beet growers' interests, the RRVSBGA voted overwhelmingly to raise its members' dues that year. The growers also continued badgering American Crystal to increase the valley's quota.[6]

American Crystal recognized the pressure building from the valley's agricultural interests and attempted to curb the growers' rising assertiveness. H. A. Tvedten, a longtime American Crystal official in the valley and manager of the Moorhead facility in the heart of RRVSBGA country, reported at the close of the 1967 campaign that the "growers wanted more acres than we could possibly give them. Considering the trend of the times and knowing the thinking of their leadership, we know that as each year passes their demands will be greater." In response to grower complaints about the company's regulation to fallow sugar beet acres the year prior to planting, American Crystal began to experiment with growing beets on nonfallow land. In 1967, the Moorhead factory district allowed growers to plant 15 percent of their acres on nonfallowed soil, although the percentage was not to exceed a total of twenty-five acres of any grower's contracted acreage. The following year the Crookston facility allowed some nonfallowed land to be planted with sugar beets. More to the heart of what the growers wanted, the company invested around six million dollars to expand the processing capacity of the Moorhead plant. When completed in 1970, the Moorhead facility had increased its processing ability by about 25 percent.[7]

To the valley's growers, however, the future for American Crystal seemed dim. Where Great Western and Holley were expanding their facilities and merging with other companies, American Crystal appeared to be stagnant, if not in decline. In addition, soft drink producers were turning more to corn sweeteners, which increased competition for all sugar producers. At a time when the nation's and, indeed, the world's sugar consumption was growing, American Crystal's sales had flattened out by 1970. The East Grand Forks plant, over forty years old, was showing its age, but the company seemed reluctant to improve its capacity as it had with the Moorhead plant. During the winter of 1970–71, American Crystal announced that it would soon close the Chaska facility, another deteriorating factory, rather than investing in modernizing it. In the short run, this meant more acreage allotments could be transferred to the valley from southern Minnesota because of the increased capacity of the Moorhead factory. For valley growers and business interests, however, shutting down the Chaska operation called into question the future of American Crystal. If the processing capacity was not raised by building new plants or modernizing older ones, growth in the valley's sugar industry would still be stymied. Therefore, by the end of the 1960s, the gulf between the growers and American Crystal had widened. The Mexican migrant workers' role in the valley's sugar equation was changing as well.[8]

THE EFFECTS OF THE FLUCTUATIONS in the valley's sugar acreage in the late 1960s also put the labor procurement process in disarray. The spurt in acreage for 1968 forced the labor agency in Texas to suddenly recruit more than one thousand additional betabeleros from what it had provided the previous year; more than 6,900 Mexican migrants came to the valley from Texas in 1968. The labor agency sent virtually the same number the following year, but in response to the acreage cutbacks in 1970, American Crystal directed Axelson and his recruiters to reduce the number of migrants by 20 percent. Many betabeleros suddenly found their services no longer needed. Fearing this would lead to a flood of freelancers descending on the valley, Axelson sent a letter to all growers warning them not to hire noncontract field laborers. Nonetheless, over one thousand migrant workers without contracts showed up in the valley that year. For most of them, it proved to be a wasted journey.[9]

The sudden reduction in migrant workers was not solely the result of the decrease in acreage. In 1969, American Crystal introduced a new electric thinner, distributing seven to its growers in the valley. The new machines performed impressively. Used in conjunction with chemical herbicides, they significantly reduced the amount of field cultivation required as long as the fields were relatively dry. At least ninety-six growers purchased the new thinner for $7,500 for the following year. The manager of the Crookston factory, G. E. Claassen, gushed over the electric thinner that "sugarbeet agriculture will experience its greatest accomplishment since the adoption of the mechanical harvester." In 1970, managers for the valley plants reported that migrant workers could cultivate on average nearly thirty acres because the new mechanical thinners that were being introduced made weeds less of a problem and, therefore, field work was less time-consuming. In the future fewer betabeleros would be needed for cultivation in the valley as long as the acreage devoted to sugar beets remained steady.[10]

For those Mexican migrant workers with contracts, increased acreage meant their highest earnings ever. For example, one factory manager in 1969 figured the migrant workers in his area cultivated twenty-seven acres on average while being paid $25.50 per acre. The following year, average pay climbed to twenty-seven dollars per acre, with one manager noting his field laborers frequently took care of up to thirty-four acres. Adjusted to an hourly wage, some betabeleros were earning five dollars per hour, well above the federal minimum wage then in effect. Therefore, for many migrant workers the valley was a very desirable place to work, and the subsequent cut in job opportunities sorely hurt those betabeleros affected. In 1971, managers complained about freelancers still appearing in the valley, and they reported some growers hiring them at reduced pay. All growers gained leverage over labor created from the oversupply of Mexican migrants in the valley; those growers willing to run the risk (they forfeited federal government support payments if caught) of paying less than the federal-mandated wage gained an even greater position over betabeleros. The pendulum had swung to the growers' advantage.[11]

Another factor in the changing sugar beet labor market in the late 1960s involved the continued use of local teenage workers through the Youth Beet Program. That the YBP had fallen short of its goals to date led the program officials to change tactics. In the Fargo district, which had continuously come up short because of the high turnover rates, recruiters focused their efforts on smaller towns in the area, such as Kindred and Casselton, on the assumption that they would attract youths less accustomed to urban amenities and with fewer job opportunities. The Grand Forks YBP district recruited less in high schools, turning to junior high students (at least age fourteen), who would have fewer summer employment chances. All YBP districts hired more teachers as crew leaders, figuring the instructors would be more adept at supervising the teenagers.[12]

These new methods had mixed results. Average acreage did climb slightly; Fargo district teens averaged five acres in 1971, and Grand Forks area youths, almost five and one-half acres. These figures remained way below that of the betabeleros, however, since the youth turnover rates were still very high. Most of the teenagers just did not stay on the job long enough to become skilled field cultivators. In 1971, the turnover rate was nearly 100 percent in the Fargo district, causing the YBP official there to lament that "the work was just too difficult [for the teens]." Even in the Grafton district, which once seemed so promising to North Dakota officials, the YBP reported its teenagers averaged only seven acres, and the turnover rate was 40 percent.[13]

The YBP struggled on into the 1970s and, with other contingents of field laborers appearing in the region, created a labor market that was increasingly fluid and advantageous to growers. A Grand Forks bank sponsored the Summer Youth Program, which supplied teenage workers to sugar beet growers. Social service agencies in Grand Forks and Fargo, such as the Salvation Army, hired out crews to growers from the ranks of the urban unemployed. Another agency received a federal grant to start the Hitch-Hike Program for rural youth, and some of these young people worked for sugar beet growers. In the northern valley some YBP teams quit the program but then hired themselves out as independent crews, figuring they could do better working on their own. Some sugar beet growers were able to take advantage of the disintegrating seasonal employment structure by not paying required wages. Many growers turned to non-Mexican crews, however, in order to avoid the increased public attention and government regulations regarding the betabeleros' working and living conditions.[14]

SOCIAL SERVICES AVAILABLE FOR MIGRANT WORKERS and their families grew notably during this period, especially in the area of children's education. In 1965, only four migrant summer school programs existed in the valley, but by 1969, at least eleven operated throughout the region, all under the auspices of Migrants Inc. After receiving a tremendous boost in 1967 from a federal grant of almost $200,000— part of the Johnson administration's Great Society program—enrollment in valley day care, Head Start, and elementary education programs grew from about six hundred migrant children in 1967 to over two thousand children in 1969. Furthermore, these summer schools and valley school districts worked together to send records back to schools in Texas, which helped place migrant children in their appropriate grades when they returned to the Lone Star State.[15]

The summer schools also offered numerous benefits for adults. They primarily hired females—from teenagers to grandmothers— although some males also received employment. Serving as interpreters, teachers' aides, day care workers, and support staff, in 1969 over 140 members of migrant families worked in the six-week schools. Their income significantly augmented the total earnings for their family. In addition, many of the schools offered adult vocational training classes and English-language courses. The school in Casselton, for example, offered evening classes in English for migrant parents and a welding course designed for migrant males. All of the schools hosted weekend social functions, such as picnics and dances, for the families.[16]

In 1970, North Dakota's Department of Public Instruction took over the migrant summer school program from Migrants Inc. and began to expand the program rapidly. Whereas six schools had operated on the North Dakota side of the Red River in 1969, there were eight in 1971.

More courses of studies were implemented, such as typing, industrial arts, and woodworking, and health services were expanded to include student vision and audio screening tests. The schools had arrangements with doctors, dentists, and optometrists to whom they could refer students when necessary. An experimental mobile Head Start program functioned for two years, although it was eventually deemed ineffective. Recognizing that most migrant youths left the summer education programs in their early teens to work in the fields, the schools offered more evening vocational training classes to these students; by 1973 the program provided daytime automotive mechanic and business education courses to encourage these young people to think of a life beyond seasonal agricultural work. The North Dakota migrant education program continued to hire large numbers of family members to work in the programs, but it also engaged parents by creating Parent-Teacher Associations in each school and having two migrant adults from each school region elected to a State Advisory Migrant Council. The North Dakota schools organized more evening social programs for adults; these drew as many as eight hundred Mexican workers and family members to weekend fiestas. The net result was more children in the program; in North Dakota enrollments climbed from 950 in 1970 to 1,150 two years later, a figure representing over 80 percent of age fourteen and younger Mexican children in North Dakota that year.[17]

The socials services offered in the valley went beyond educational opportunities. Besides its federal educational grant, Migrants Inc. had an operating budget of another $250,000 that it funneled into various health services throughout the valley. These health programs included at-home visits, referrals to physicians, and mobile X-ray units (for tuberculosis testing). In 1968, Migrants Inc. started a dental clinic for migrants in Clay and Wilkin counties and opened an evening Medical Family Center in Moorhead. Individual counties offered other services for migrant families, such as transportation, counseling, and, beginning in 1968, a Food Stamp Plan. Minnesota's state government provided even more benefits for migrant workers in the early 1970s. The state's minimum wage law was extended to seasonal farm workers in 1973, and the following year migrant farm workers gained coverage under the Minnesota workman's compensation law.[18]

Migrant housing also continued to be a major focus of concern for state officials, Migrants Inc., and American Crystal. Minnesota implemented new housing regulations in 1969 that were more in line with the extensive federal guidelines recommended two years previously. Those owning or operating migrant housing had to secure State Board of Health permits. Housing sites had to be well drained, located away from traffic or other hazards, cleared of any harmful plants (especially poison ivy), and have room for outdoor recreation. A sanitary water source was to be close to each house, and if the water came from a trucked-in tank, it had to be treated with chlorine. Housing construction standards included ceilings at least seven feet high, fifty square feet of sleeping space for each occupant, sixty square feet combined for cooking and eating for each occupant, and separate sleeping rooms for each sex and each family. Houses had to have electricity, with light fixtures and at least one electrical outlet in each room. Standards were set for indoor and outdoor toilets, including that they "shall be well-lighted, ventilated, clean, and sanitary." Minnesota's migrant housing regulations, in seven typed, single-spaced pages, also provided requirements for heating, cooking, washing, bathing, refuse disposal, window screens, sleeping, safety, fire, and first aid. It was these sorts of regulations that many sugar beet growers found onerous.[19]

Indeed, growers were being pressured from many directions to upgrade and maintain housing for their betabeleros. Each year, state inspectors from both Minnesota and North Dakota arrived in the valley to check on migrant resident facilities. Growers with below-standard housing were advised to make improvements, and inspectors returned to check if the work was completed. American Crystal fieldmen continued to examine housing and urged growers to keep theirs in good repair, noting that decent housing was a major factor in migrant workers' loyalty to the region's sugar industry. In fact, the manager of the Drayton factory complained in 1970 that Minnesota's state inspectors were not being as diligent in enforcing the migrant housing regulations as they should be, relying too often on grower self-evaluation forms. In some respects, American Crystal had become another adversary in the eyes of some growers when it came to migrant housing, and this contributed to the gulf between them and the company.[20]

Area newspapers also published stories on migrant worker housing, therefore putting more pressure on the growers. In 1967, the *Grand Forks Herald* ran a series on migrant housing in that district that resulted, according to the company's East Grand Forks manager, in "poor publicity" for some sugar beet growers. Likewise, the *Fargo Forum* ran a long piece titled "The Migrants" that described housing at one site. The newspaper reported that the facility did not meet state regulations, as it was only "14 by 14 feet, wooden frame, one doorway, three windows, one room. . . . two beds for the parents and four young children." The house did have a gas stove and an electric refrigerator, but for cleaning up there was only a water pump outside. The family took sponge baths "in a wash tub on the floor." There were two outdoor privies to serve a total of five families. Accompanying photos revealed clean houses, but an interior shot made it clear just how crowded the living conditions were. The reporter also concluded that the group of houses at this farm were "better than average." According to officials, however, the migrant housing situation was improving. In North Dakota in 1972, officials conducted inspections on fifty-five farms that had previously been found noncompliant with regulations and discovered that only three still failed to meet government standards. One *betabelera* remembered that the mobile home provided to her family was carpeted and included an air conditioner. In fact, "that house was better than the one we had down here [in Texas]."[21]

The attention paid to Mexican migrants by many residents in the valley during the late 1960s mirrored a climate of greater awareness and concern about racial matters throughout the region. Fargo residents had been stunned earlier in the 1960s when the Citizens Council of Mississippi had suggested that their city become a relocation site for southern blacks since North Dakota had so few. The implication being, from the Citizens Council's proposal, that overwhelmingly white North Dakotans had no concept of relating to other racial groups or were unaware of their own racist behaviors. Black servicemen stationed at the air base in Grand Forks also reported discrimination in housing in the region. Valley residents were reminded by the newspapers that North Dakota had had a very active, visible Ku Klux Klan in the 1920s.[22]

In response, various race- and ethnic-related social actions occurred in the late 1960s. Several communities in the region participated in

Operation Friendly Town, a program in which church groups each summer "adopted" children from Chicago's ghetto areas. The children, mostly black or Puerto Rican, escaped the poverty they lived in for a few weeks, and valley hosts learned more about cultures that otherwise would be alien to them. Moorhead State College (now Minnesota State University Moorhead) launched a program in 1968 to actively recruit fifty "underprivileged Negro students," an effort that was quickly expanded to include Native Americans as well. The Moorhead State initiative led directly to the creation of a joint Fargo-Moorhead committee to deal with racial prejudice in these border cities. Newspaper articles such as "The Migrants" suggested to readers that the growers' poor treatment of Mexican migrants fit into an overall climate of racial prejudice and discrimination that needed to be rooted out of the region. This level of social awareness by the white community reflected, however, only some of the important changes coursing through Mexican migrant communities in the late 1960s that were also reshaping the relationships among American Crystal, the betabeleros, and the growers in the valley.[23]

IN SOUTH TEXAS, Mexican citizens worked assertively to improve their lives on various levels during the latter years of the 1960s and into the early 1970s. An important catalyst to this development came from Mexican American college students throughout the country, especially in the Southwest. As more Mexican youths graduated from high school, they took advantage of numerous federal and university programs designed to enhance Mexican American enrollment numbers in higher education. These college students were influenced toward more activism by various agents. Certainly César Chávez and his United Farm Worker union had by now inspired a generation of Mexican university students. The African American civil rights campaign, Reies López Tijerina's efforts to restore Mexican land claims in the Southwest, the New Left, the antiwar movement, and the related sixties' counterculture further motivated Mexican college students. As Mexican youths became more assertive, they adopted the term *Chicano/a* (once a pejorative) to describe themselves, and they made the Plan of Aztlán their guide. As David G. Gutiérrez defined it, the dream of Aztlán venerated a pre-Columbian New World, a rejection of contemporary American society, and a motivation "to build a political program based on that [Chicano] identity."[24]

In Texas, Mexican college students and other youths rejected the more establishment, middle class–oriented LULAC and PASO and joined the Mexican American Youth Organization (MAYO), formed in 1967. Though initially concerned mainly with education-related issues, in 1969 MAYO launched the Winter Garden Project—an effort to gain political ascendancy for Mexicans in the area of South Texas where their numbers were greatest. These young people organized into a political party, La Raza Unida Party (RUP), for the 1970 elections and devoted themselves to grassroots campaigning, and the results stunned Texas political observers. In most of the elections in which RUP candidates contested in 1970, they won. Most impressive were the electoral victories in Cotulla, Carrizo Springs, and especially Crystal City, where RUP candidates won control over both the city council and the school board. Two years later, the RUP participated in elections throughout Texas (winning several more in South Texas) and earning 6 percent of the vote in the governor's race. As a political entity, RUP was active in seventeen other states by the early 1970s.[25]

As RUP gained political strength and visibility, MAYO continued its community organization efforts, and Mexicans in general increased their political participation. Those Mexicans living in South Texas began to see some social improvements and greater economic opportunities in their neighborhoods. By 1968, three of the larger cities in southern Texas—Austin, San Antonio, and Corpus Christi—passed open housing ordinances, ending bans on Mexicans residing in certain parts of town. In 1969, Texas passed legislation dismantling the last vestiges of the segregated school systems, the laws that restricted sports competition between different races. In Crystal City after the 1970 elections, the fire department hired its first Mexicans, more Mexicans became police officers, a community health center and a jobs training program were funded by the city council, and an urban renewal grant was approved by the federal government. More educational opportunity and political influence paid off in economic rewards. In 1950, about 50 percent of Mexicans in Texas were employed as "unskilled workers," but by 1970 that figure had dropped to barely 30 percent; conversely, whereas only 21 percent had a white collar job in

1950, in 1970 almost 33 percent did. With more manufacturing jobs moving into Texas, by 1970 about 35 percent of Mexicans had found work in skilled trades or as machine operators in factories.[26]

Many Mexican migrant workers did not reap immediate benefits from the political activism of MAYO and RUP or the new employment chances, but the increased activism among Mexicans did spill over into farm worker causes. Impromptu farm worker strikes occurred throughout the Nueces Strip in the late 1960s and into the 1970s. For example, in 1972 over one hundred Mexican men and women walked out of the packing sheds at one of Zavala County's major agribusinesses, Warren Wagner Farms, when their pay was reduced. The RUP supported the strikers and eventually not only got their wages restored but also secured a modest pay hike for the workers in the agreement. In an attempt to build on this experience, RUP created Obreros Unidos Independientes (Independent United Workers), a union that was eventually recognized in 1973 at Del Monte's plant in Crystal City. Farm workers in South Texas continued to be courted by unions as they migrated to the Midwest. The Farm Labor Organizing Committee (FLOC) remained active in organizing Mexican migrants in Ohio and Indiana during this period, although the union did not mount another direct action against an agribusiness until 1976. The Chávez-led UFW affiliated with the AFL-CIO in 1966 to promote the organization of migrant workers outside of California. Renamed the United Farm Workers Organizing Committee (UFWOC), its representatives started several migrant farm worker union campaigns in Great Lakes states in the early 1970s. These efforts, however, generally came up short during this era. For example, UFWOC strikes against cucumber growers in Michigan and the Michigan Sugar Company (a sugar beet operation) failed. Shortly thereafter, UFWOC withdrew most of their organizers from the Midwest.[27]

None of these labor activities seemed, however, to have had any major influence on American Crystal's operations during this period, other than raising some growers' apprehensions. Whereas labor agency recruiters had clearly been concerned about possible union activities among betabeleros earlier in the 1960s, company records and oral histories are silent about possible union efforts at the end of the decade.

The only mention of union organizers occurred in 1969 when Axelson reported that the labor hearing in San Antonio to set sugar beet field wages for that year attracted "not a single 'do-gooder' nor anyone from MAYO or any of the other radical groups." Of course, for betabeleros in the valley, the late 1960s labor scene was very uncertain. It must have seemed to them that American Crystal expanded acreage and hired more workers one year only to reduce acres and recruit fewer workers the next. The presence of YBP crews also must have been threatening to Mexican migrants. Therefore, union-minded betabeleros had to fear the consequences of becoming activists. Another reason for betabeleros not to rock the boat was, however, that sugar beet wages had gone up considerably during this era. In 1972, the federally mandated acreage piece rates were keyed to convert to about $2.15 per hour, the national minimum wage. An experienced betabelero with three family members as coworkers could earn $3,200 for eight weeks' labor (plus many growers still offered an incentive bonus), a wage much greater than those in other seasonal field labor jobs available in the Midwest. When one factored the relatively high wages with the improved social services being offered in the valley, most South Texas betabeleros had less incentive to listen to union organizers.[28]

A lack of labor union sentiment did not mean that betabeleros were not influenced by the other political and economic developments taking place in South Texas. For one thing, betabeleros were more assertive in their work expectations in the valley. In 1968, the manager of the East Grand Forks factory noted that Mexican migrant workers were "becoming harder to deal with each year. Many groups almost refused to work anything but clean fields [machine thinned and treated with herbicides] and they demanded the very top rate and many times a bonus." Clean fields meant that workers always hoed in an upright position, cleared weeds from an acre faster, and, consequently, made more money. The Drayton factory manager also claimed his field laborers were "getting more demanding each year... they always want more money than [the] contract calls for and they usually get it." Two years later, the Drayton manager complained, "Unless mechanical and chemical means to control weeds have been used, many labor groups have refused to work." Therefore, while the overall advantage had passed to the growers by now, betabeleros did not just surrender. Dependable, hard-working field laborers were still in demand by most growers, and such workers might use that to their advantage.[29]

American Crystal realized other new developments occurring with its betabeleros. The number of returnees began to decline in the late 1960s because they had other opportunities. In a study the American Crystal Labor Agency conducted in 1967–68, 318 families of betabeleros who had worked in 1967 did not return the following year because "the main breadwinners had obtained year-round work [other than sugar beets]." Another sixty-eight families did not re-sign contracts because either they "went with another company [agribusiness]" or they had taken advantage of one of the available government programs, such as Job Corps. Over two hundred betabeleros could not be located, suggesting they had moved where other employment or educational opportunity beckoned. The number of betabeleros coming with their families began to drop as well. American Crystal noted in most cases that this reflected a family's decision to keep children at home in Texas so they might attend school without disruption. The number of younger female migrant workers declined. Axelson reported in 1968 that younger Mexican women, especially those graduating from high school, were securing service jobs: "These girls are making up to $1.60 an hour... and besides they don't have to travel."[30]

American Crystal's labor agency also noted that more betabeleros were settling in the valley—some remaining available for seasonal farm work, some securing permanent farm employment, and others finding urban jobs. Certainly, the 1970 U.S. census found a much larger population, based at least on the "Spanish-speaking" category. In Minnesota over 23,000 were counted as such by census takers, of whom over 4,500 had been born in Mexico. A separate 1973 study found that over 10,000 "Hispanos" resided in St. Paul alone. North Dakota's Spanish-speaking population was only slightly more than 2,000, but at least one-half of those were concentrated in the Red River Valley counties. In 1970, on both sides of the river, the Spanish-speaking population numbered at least 1,600. This rise mirrored the growing Mexican population throughout the Midwest, especially in the states that drew large numbers of Mexican migrant workers from Texas. Wisconsin, Illinois, Ohio, and Michigan also witnessed an influx of Mexican residents between 1960 and 1970, many of whom were being hired in manufacturing or meatpacking jobs.[31]

Though these new residents fit uneasily into their adopted homeland in the valley, on the surface the valley's residents, at least culturally, appeared more accepting of things associated with Mexico and Mexicans. Fargo's first eatery with what it advertised as Mexican food, the Taco Shop (still operating in 2008), opened in the early 1960s; the owners also made tortillas that they supplied to area schools and grocery stores. In fact, Fargo public schools began to include tacos in their lunch menus, and the newspaper printed recipes for Mexican food. Grocery stores started to stock more pinto beans, peppers, and special flours for making tortillas, too. Area students traveled in groups to Mexico; high schools and colleges began to offer Spanish-language classes; and in 1968 the YWCA in Fargo kicked off a program to offer Spanish courses for adults. In addition, local newspapers offered a steady stream of human interest articles, especially during the summer, about migrants, migrant schools, and those who provided services to the betabeleros.[32]

Despite these indications of acceptance, social interactions between Mexicans and the valley's Anglos were not abundant. As one newspaper reporter wrote: "An invisible barrier exists between the permanent residents of the Red River Valley and their [Mexican] migrant neighbors." Betabeleros and their families for the most part remembered valley residents during the 1960s and 1970s as not blatantly racist or prejudiced, but the Anglos were certainly "standoffish" and quick to stereotype Mexicans. The son of a Mexican migrant worker who taught in one of the migrant schools each summer recalled that, upon first meeting him, Anglos in the valley always assumed that he, too, was a betabelero. Another valley Mexican migrant teacher had difficulties renting a motel room for his family, although, when he protested, the manager relented and provided them with a room. A Mexican migrant's son related overhearing an Anglo at a fair in Barnesville asking another, "Are those Mexicans suppose to be here?" For the region's sugar beet growers, an ambivalence toward Mexican migrant workers also began to emerge in the late 1960s and became one of the factors leading the RRVSBGA to determine the time had come for a drastic change in the sugar beet industry.[33]

SOME GROWERS had clearly become disenchanted with depending on Mexican migrant workers for their field labor needs. Company documents from the late 1960s onward indicated that growers were unhappy about two main aspects regarding betabeleros: the increase in government regulations regarding migrant living conditions and the escalating wages betabeleros earned. For example, at the end of the 1968 growing season, the East Grand Forks manager reported that growers "were very disgusted after adding up the costs" for labor and migrant housing. In 1970, the manager at Crookston registered grower complaints about state regulations that required showers be installed in migrant housing. In 1971, the Drayton manager wrote, "The demands of labor sometimes irks the grower." To be sure, American Crystal saw a silver lining in grower dissatisfaction with migrant labor costs, as the company used it to promote more mechanization. The manager at Moorhead predicted in 1969 that "more regulations and tougher regulations by the Federal and State agencies in the handling of Migrant Labor will give us a valuable assist in our Mechanization Program, as growers will find it impossible or too expensive to meet these regulations."[34]

These attitudes toward migrant workers and government regulations were shared by other farmers in the Midwest, as well. Studies found that "farmers sometimes are critical of 'outsiders' and 'do-gooders' who are concerned" about the living and working conditions of migrants. Moreover, social science researchers noted, "antagonism has been expressed by the farmers toward county and state health departments" inspecting migrant housing and labor camps. Interestingly, one study concluded that growers not very familiar with Mexican people, or who interacted with them less often, were more likely "to respond negatively to migrants." Conversely, growers who had a more paternalistic relationship with Mexican migrant workers tended to have a more favorable attitude.[35]

Obviously, American Crystal's rapid increase in contracted grower numbers in the valley during the 1960s meant that a larger percentage of growers had little or no previous experience with Mexican workers. As a result of the opening of the Drayton factory in 1964, the company carried contracts with 360 more valley growers by 1968— a jump of over 20 percent. In the early 1970s it added more growers.

Most of these new sugar beet producers, like the problematic Richland County growers during the expansion in 1961, had no migrant housing in place. Therefore, these new growers were more likely to either need to invest considerable sums of money to erect regulation housing on their property or reject migrants in favor of YBP crews. Growers who chose not to use Mexican migrants were, however, still assessed the fee to help cover the costs of the labor agency in Texas, a factor that must have irritated them and further soured their attitude toward Mexican migrant workers.[36]

Not all growers held this negative view of migrant workers, as many maintained paternalistic ties to their betabeleros throughout this era. One grower recalled that, after he got a new television during the 1960s, he would come home to find his own children and "a half a dozen" migrant children all gathered around the set "wanting to see cowboys." The children all played together in the yard, and his wife stayed busy during the summer months "making cold drinks and ice cream bars" for them. Another Mexican migrant worker was hired full time by a grower after he had worked seasonally for the landowner over many summers. When this betabelero developed a kidney disease, the sugar beet grower helped with his medical bills. A betabelero's wife related that a grower for whom her husband worked bought a new mobile home for their use and installed an air conditioner and carpeting in it—items not required in any of the government migrant housing regulations.[37]

Nonetheless, the reliance on YBP workers, the availability of betabeleros who now resided in the region, and a greater dependence on mechanical thinners with chemical herbicides all contributed to a reduction in the number of migrants needed from Texas during the early 1970s. Between 1969 and 1973, the number of betabeleros recruited in Texas dropped by almost two thousand. That year, barely five thousand were dispatched to the valley, a figure approaching the level needed before the Cuban embargo, despite the fact that sugar beet acreage had almost doubled since then. The reduction allowed the company to cut back significantly on the labor agency's operation. In 1973, Axelson's group recruited in only eleven counties, maintained four offices (San Antonio, Alamo, Laredo, and Crystal City), and employed only six recruiters. These reductions encouraged the manager of the Moorhead district to advocate in 1972 that the company close the labor agency: "My point is that there are enough migrants [settled in the region] and local youth who want to work so that we figure it is a good time to get out of the labor business." Many growers in the valley agreed with that conclusion. A reevaluation of how labor was procured was not, however, the only thing on the mind of the growers by then. Through the leadership of the RRVSBGA, a majority of them desired a complete restructuring of the valley's sugar beet industry by taking over the processing facilities—buying out American Crystal.[38]

THE IMPETUS FOR PURCHASING AMERICAN CRYSTAL came from a new cadre of leaders in the RRVSBGA. Generally, Aldrich "Al" C. Bloomquist received the most credit for developing the successful strategy the growers implemented to buy American Crystal. Bloomquist was hired as the association's executive secretary in 1962 after many years as a public relations specialist with the Western Beet Sugar Producers, a group financed by some of the giants in the sugar industry, such as Great Western, Holley, Utah-Idaho Sugar, and American Crystal. Bloomquist's position with the Western Beet Sugar Producers had given him considerable knowledge of the industry. During this time he had also traveled to Europe, where he gained insight into the Dutch Sugar Union, a farmers' cooperative that controlled the sugar beet factories in that country. Once installed as executive secretary of the RRVSBGA, Bloomquist quickly became a forceful advocate for the sugar beet growers—and those who wanted to be—throughout the valley. He had helped negotiate better contracts for the growers with American Crystal, and he had been a key member of the Drayton Economic Development Council that had maneuvered the company into building the new facility there. Bloomquist received significant support from the second and, in some cases, third generation of valley growers—the offspring of the growers who had retired in the 1950s and those added by the expansion associated with the Cuban embargo in the early 1960s. Benefiting from their parents' relative prosperity and often holding college degrees, these new growers were more willing to think as innovators and to imagine a sugar industry that they controlled.[39]

While American Crystal's deteriorating position among the other major sugar-producing firms increasingly led to tension between the company and its valley growers, the movement to purchase the factories gained tremendous momentum when the factory workers at American Crystal's processing plants went on strike during the harvest in 1971. The company's hourly factory employees had been unionized after World War II, and while there had been some problems in the past, there had never been a strike. With the plants idled at this crucial time, growers feared rightly that their entire crop, predicted to be a record 2.3 million tons, might rot. Heavy rains further put the crop in jeopardy as the sugar beets sat in soggy fields. One grower bemoaned that "we're kinda pawns caught in the middle." The strike lasted only a week but left many growers with frayed nerves.[40]

Less than two months later at the RRVSBGA annual meeting in Moorhead, the growers heard Robert Sakata, chairman of the board of the Great Western Producers Cooperative, explain how that growers' organization was going about its quest to buy Great Western Sugar Company for $120 million. In essence, over five thousand growers had pooled their resources to purchase Great Western and run it as a co-op. Sakata participated in a panel discussion, "Looking at Sugarbeets and Beet Sugar in the Years Ahead," and stirred growers with the notion that the "sugarbeet industry can best be guided by those who are the rightful owners of the raw product."[41]

From there Bloomquist and his supporters among the association moved rather quickly. Early in 1972, Bloomquist met with American Crystal's president in Denver to inquire as to whether the board of directors might be willing to sell the entire sugar operation. The answer was affirmative. Next, Bloomquist and the other officers navigated the RRVSBGA through the process of forming a corporation (required in order to make the purchase), overcoming in the process a significant opposition by a sizeable group of growers who deemed the venture too risky. In fact, about one-third of the association's membership opposed the purchase of American Crystal, not because they were against change but because they believed too many of American Crystal's facilities were outmoded. They urged the association to ignore American Crystal and build their own modern processing plants. Nonetheless, the RRVSBGA devised a scheme by which growers purchased stock in a corporation—called Crystal Growers Corporation—based on a plan in which growers invested one hundred dollars for each contracted acre of sugar beets they controlled. Thus, a grower with a one-hundred-acre contract committed ten thousand dollars to the corporation. The growers could also buy an option at the same rate for more acres, up to 25 percent more than they currently grew, from a projected increase that a team of consultants had estimated to be the real sugar beet capacity of the factories in the valley. Most growers took the opportunity to make this extra investment because this was what the whole enterprise was all about: more acres of sugar beets for each grower. For most of them, this meant borrowing considerable sums of money to purchase their shares in the venture; however, by the autumn of 1972, over 1,300 growers had signed on to the plan. As one young grower explained, though he was nervous about what might happen, "You have to take some chances in this business. When you buy some land, you're scared. When you buy some machinery, you're scared." His debt from the buyout of American Crystal amounted to over thirty thousand dollars.[42]

To many observers it must have appeared as though the valley had gone sugar crazy in 1972. Part of this was fueled by the federal government's decision to increase the domestic quota that year by 400,000 tons in order to curb sugar prices that were again on the rise. Other groups of farmers in the region also attempted to cash in on the sugar bonanza. Growers in the central part of the valley around Hillsboro, North Dakota (forty-five miles north of Fargo), some of whom were opposed to buying American Crystal, formed their own co-op—the Red River Valley Cooperatives Inc.—and contracted with a German firm to construct a new factory capable of processing beets from fifty thousand acres. The Red River Valley Co-op broke ground on the plant in September. Farmers in the southern end of the valley, long kept out of the sugar beet business, had previously organized into the Southern Red River Valley Sugarbeet Corporation. In July 1972, they signed a contract with a Texas firm to build a processing plant near Wahpeton, North Dakota (about forty-five miles south of Fargo), that also could support another fifty thousand acres of sugar beets.[43]

Meanwhile, the negotiations and other legal machinations between the RRVSBGA and American Crystal continued. In February 1973, 76 percent of the growers approved the final plans for the purchase, which still needed some financial backing from banks in the region.

With that in place, the Crystal Growers Corporation bought an eight-acre tract of land in Moorhead to erect a new two-story building to serve as the headquarters for the new American Crystal Sugar Company. In June the growers' takeover of American Crystal was finalized in meetings held in Moorhead. That autumn, the sugar beet growers harvested a crop of beets to be turned into granulated sugar that, in essence, was white gold belonging to them. The old triangular structure of company, growers, and migrants had disappeared, and a new sugar industry matrix in the valley was unfolding.[44]

SWEEPING CHANGES RAPIDLY FOLLOWED in the valley's sugar industry after the acquisition of American Crystal by the growers. Several key officials with American Crystal's headquarters in Denver decided to relocate to the valley and made the transition to a grower-owned operation easier than it might otherwise have been. Most of the factory managers stayed, too. Before the year ended, the new owners elected to invest in renovating and expanding the capacity of the East Grand Forks facility. More piling stations were added, and restrictions that growers use only company sugar beet seed were lifted.[45]

Two very important developments occurred the following year. First, during the summer of 1974, Congress did not renew the quota-based Sugar Act of 1948; a federal quota on domestic production was eliminated that had governed the industry since the New Deal. Demand for sugar, both in the United States and internationally, had increased substantially during the early 1970s. This had forced prices upward, playing an important role in the ongoing inflationary surge of the period (compounded with the oil embargo of 1973–74). Another factor contributing to the legislative decision not to extend the sugar act sprang from the political turmoil created by the Watergate crisis. Consequently, sugar prices spiked by as much as 300 percent that year, leading to a tremendous profit windfall for the valley's growers and their cooperative. Indeed, many growers took these earnings and significantly reduced the debt they had amassed during the purchase of American Crystal. It also meant, of course, that the growers could expand their sugar beet acreage. In fact, the elimination of sugar quotas (only partially restored in 1981) proved to be an incredible stroke of fortune for the new American Crystal and the growers. The other development in 1974 for the sugar industry in the valley was American Crystal's decision to close the labor agency in Texas.[46]

The necessity of having a labor agency located in San Antonio had faded in the early 1970s. The availability of more Mexicans residing in the valley, the pool of labor generated by the YBP and other sponsoring groups, machines, and chemicals meant less migrant workers were needed. Though the labor agency had already slashed its operation by the time the RRVSBGA took over American Crystal, the growers still paid dues to keep it operating. These costs were minimal—about $250 for a one-hundred-acre sugar beet plot—but for growers investing heavily in their shares for American Crystal, it was an additional expense. Furthermore, the labor agency's method of contracting with betabeleros, overseen by the federal government, obliged growers to provide approved housing, likewise an expensive irritant. Many growers already tried to get around this by hiring freelancers, a rising source of conflict between the growers and the labor agency personnel in Texas. Indeed, by 1974 the new owners of American Crystal and the labor agency were at odds over freelancers and other matters, prompting Axelson to complain that "if these growers would get it through their heads that we are here to work with them and are not their enemies," relations would be smoother. The growers were now in charge, however, and the advantage rested with them. The labor agency shipped about only 3,400 Mexican migrants to the valley for the 1974 season. The next winter the American Crystal Labor Agency did not reopen for business. The era of the valley sugar industry's vital reliance on Mexican migrant workers from Texas had ended.[47]

What was also manifest in this decision to close the labor agency was that migrant workers lost many benefits. True, wages remained under the control of the federal government despite the demise of the Sugar Act of 1948, and betabeleros received a 7 percent increase in 1974. Each worker now had to negotiate his or her employment with the grower, however, and a desperate migrant might accept less money from an unscrupulous grower avoiding the federal minimum. No longer did betabeleros receive monetary advances or travel allowances unless a grower chose to provide them. If they had a vehicle breakdown or an illness on their travels to and from the valley, the betabeleros were on their own. The purchase of automobile liability insurance, once provided by the labor agency, was left up to the migrant workers. Housing was no longer a given; many growers chose not to offer housing, thus avoiding the expenditure of funds to keep domiciles up to standard and forcing Mexican migrants to find whatever housing they could in nearby towns. Paying rent further eroded betabelero earnings. Fieldmen were no longer the arbiters of disputes—migrant workers would have to turn to other agencies if they thought they had been cheated or treated badly by a grower. Indeed, one fieldman related that the biggest change in his duties during his entire career (1949 to 1990) came when he no longer served as a middleman between the migrant workers and the grower. Putting it simply, he stated that "it [his job] was much easier" when he no longer had to adjudicate problems that had arisen between a grower and a laborer. While some betabeleros continued to benefit somewhat from the paternalistic relationship forged with particular growers, the situation for most Mexican migrant workers in the valley's sugar beet fields became more precarious.[48]

The sugar beet industry continued to grow and prosper in the valley over the next two decades. The grower-owned American Crystal added another sugar-processing plant in Hillsboro in 1975 and a new facility, to replace the original, in East Grand Forks the following year. The company shed sugar-processing factories in other areas, focusing its efforts in the Red River Valley. The Rocky Ford, Colorado, plant closed in 1979; three years later American Crystal sold the Clarksburg, California, facility. By the early 1990s the valley had become the largest sugar beet–processing region in the United States. During this period the number of growers nearly doubled, as did the total acreage. In 1991, American Crystal paid $47.31 a ton to growers, establishing a new payment record.[49]

While the number of Mexican migrant workers needed in the industry declined through the 1980s, the permanent Mexican population in the valley increased. Relying significantly on herbicides, growers employed fewer field workers. By the mid-1980s about one-third of the growers employed no migrant workers at all, and those who did required fewer betabeleros than before. Nonetheless, the Mexican population in the area continued to grow as others followed family and friends who had established residence. Clearly recognizable Mexican communities formed in Crookston, Grand Forks–East Grand Forks, and Fargo-Moorhead. In fact, in 1990, Mexicans totaled 3 percent of the Fargo-Moorhead population. Members of the Mexican community found assimilation a slow process, however. A 1990s study concluded that, while many Mexican residents viewed their life in the valley as good, most did not believe the Anglo community fully accepted them. The racism and prejudice they experienced was not usually overt, though they "felt the sting of rejection" when they shopped in department stores or ate in some of the more upscale restaurants in the area. Some found life in the north not at all satisfactory. One betabelero family that had settled in the valley during the 1950s decided to go back to Texas forty years later because they wanted to live "with more Mexicans."[50]

SHORTLY AFTER THE LABOR AGENCY CEASED OPERATIONS, Adolfo Aguilar, who had recruited for American Crystal in Laredo since World War II, received a plaque and gifts from Stewart Bass, recently appointed vice president for the new American Crystal. Bass had been with American Crystal since the 1950s and had assisted the labor agency periodically during the spring recruitment campaigns. Bass and Aguilar knew each other well, and Aguilar wrote to thank Bass for the items the company had sent him in recognition for his services. In his letter Aguilar referred to himself as "this Border Mex (as Sully [M. C. Sullivan] use to call me)," attesting to the closeness that had once existed between the man who directed the labor agency for two decades and the Laredo recruiter. Aguilar was clearly touched by Bass's gesture and wanted him to know how "proud" he was for having "worked for this great company half of [his] life." In Aguilar's mind it was obvious that what he did for American Crystal was something of merit, and in some ways it clearly was. The interrelationship among American Crystal, growers, and betabeleros had benefited them all, albeit some more than others. In the future, however, the reciprocity created from necessity—that company, growers, and migrant workers all to a degree needed each other—for the most part vanished.[51]

Notes

INTRODUCTION

1. Lloyd Beiswinger, interview, July 10, 1990, transcript, Minnesota Farm Economy Red River Valley Sugarbeet Industry Oral History Project, Northwest Minnesota Historical Center, Minnesota State University Moorhead (hereafter RRVSBIOHP).

2. Ibid.

3. Ibid.

4. Jesus Sanchez Jr., interview, July 25, 1990, transcript, RRVSBIOHP.

5. Ibid.

6. Ibid.

7. Ibid.

8. Emmett Gunderson, interview, July 26, 1991, transcript, RRVSBIOHP.

9. Ibid.

10. Ibid.

11. Ibid.

12. R. H. Cottrell, ed., *Beet-Sugar Economics* (Caldwell, ID: Caxton Printers, 1952); Sidney W. Mintz, *Sweetness and Power: The Place of Sugar in Modern History* (New York: Penguin Books, 1985), 188, 207; D. Jerome Tweton, "The Business of Agriculture," in *Minnesota in a Century of Change*, ed. Clifford E. Clark Jr. (St. Paul: Minnesota Historical Society Press, 1989), 287–89.

13. Stanley Norman Murray, *The Valley Comes of Age: A History of Agriculture in the Valley of the Red River of the North, 1812–1920* (Fargo: North Dakota Institute for Regional Studies, 1967), 3–4.

14. Ibid., vii, 4–7.

15. "Weather Almanac," *Fargo Forum*, www.in-forum.com (accessed June 29, 2008). This newspaper went by a variety of names. I have consistently used the most common, *Fargo Forum* (hereafter FF).

16. Mintz, *Sweetness and Power*, 188, 207; Dennis Nodín Valdés, "Betabeleros: The Formation of an Agricultural Proletariat in the Midwest, 1897–1930," *Labor History* 30 (Fall 1989): 536–62.

CHAPTER 1

1. Elwyn B. Robinson, *History of North Dakota* (Lincoln: University of Nebraska Press, 1966), 133–40.

2. Murray, *The Valley Comes of Age*, 63–66; Claire Strom, *Profiting from the Plains: The Great Northern Railway and Corporate Development of the American West* (Seattle: University of Washington Press, 2003), 13–18.

3. Theodore C. Blegen, *Minnesota: A History of the State* (Minneapolis: University of Minnesota Press, 1975), 448–53.

4. Robinson, *History of North Dakota*, 133–40; Murray, *The Valley Comes of Age*, 129–35. The most thorough history of the Bonanza farms is Hiram Drache's *Day of the Bonanza: History of Bonanza in the Red River Valley* (Fargo: North Dakota Institute for Regional Studies, 1964).

5. Robinson, *History of North Dakota*, 154–55; Murray, *The Valley Comes of Age*, 158–60.

6. Strom, *Profiting from the Plains,* 40–63; Robinson, *History of North Dakota,* 251–54; Murray, *The Valley Comes of Age,* 161–64, 175–78, 204–7.

7. Robinson, *History of North Dakota,* 251–54; Lloyd Beiswenger, interview, July 10, 1990, transcript, 4–5, RRVSBIOHP; Leslie Anderson, Virginia Anderson, and Lee Lykken, interview, December 15, 1992, transcript, 4–6, RRVSBIOHP.

8. Terry L. Shoptaugh, *Roots of Success: History of the Red River Valley Sugarbeet Growers* (Fargo: North Dakota Institute for Regional Studies, 1997), 13–15; James J. Hill to J. H. Worst, May 24, 1897, Great Northern Railroad Papers, Minnesota Historical Society collections (hereafter MHS).

9. Robinson, *History of North Dakota,* 367–69.

10. Alfred S. Eichner, *The Emergence of Oligopoly: Sugar Refining as a Case Study* (Baltimore, MD: Johns Hopkins University Press, 1969), 343; Shoptaugh, *Roots of Success,* 15–16.

11. Shoptaugh, *Roots of Success,* 11; Eichner, *Emergence of Oligopoly,* 30–36, 343; James E. Fogerty, "From California to the Red River: The Saga of American Crystal Sugar" (unpublished manuscript, Minnesota Historical Society, n.d.), 1, 5, 7–8; Gutleben Historical Scrapbooks, "James M. Booth: An Autobiography," 4, 7, Series 3, American Crystal Sugar Company, Minnesota Historical Society collections (hereafter ACSC/MHS).

12. Fogerty, "California to the Red River," 5.

13. Susan M. Diebold, "The Mexicans," in *They Chose Minnesota: A Survey of the State's Ethnic Groups,* ed. June Drenning Holmquist (St. Paul: Minnesota Historical Society Press, 1981), 92; Fogerty, "California to the

Red River," 15; Shoptaugh, *Roots of Success,* 15–18.

14. Fogerty, "California to the Red River," 1–2, 6–9; Shoptaugh, *Roots of Success,* 19.

15. Fogerty, "California to the Red River," 12, 15; Shoptaugh, *Roots of Success,* 19–20.

16. Fogerty, "California to the Red River," 15; Shoptaugh, *Roots of Success,* 20; "Denver," 502, Gutleben Historical Scrapbooks, Series 3, ACSC/MHS.

17. Shoptaugh, *Roots of Success,* 20–22; Fogerty, "California to the Red River," 10; "James M. Booth: An Autobiography," 9–10, Gutleben Historical Scrapbooks, Series 3, ACSC/MHS. Booth was in charge of the construction of the East Grand Forks facility. He stayed on as the master mechanic there until 1946 when he left to help construct American Crystal's new factory in the Red River Valley at Moorhead, Minnesota.

18. Shoptaugh, *Roots of Success,* 40–41.

19. "Invitation and Program, Formal Opening Ceremonies of the Plant of the American Beet Sugar Co.," and "James M. Booth: An Autobiography," 10, Gutleben Historical Scrapbooks, Series 3, ACSC/MHS.

20. Jim Norris, "Bargaining for Beets: Migrants and Growers in the Red River Valley," *Minnesota History* 58, no. 4: 198–99.

21. Ibid., 198.

22. Sara A. Brown and R. O. Sargent, "Children in the Sugar Beet Fields of the North Platte Valley, 1923," *Nebraska History* 67 (1986): 256–57, 266–67; William John May Jr., *The Great Western Sugarlands: The History of the Great Western Sugar Company and the Economic Development of the Great Plains* (New York: Garland Publishing,

1989), 356–57, 367; Manuel Contreras, interview, July 16, 1975, transcript, 21, Mexican American Oral History Project, MHS.

23. Brown and Sargent, "Children in the Sugar Beet Fields," 266–67; *The Sugar Beet*, June 1929, 22, ACSC/MHS; Shoptaugh, *Roots of Success*, 30–31.

24. Brown and Sargent, "Children in the Sugar Beet Fields," 268–69; Shoptaugh, *Roots of Success*, 35–37.

25. Valdés, "Betabeleros," 538–39, 544–47; Mae M. Ngai, *Impossible Subjects: Illegal Aliens and the Making of Modern America* (Princeton, NJ: Princeton University Press, 2004), 38–39.

26. Valdés, "Betabeleros," 549–50; Dennis Nodín Valdés, *Al Norte: Agricultural Workers in the Great Lakes Region, 1917–1970* (Austin: University of Texas Press, 1991), 4–7; Ngai, *Impossible Subjects*, 19–55.

27. *The Sugar Beet*, July 1924, 8, ACSC/MHS; Ngai, *Impossible Subjects*, 64–68; Francisco Guzman and Dolores Guzman, interview, July 17, 1975, transcript, 3, Mexican American Oral History Project, MHS; George O. Coalson, *The Development of the Migratory Farm Labor System in Texas: 1900–1954* (San Francisco: R and E Research Associates, 1977), 13.

28. Ngai, *Impossible Subjects*, 62, 67–69.

29. Manual Contreras, interview, July 16, 1975, transcript, 4–5, Mexican American Oral History Project, MHS.

30. Juan R. García, *Mexicans in the Midwest, 1900–1932* (Tucson: University of Arizona Press, 1996), 5–10, 19–21, 25–48; Diebold, "The Mexicans," 94. See also Zaragosa Vargas, *Proletarians of the North: A History of Mexican Industrial Workers in Detroit and the Midwest, 1917–1933* (Berkeley and Los Angeles: University of California Press, 1989), 54–85, for a more detailed narrative on Mexicans in the automobile industry.

31. Sarah Deutsch, *No Separate Refuge: Culture, Class, and Gender on an Anglo-Hispanic Frontier in the American Southwest, 1880–1940* (New York: Oxford University Press, 1989), 133–34, 154–55; Coalson, *Migratory Farm Labor System in Texas*, 35–36; Jesus Mendez, interview, July 15, 1976, transcript, 1, Mexican American Oral History Project, MHS.

32. The most comprehensive account of this process is David Montejano, *Anglos and Mexicans in the Making of Texas, 1836–1986* (Austin: University of Texas Press, 1992), 105–78; Paul Schuster Taylor, *An American-Mexican Frontier: Nueces County, Texas* (New York: Russell and Russell, 1971), 72, 84–85.

33. Selden C. Menefee, *Mexican Migratory Workers of South Texas* (Washington, D.C.: U.S. Government Printing Office, 1941), 1–3. The quotation is from John Staples Shockly, *Chicano Revolt in a Texas Town* (Notre Dame, IN: University of Notre Dame Press, 1974), 14.

34. Douglas E. Foley et al., *From Peones to Politicos: Ethnic Relations in a South Texas Town, 1900 to 1977* (Austin, TX: Center for Mexican American Studies, 1977), 13–14, 82–83.

35. Montejano, *Anglos and Mexicans*, 220–28; Teresa Palomo Acosta and Ruthie Winegarten, *Las Tejanas: 300 Years of History* (Austin: University of Texas Press, 2003), 116–17; Patrick J. Carroll, *Felix Longoria's Wake: Bereavement, Racism, and the Rise of Mexican American Activism* (Austin: University of Texas Press, 2003), 24–26; Menefee, *Mexican Migratory Workers*, 44–45. See also Emilio Zamora, *The World of the Mexican Worker in Texas* (College

Station: Texas A&M University Press, 1993), 10–54.

36. Beet Contracts (Box 3), East Grand Forks, 1925–42, Contracts, 1925–29, Series 34, ACSC/MHS.

37. Valdés, Al Norte, 15; East Grand Forks Manager's Report, 1930, Box 20, American Crystal Statistical Records, Records of the Red River Valley Sugarbeet Growers Association, Northwest Minnesota Historical Center, Minnesota State University Moorhead (hereafter RRVSBGA).

38. Frank Tobias Higbie, *Indispensable Outcasts: Hobo Workers and Community in the American Midwest, 1880–1930* (Urbana: University of Illinois Press, 2003), 25, 41–46, 160–64.

39. Norris, "Bargaining for Beets," 198–99; *The Sugar Beet*, March 1927, 17–22, ACSC/MHS; Diebold, "The Mexicans," 92.

40. Michael M. Smith, "Beyond the Borderlands," *Great Plains Quarterly* 1 (1981): 244–45; Brown and Sargent, "Children in the Sugar Beet Fields," 262–63.

41. *The Sugar Beet*, 1925–31, especially "Your Beet Labor," April 1929, 7–8, ACSC/MHS; Leslie and Virginia Anderson and Lee Lykken, interview, December 15, 1992, transcript, 21–22, RRVSBIOHP; Brown and Sargent, "Children in the Sugar Beet Fields," 288–95.

42. Smith, "Beyond the Borderlands," 241–42; Diebold, "The Mexicans," 93; Dionicio Nodín Valdés, Barrios Norteños: *St. Paul and Midwestern Mexican Communities in the Twentieth Century* (Austin: University of Texas Press, 2000), 48–53.

43. Financial Statements and Statistical Reports, East Grand Forks, 41–42, Series 15, ACSC/MHS.

44. Montejano, *Anglos and Mexicans*, 209–10; Smith, "Beyond the Borderlands," 245; Ngai, *Impossible Subjects*, 54–55.

45. Montejano, *Anglos and Mexicans*, 210–12; Coalson, *Migratory Farm Labor System in Texas*, 36–37.

CHAPTER 2

1. Robinson, *History of North Dakota*, 399–402; Annual Reports, 1931–35, Box 1, Series 2, ACSC/MHS.

2. Robinson, *History of North Dakota*, 398; Statistical Reports, East Grand Forks Manager's Report, 1931, 207–11; 1932, 161–67; 1933, 184–87; and 1934, 206–8, Box 20, American Crystal Sugar Statistical Records, RRVSBGA.

3. Robinson, *History of North Dakota*, 398–99; Statistical Reports, East Grand Forks Manager's Report, 1931, 207–11, and 1932, 161–67, Box 20, American Crystal Sugar Statistical Records, RRVSBGA; "Hopper Fighters Keyed to Launch Drive," FF, May 8, 1934; "Hopper Horde Hatches Early," FF, May 9, 1934; "Weather Hits Clay's Crops," FF, May 14, 1936; Meta and Ester Engel, interview, October 29, 1990, transcript, 15, Minnesota Farm Economy, RRVSBIOHP.

4. Annual Reports, 1931–35, Box 1, Series 2, ACSC/MHS; Financial Statements and Statistical Reports, 1930–32, Box 75, Series 15, ACSC/MHS.

5. *El Cultivo del Betabel*, Box 149, Series 20, ACSC/MHS (the quote is on page 2).

6. Statistical Reports, East Grand Forks Manager's Report, 1931, 207–11; 1932, 161–67 (quotes from page 163); 1933, 184–87; and 1934, 206–8, Box 20, American Crystal Sugar Statistical Records, RRVSBGA; "Rates Paid Beet Workers 1931 to 1935, Incl.," Box 16, Series 11, ACSC/MHS; Governor's Interracial Commission, *The Mexican in*

Minnesota (St. Paul: State of Minnesota, 1948), 8.

7. Francisco E. Balderrama and Raymond Rodríguez, *Decade of Betrayal: Mexican Repatriation in the 1930s* (Albuquerque: University of New Mexico Press, 1995), 49–64, 120–22, 216–17. For a discussion on the debate over the numbers repatriated, see Jorge Durand and Douglas S. Massey, "Mexican Migration to the United States: A Critical Review," *Latin American Research Review* 27 (1992): 4–5.

8. Valdés, Barrios Norteños, 96–98; Valdés, Al Norte, 30–32.

9. Coalson, *Migratory Farm Labor System in Texas*, 56–57; Balderrama and Rodríguez, *Decade of Betrayal*, 79; Norris, "Bargaining for Beets," 199–200.

10. Norma Linda Longoria, "The Depression Years for Mexican Americans in Edinburg, Texas" (unpublished manuscript, Lower Rio Grande Historical Collection, University of Texas–Pan American, 1985), 3; Irene Ledsma, "The New Deal Public Works Programs and Mexican Americans in McAllen, Texas, 1933–1936" (master's thesis, Pan American University, 1977), 6–16; "Valley Agricultural Development," *Mercedes Tribune,* September 17, 1937 (Hidalgo County Historical Museum, Agricultural Labor Scrapbooks).

11. David B. Danbom, *Born in the Country: A History of Rural America* (Baltimore, MD: Johns Hopkins University Press, 1995), 206–10; Pete Daniel, *Breaking the Land: The Transformation of Cotton, Tobacco, and Rice Cultures since 1880* (Urbana: University of Illinois Press, 1986), 83–90, 104–8, 146–47.

12. For Roosevelt, foreign policy to Latin America, Cuba, and their sugar, see Louis A. Pérez, *Cuba: Between Reform and Revolution* (New York: Oxford University Press, 1995), 251–55, 260–71; National Recovery Administration, *Labor Provisions for the Beet Sugar Industry* (Washington, D.C.: U.S. Government Printing Office, 1933), 1–4; Kent Hendrickson, "The Sugar Beet Laborer and the Federal Government," *Great Plains Journal* 3 (1964): 47–48.

13. Background on the Costigans can be found in the statement of Mrs. Mabel Costigan, 18–20, and a written statement titled "One Test of Our Democracy," Transcript of Public Hearing, Ft. Collins, August 17, 1950, Box 4, RG 220, President's Commission on Migratory Labor, Harry S. Truman Library, Independence, Missouri (hereafter PCML/HSTL).

14. Statement of Mrs. Mabel Costigan, 19–20, Transcript of Public Hearing, Ft. Collins, Colorado, August 17, 1950, Box 4, RG 220, PCML/HSTL; Shoptaugh, *Roots of Success*, 45–47; Hendrickson, "Sugar Beet Laborer," 52–53.

15. Shoptaugh, *Roots of Success*, 47–48; Statistical Report 1937, 2 and 55, Box 75, Series 15, ACSC/MHS.

16. Statistical Report 1937, 2 and 50–56, Box 75, Series 15, ACSC/MHS.

17. Valdés, Al Norte, 47–50; Hendrickson, "Sugar Beet Laborer," 53–56; "Sugar Beet Growers Are Notified of Child Labor Compliance Plans," U.S. Department of Agriculture Press Release, Subject Files, Box 16, Series 11, ACSC/MHS.

18. Phyllis Palmer, "Outside the Law: Agricultural and Domestic Workers under the Fair Labor Standards Act," *Journal of Policy History* 7 (1995): 419–23.

19. Crop Information Reports, 1936–39, Box 15, RRVSBGA.

20. Daniel, *Breaking the Land,* 174–75; Coalson, *Migratory Farm Labor System*

in Texas, 56–57; Valdés, *Al Norte*, 52–53; Jesus and Ramona Mendez, interview, July 16, 1976, transcript, 2, Mexican American Oral History Project, MHS.

21. Harold A. Shapiro, "The Pecan Shellers of San Antonio, Texas," *Southwestern Social Science Quarterly* 32 (March 1952): 229–31, 234–39, 242.

22. Menefee, *Mexican Migratory Workers*, 5–6, 8–10, 13–19.

23. Valdés, *Al Norte*, 54–55. American Crystal's labor procurement methods for the 1930s are partially reviewed in "Texas Labor Procurement Data," Annual Report, 1946, Series 8, RRVSBGA.

24. Norris, "Bargaining for Beets," 200; Menefee, *Mexican Migratory Workers*, 21; quote is from Taylor, *American-Mexican Frontier*, 142.

25. Crop Information Report, 1936, Box 15, RRVSBGA; "AAA Announces 'Fair' 1938 Sugar Beet Rates," U.S. Department of Agriculture Press Release, Subject Files, Series 11, Box 16, ACSC/MHS; Menefee, *Mexican Migratory Workers*, 24; Valdés, *Al Norte*, 52–53.

26. Shoptaugh, *Roots of Success*, 64–68.

27. D. Hunt, "Mechanizing the Sugar Beet Harvest," *Journal of the West* 30 (April 1991): 86; Statistical Reports, East Grand Forks Manager's Report, 1937 and 1938, Box 20, American Crystal Sugar Statistical Records, RRVSBGA.

28. Valdés, *Al Norte*, 33–34; Coalson, *Migratory Farm Labor System in Texas*, 37.

29. Shoptaugh, *Roots of Success*, 50–52.

30. Ibid., 48–56.

31. "Beet Men to Meet Monday," FF, June 13, 1940.

32. "Seek to Bar Mexicans," FF, June 17, 1938.

33. Crop Information Reports, 1937 and 1939, Box 15, RRVSBGA.

34. Statistical Reports, 1939–42, Box 75, Series 15, ACSC/MHS; Annual Rates of Grower Earnings, Crop Information Reports, 1943, Box 15, RRVSBGA; Robinson, *History of North Dakota*, 424–25.

35. Robinson, *History of North Dakota*, 425; Crop Information Reports, 1939–41, Box 15, RRVSBGA.

36. Crop Information Reports, 1941, Box 15, RRVSBGA; "Labor Shortage Creates Harvest Problem in N.D.," FF, July 13, 1941; "Asks CCC Boys Release for Harvest If Needed," FF, August 15, 1941.

37. Victor B. Nelson-Cisneros, "UCA-PAWA Organizing Activities in Texas, 1935–50," *Aztlan* 9 (1978): 73–74; Valdés, *Al Norte*, 38–49; Governor's Interracial Commission, *The Mexican in Minnesota*, 23–24; Manager's Report Chaska District, 265, Statistical Report 1937, Box 75, Series 15, ACSC/MHS.

38. Rocky Ford Manager's Report, 1942, Statistical Reports 1942, Box 75, Series 15, ACSC/MHS.

39. Crop Information Reports, 1942, Box 15, RRVSBGA; "Aid Beet Growers, Murray Demands," FF, August 28, 1942.

40. Crop information Reports, 1942, Box 15, RRVSBGA; Annual Reports, County Extension Service, 1942, Polk County, 5–15, Minnesota State Archives, MHS.

41. Danbom, *Born in the Country*, 230; Robinson, *History of North Dakota*, 428–29.

42. Manuel García y Griego, "The Importation of Mexican Contract Laborers to the United States, 1942–1964: Antecedents, Operation, and Legacy," in *The Border That Joins: Mexican Migrants and U.S. Responsibility*, ed. Peter G. Brown and Henry Shue (Totowa, NJ: Rowan and Littlefield, 1983), 54.

43. García y Griego, "Importation of Mexican Contract Laborers," 56–60;

Johnny Mac McCain, "Contact Labor as a Factor in United States–Mexican Relations, 1942–1947" (PhD diss., University of Texas at Austin, 1970), 351–58.

CHAPTER 3

1. Coalson, *Migratory Farm Labor System in Texas*, 36–37; Menefee, *Mexican Migratory Workers*, 31.

2. "Detail of Labor Procurement for the Eastern Factories from the State of Texas for the Season of 1943," 1–3, Box 14, Labor, RRVSBGA; Coalson, *Migratory Farm Labor System in Texas*, 67–68.

3. "Details of Labor Procurement, 1943," 4–5, Box 14, Labor, RRVSBGA.

4. Ibid., 6–7.

5. Annual Reports, 1944 and 1945, American Crystal Labor Agency: Texas Recruitment, Box 14, Labor, RRVSBGA; Leslie and Virginia Anderson, and Lee Lykken, interview, December 15, 1992, transcript, 11, 16, RRVSBIOHP; Shoptaugh, *Roots of Success*, 74–76; "Plans Laid for Intensive Registration of Farm Help," FF, July 16, 1943; "Minnesota Migrant Report, 1943," 4, and "Minnesota Migrant Report: Summary of 1944 Activities," 1, Home Missions Council of North America, Church Women United in Minnesota, Records 1907–83, MHS.

6. Polk County, 1944, 23–24, Annual Reports, County Extension, MHS.

7. Menefee, *Mexican Migratory Workers*, 43; Valdés, Al Norte, 107–13; "The New York Migrant Program," Student Files 14–14, PCML/HSTL; Cindy Hahamovitch, *The Fruits of Their Labor: Atlantic Coast Farmworkers and the Making of Migrant Poverty, 1870–1945* (Chapel Hill: University of North Carolina Press, 1997), 166; Coalson, *Migratory Farm Labor System in Texas*, 71–72.

8. "Mexican Migrant Service in the Red River Valley," Polk County Schools, Department of Education Records, Minnesota State University Moorhead; Diebold, "The Mexicans," 97; "Minnesota Migrant Report," 1943–44, Church Women United in Minnesota, Records, 1907–83, MHS.

9. "School for Migrants, June 14–August 6, 1943," 1–2, Department of Education Records, Minnesota State University Moorhead.

10. "School for Migrants, June 14–August 6, 1943," 5, 14, 27, 38–42, Department of Education Records, Minnesota State University Moorhead; "Minnesota Migrant Report, 1943," 5–6, Church Women United in Minnesota, Records, 1907–83, MHS.

11. "Migrant Center Is Ready for Mexican Children," FF, May 30, 1943; "Migrant Center Will Close Today," FF, August 6, 1943; "Minnesota Migrant Report, 1944," 2–4, Church Women United in Minnesota, Records, 1907–83, MHS; Diebold, "The Mexicans," 97.

12. Robinson, *History of North Dakota*, 424–25; Shoptaugh, *Roots of Success*, 72; Statistical Reports, 1942–45, Box 75, Series 15, ACSC/MHS; Crop Information Reports, 1942–45, Boxes 15–16, RRVSBGA.

13. Shoptaugh, *Roots of Success*, 71; "Plant to Boost Beet Acreage in Valley by 12–14,000 Acres," FF, April 17, 1946.

14. Shoptaugh, *Roots of Success*, 83–85.

15. Hunt, "Mechanizing the Sugar Beet Harvest," 78, 84–86.

16. "Shortage of Bread Hits F-M Stores," FF, April 30, 1946; "Pork, Beef Prices Up on Monday," FF, March 29, 1946; "It Looks Like a Long, Dry Summer for Beer Drinkers," FF, May 15, 1946; "Sewer System Inadequate," FF, March 26, 1946; "Big Paving Job Ahead," FF, March 27, 1946; "Plans Well Under Way," FF, March 28, 1946.

17. "Plant to Boost Beet Acreage in Valley," FF, April 17, 1946.

18. "Introducing M. C. Sullivan," *Crystal-ized Facts*, January 1952, 25, Box 5, Crystal-ized Facts, RRVSBGA; Stewart Bass, interview, March 23, 2000, transcript, 13, RRVSBIOHP.

19. "Texas Labor Procurement Data, Annual Report, 1946," Box 14, Labor, RRVSBGA.

20. Ibid.

21. Coalson, *Migratory Farm Labor System in Texas*, 78–84.

22. Johnny Mac McCain, "Texas and the Mexican Labor Question, 1942–1947," *Southwestern Historical Quarterly* 85 (1981): 50–51; García y Griego, "Importation of Mexican Contract Laborers," 60–61.

23. McCain, "Texas and the Mexican Labor Question," 61; Coalson, *Migratory Farm Labor System in Texas*, 81–83; García y Griego, "Importation of Mexican Contract Laborers," 61.

24. García y Griego, "Importation of Mexican Contract Laborers," 62.

25. David G. Gutiérrez, *Walls and Mirrors: Mexican Americans, Mexican Immigrants, and the Politics of Ethnicity* (Berkeley and Los Angeles: University of California Press, 1995), 75–78; Montejano, *Anglos and Mexicans*, 242–44.

26. John Staples Shockley, *Chicano Revolt in a Texas Town* (Notre Dame, IN: University of Notre Dame Press, 1974), 10–11; Maria Ramos, "The Brownization of Pharr-San Juan-Alamo (1945-70)" (unpublished manuscript, Lower Rio Grande Historical Collection, University of Texas–Pan American, 1993), 5–9; Alvaro Zamora, interview, July 22, 1991, transcript, 7, 16, Minnesota Farm Economy, RRVSBIOHP; Norris, "Bargaining for Beets," 206.

27. For a complete account of the Longoria story, see Carroll, *Félix Longoria's Wake;* Gutiérrez, *Walls and Mirrors*, 154–55.

28. Carroll, *Félix Longoria's Wake*, 160–63; Pauline R. Kibbe, *Latin Americans in Texas* (Albuquerque: University of New Mexico Press, 1946); Gutiérrez, *Walls and Mirrors*, 164, 182.

29. Shoptaugh, *Roots of Success*, 79–80; "Issue Sewage Plant Permit for Moorhead Sugar Factory," FF, April 5, 1946; "New 'Town' Near Moorhead Named for Sugar Plant Head," FF, April 8, 1946; "Plant to Boost Beet Acreage in Valley by 12–14,000 Acres," FF, April 17, 1946; "CPA Okays Sugar Plant Application," FF, April 23, 1946.

30. Shoptaugh, *Roots of Success*, 79; "Delay in Plant Construction Cancels New '47 Beet Acreage," FF, August 26, 1946; "Polio Quarantine Lifted in Fargo," FF, October 7, 1946.

31. Shoptaugh, *Roots of Success*, 79–80, 110–11; "Dedication of Beet Plant to Be on Network," FF, July 2, 1948; "Grand Opening Program (Moorhead Plant)," Red River Valley, 1945–53, Box 19, Series 11, ACSC/MHS; Crop Information Reports, 1947 and 1948, Box 15, RRVSBGA. While the Sugar Act of 1948 did provide for increases, it otherwise differed very little from the 1937 law. See Cottrell, *Beet-Sugar Economics*, 271–82.

32. "State's Farm Income for '49 Third Highest," FF, September 8, 1950; "Underprivileged If N.D. Family of Four Income Below $6,712," FF, April 1, 1949; Crop Information Reports, 1946–50, Box 15, RRVSBGA; "U.S. Controls Sugar Prices by Regulating Import Quotas," FF, September 26, 1949.

33. North Dakota Agricultural Advisory Council, *Post-war Agriculture in North Dakota*, Preliminary Report Number II, June 28–29, 1944, 63–68, 97; "Electricity Outdoes Aladdin on Cass County Farmstead," "'49 REA

Program May Double N.D. Families Served," "Farm Plumbing Installations Increase as REA Expands," "NW Bell Maps $700,000 Rural Phone Extension Campaign," FF, April 1, 1949.

34. Annual Reports, 1946–50, American Crystal Labor Agency: Texas Recruitment, Box 14, Labor, RRVSBGA; Governor's Interracial Commission, *The Mexican in Minnesota*, 13; "Seek 500 Men to Aid Sugar Beet Harvest," FF, October 15, 1948.

35. Council of Welfare Agencies Meeting Minutes, November 28, 1949, Folder 22, Box 1, North Dakota Institute for Regional Studies, Fargo; "Will Return 14 Workers to Mexico," FF, July 6, 1949; "Alien Laborers Being Rounded Up," FF, October 6, 1949.

36. "Mexican Kills Young N.D. Man," FF, May 7, 1940; "Mexican Free in Knife Case," FF, July 28, 1940; "Mexican Beet Worker Shot," FF, May 13, 1941; "Mexican Held in Stabbing," FF, July 13, 1943; "3 Injured, 5 Held in Brawl," FF, September 5, 1943; "Hold Mexican at Crookston for Murder," FF, May 8, 1946; "Murder Charge to Be Filed in Moorhead Stabbing Case," FF, June 30, 1947; "Suspect in Stabbing Case Is Identified," FF, July 1, 1947; "Stabbed on Street, Woman Walks with Knife Buried in Back," FF, September 16, 1949; "Knife Victim Said in Good Condition," FF, September 17, 1949; "$10,000 Bond Set in Stabbing Case," FF, September 18, 1949; "Flores Sentenced to Prison for Stabbing," FF, October 19, 1949; "Walsh Farmer Stabbed Trying to Rescue Girl," FF, September 28, 1949.

37. Minutes, Migrant Committee, 1946–47, Church Women United in Minnesota, Records, 1907–83, MHS; Governor's Interracial Commission, *The Mexican in Minnesota*, 46; "Welfare Program Set Up for 4,000 Migrant Workers," FF, June 9, 1948.

38. Blegen, *Minnesota*, 552–55; Governor's Interracial Commission, *The Mexican in Minnesota* (quote is from Youngdahl's introduction).

39. Governor's Interracial Commission, *The Mexican in Minnesota*, 7–11, 16–17, 19–21.

40. Ibid., 14–16.

41. Ibid., 30–31, 35–36, 43–46, 61–62.

42. Ibid., 63–64.

CHAPTER 4

1. Peter N. Kirstein, "Agribusiness, Labor, and the Wetbacks," *The Historian* (1978): 651–54; Donald R. McCoy and Richard T. Ruetten, *Quest and Response: Minority Rights and the Truman Administration* (Lawrence: University Press of Kansas, 1973), 306–9.

2. News release, June 3, 1950, Papers of Stephen J. Spingarn, Student Files 16-4, PCML/HSTL; Kirstein, "Agribusiness, Labor, and the Wetbacks," 655–57.

3. Kirstein, "Agribusiness, Labor, and the Wetbacks," 657–62; McCoy and Ruetten, *Quest and Response*, 309.

4. "Report to the Members of the Good Neighbor Commission of Texas," Papers of David H. Stowe, Student Files 18-1; "The 'Wetback' Problem of the Southwest," Papers of Phileo Nash, Student Files 7-13, PCML/HSTL; Statement of Grover C. Wilmoth (El Paso District Director, INS), August 5, 1950, Transcripts of Public Hearings, Box 3; Statement of John Holland (San Antonio District Enforcement Officer, INS), August 1, 1950, Transcripts of Public Hearings, Box 2, RG 220, PCML/HSTL; George O. Coalson, *The Development of the Migratory Farm Labor System in Texas* (San Francisco: R and E Research Associates, 1977), 78.

5. Coalson, *The Development of the Migratory Farm Labor System in Texas*, 82; Statement of Grover C. Wilmoth,

(El Paso District Director, INS), August 5, 1950, Transcripts of Public Hearings, Box 3, RG 220, PCML/HSTL.

6. McCoy and Ruetten, *Quest and Response*, 307; Cliff Parliman to President Truman, June 15, 1951, and Petition of Hidalgo County Farmers, June 20, 1951, Student Files 407-D; Statement of Glen White, President of Rio Grande Valley Farm Bureau Association, July 31, 1950, Transcripts of Public Hearings, Box 2, RG 220, PCML/HSTL.

7. McCoy and Ruetten, *Quest and Response*, 307–8; "Employment, Wages, and Earnings of Migratory Workers," Staff Study Number 9, Staff Studies, Box 10, RG 220; Jesus Clemente to President Truman, June 15, 1950, Student Files 407-D; Statements of D. C. Baca, A. F. Cardenas, and Chester Turner, American Federation of Labor, July 31, 1950, Transcripts of Public Hearings, Box 2, RG 220; "Wetbacks," Papers of Phileo Nash, Student Files 7–16, PCML/HSTL.

8. Statement and Questions-Answers of W. H. Hughes, Valley Chamber of Commerce, July 31, 1950, Transcripts of Public Hearings, Box 2; Statement of Dr. Hector P. Garcia, Transcript of Public Hearings, Box 7; Report, Texas Employment Commission, September 7, 1950, B3–8a, Box 7; Statement of Dr. George Sanchez, August 1, 1950; Statements of D. C. Baca, A. F. Cardenas, and Chester Turner, July 31, 1950; Statement of Harry Kroger, Committee to Aid Migrant Workers, July 31, 1950, Transcript of Public Hearings, Box 2, RG 220, PCML/HSTL.

9. Statement of James H. Lumpkin, Colorado State Employment Service, August 17, 1950; Statement of Dr. Allen Hurst, Colorado Committee on Migrant Labor, August 17, 1950; Statement of Phillips B. Smith, Great Western Sugar Company, August 18, 1950, Transcripts of Public Hearings, Box 4, RG 220, PCML/HSTL.

10. Statement of Bernard Valdez, Colorado Governor's Committee on Migrant Labor, August 17, 1950; Statement of Helen Peterson, Mayor's Commission on Human Relations, Denver, August 17, 1950; Statement of Eutimio Duran, Social Worker, Denver Public Schools, August 17, 1950, Transcripts of Public Hearings, Box 4, RG 220, PCML/HSTL.

11. Statement of Alfred Medellin, Migrant worker, August 17, 1950; Statement of Isabel Díaz, Migrant crew leader, August 17, 1950, Transcripts of Public Hearings, Box 4, RG 220, PCML/HSTL.

12. Statement of William B. Gess, Mountain States Beet Growers Association, August 18, 1950, Transcript of Public Hearings, Box 4, RG 220, PCML/HSTL.

13. Statement of Phillips B. Smith, August 18, 1950; Statement of James H. Lumpkin, August 17, 1950; Statement of William B. Gess, August 18, 1950; Statement of Dr. R. W. Roskeley, Utah State College, August 18, 1950, Transcripts of Public Hearings, Box 4, RG 220, PCML/HSTL.

14. "Report of the President's Commission on Migratory Labor," Papers of Harry S. Truman, Official File, Student File 407-E, PCML/HSTL; Kirstein, "Agribusiness, Labor, and the Wetbacks," 662–66.

15. Kirstein, "Agribusiness, Labor, and the Wetbacks," 666–67; Ellis W. Hawley, "The Politics of the Mexican Labor Issue," *Agricultural History* 40 (July 1966): 160, 163–64.

16. Written Statement, the New York Migrant Program, September 6, 1950; Written Statement of Theresa Chiesa, Colorado Migrant Committee, August 4, 1950, Student Files 14–14 and 12–8, PCML/HSTL; Dennis Nodín Valdés, *Al Norte*, 143–44.

17. Statement of Sara Snare, Child Welfare Field Supervisor (the Border Project), August 4, 1950, Transcripts of Public Hearings, Box 2; Statement of Theodore J. Radtke, Bishops Committee for the Spanish Speaking, August 1, 1950, Hearing Statements, B3–21a, Box 7; Statement of Harry Koger, Committee to Aid Migrant Workers, July 31, 1950, Transcripts of Public Hearings, Box 2, RG 220, PCML/HSTL; Jim Norris, "Growing Up Growing Sugar," *Agricultural History* 79 (Summer 2005): 302; Governor's Interracial Commission, *The Mexican in Minnesota*, rev. ed. (St. Paul: State of Minnesota, 1953), 34–35, 41, 56–57; "X-rays Thursday for Migrants," FF, June 20, 1951.

18. Statistical Reports, 1949–1954, Boxes 75 and 76, Series 15, ACSC/MHS.

19. Ibid.

20. Gilbert C. Fite, *American Farmers: The New Minority* (Bloomington: Indiana University Press, 1981), 102–19; see also Judith Fabry, "Agricultural Science and Technology in the American West," in *The Rural West since World War II*, ed. R. Douglas Hurt (Lawrence: University Press of Kansas, 1998), 169–89; Danbom, *Born in the Country*, 234–48.

21. Robinson, *History of North Dakota*, 444–52.

22. Statistical Reports, 1950–54, Box 76, Series 15, ACSC/MHS; William Brekken, interview, July 17, 1989, transcript, 8, RRVSBIOHP.

23. O. A. Holkesvig to J. A. Summerton, October 15, 1952, and Holkesvig to P. H. Johnson, April 13, 1953, Subject Files, Red River Valley, 1945–53, Box 19, Series 11, ACSC/MHS; "400,000-Bag Warehouse Set at Crookston by Sugar Firm," FF, May 14, 1952; "Sugar Plant to Go Up at Crookston," FF, May 20, 1952; "Sugar Firm to Survey Valley for Beet Plant Sites," FF, June 16, 1953; "Holley Sugar Officials Survey Valley Beet Potential," FF, June 25, 1953.

24. "J. B. Bingham, Sugar Firm Manager, Dies," FF, September 18, 1950; "Wet Weather Slows Sugar Beet Harvest," FF, September 13, 1954; "Crews Prepare Grounds for Beet Fete, Roundup," FF, September 16, 1954; "Youngsters Ignore Weather to Parade in Moorhead Fete," FF, September 18, 1954.

25. Annual Reports, 1949–54, American Crystal Labor Agency: Texas Recruitment, Box 14, Labor, RRVSBGA.

26. Ibid.

27. Ibid. (direct quote is in the 1952 report); "Beet Workers Flown to Area," FF, June 5, 1951.

28. Annual Report, 1953, American Crystal Labor Agency: Texas Recruitment, Box 14, Labor, RRVSBGA.

29. *Crystal-ized Facts*, January 1948, 13–15; April 1952, 19–20; Spring 1953, entire issue, Box 5, Crystal-ized Facts, RRVSBGA; Crop Information Reports, 1950 and 1954, Box 16 Crop Information, RRVSBGA.

30. Numerous articles on the snowfall and flooding were in the *Fargo Forum* during 1950. The situation is summed up well in "Over 8,300 Families Hit by N.D., Minnesota Floods," FF, July 10, 1950; Annual Report, 1950, American Crystal Labor Agency: Texas Recruitment, Box 14, Labor, RRVSBGA; "Beet Harvest Set to Begin Here Sept. 18," FF, September 11, 1950; "Freeze Due to Follow First Snowfall," FF, October 2, 1950; "More Frost Due Tonight for Valley," FF, October 3, 1950; "Harvest Worker Need Increases," FF, October 6, 1950; "300 Moorhead High Students Picking Spuds," FF, October 11, 1950.

31. Norris, "Bargaining for Beets," 207; "Can I Afford a Mechanical Harvester," *Crystal-ized Facts*, July 1951, 19–22, Box 5, Crystal-ized Facts, RRVSBGA; Shoptaugh, *Roots of Success*, 94–95;

Harlow and Telbert Grove, interview, September 6, 1990, transcript, 13, RRVSBIOHP.

32. Octavio Ignacio Romero V, "Donship in a Mexican-American Community in Texas," *American Anthropologist* (December 1960): 968–69; Ozzie G. Simmons, *Anglo-Americans and Mexican Americans in South Texas* (New York: Arno Press, 1974), 232–36, 243; Foley et al., *From Peones to Politicos*, 82–83; Arthur J. Rubel, *Across the Tracks: Mexican-Americans in a Texas City* (Austin: University of Texas Press, 1966), 211.

33. "Labor Prospects for 1950," *Crystal-ized Facts*, April 1950, 13; "Handling of Field Labor," *Crystal-ized Facts*, April 1952, 17–18; "Beet Field Labor Experiences," *Crystal-ized Facts*, July 1952, 5–6, Box 5, Crystal-ized Facts, RRVSBGA.

34. "Labor Prospects for 1953," *Crystal-ized Facts*, Spring 1953, 20; "Labor Prospects for 1950," *Crystal-ized Facts*, April 1950, 13; "Contact Your Labor during the Winter," *Crystal-ized Facts*, October 1948, 39, Box 5, Crystal-ized Facts, RRVSBGA.

35. "Have Growers Any Responsibility in Recruiting Beet Workers," *Crystal-ized Facts*, September 1947, 32–33; "Field Labor for 1949," *Crystal-ized Facts*, January 1949, 27; "Let's Consider Your Labor House," *Crystal-ized Facts*, Spring 1955, 17–18; "Labor Prospects for 1953," *Crystal-ized Facts*, Spring 1953, 20; "Beet Field Labor Experiences," *Crystal-ized Facts*, July 1952, 5–6, Box 5, Crystal-ized Facts, RRVSBGA; Norris, "Bargaining for Beets," 204.

36. Wilburn Brekken, interview, July 17, 1989, transcript, 9–10; Meta and Esther Engel, interview, October 29, 1990, transcript, 27–29; Harold Helmeke, interview, April 9, 1990, 27–30; Leslie and Virginia Anderson and

Lee Lykken, interview, December 15, 1992, transcript, 19–20, RRVSBIOHP.

37. Meta and Esther Engel, interview, October 29, 1990, transcript, 28–29; Leslie and Virginia Anderson and Lee Lykken, interview, December 15, 1992, transcript, 16; Stewart Bass, interview, March 23, 2000, transcript, 10; Yolanda Lara Arauza, "The Settlement and Assimilation of Mexicans" (master's thesis, North Dakota State University, 2000), 59; Harlow and Telbert Grove, interview, September 6, 1990, transcript, 23, RRVSBIOHP.

38. Leslie and Virginia Anderson and Lee Lykken, interview, December 15, 1992, transcript, 21–22; Harold Helmeke, interview, April 9, 1990, transcript, 27; Meta and Esther Engel, interview, October 29, 1990, transcript, 28; Harlow and Telbert Grove, interview, September 6, 1990, transcript, 22–23, RRVSBIOHP.

39. Leslie and Virginia Anderson and Lee Lykken, interview, December 15, 1992, transcript, 19–20, 22; Harlow and Telbert Grove, interview, September 6, 1990, transcript, 23–24; Douglas Sillers, interview, August 24, 1990, transcript, 27, RRVSBIOHP; "Beet Field Labor Recruiting in 1952," *Crystal-ized Facts*, October 1952, 24–25, Box 5, Crystal-ized Facts, RRVSBGA.

40. Jesus Sanchez Jr., interview, July 25, 1990, transcript, 5, 14–15, RRVSBIOHP; Norris, "Bargaining for Beets," 204; Elva Treviño Hart, *Barefoot Heart: Stories of a Migrant Child* (Tempe, AZ: Bilingual Press/Editorial Bilingüe, 1999), 19.

41. Douglas Sillers, interview, August 24, 1990, transcript, 24; Stewart Bass, interview, March 23, 2000, transcript, 8, RRVSBIOHP; Arauza, "The Settlement and Assimilation of Mexicans," 59; Norris, "Bargaining for Beets," 204.

CHAPTER 5

1. Portions of this chapter appeared first in Norris, "Growing Up Growing Sugar." William Madsen, *Mexican-Americans of South Texas* (New York: Holt, Rinehart and Winston, 1964), 29–32; Florence Mason, *Survey of the City of Laredo, Texas* (unpublished manuscript), Folder 12, Box 83, George I. Sanchez Papers, Nettie Lee Benson Latin American Library, University of Texas at Austin; Marc Simon Rodriguez, *"Obreros Unidos:* Migration, Migrant Farm Worker Activism, and the Chicano Movement in Wisconsin and Texas, 1950–1980" (PhD diss., Northwestern University, 2000), 45–60; Shockley, *Chicano Revolt in a Texas Town,* 19.

2. "Experience with Labor in 1950," January 1951, *Crystal-ized Facts,* 16–17, and "Beet Labor Performance in 1951," January 1952, *Crystal-ized Facts,* 17–19, Box 5, Crystal-ized Facts, RRVSBGA.

3. Ngai, *Impossible Subjects,* 155–56; García y Griego, "Importation of Mexican Contract Laborers," 64–66; Gutiérrez, *Walls and Mirrors,* 163–68; Zaragosa Vargas, "In the Years of Darkness and Torment: The Early Mexican-American Struggle for Civil Rights, 1945–63," *New Mexico Historical Review* 76 (October 2001): 390–96; Montejano, *Anglos and Mexicans,* 298–300.

4. Shockley, *Chicano Revolt in a Texas Town,* 18–19; Rodriguez, *"Obreros Unidos,"* 112–13.

5. Rodriguez, *"Obreros Unidos,"* 49–56; Madsen, *Mexican-Americans of South Texas,* 32–34.

6. Governor's Interracial Commission, *The Mexican in Minnesota,* rev. ed., 53; Shockley, *Chicano Revolt in a Texas Town,* 11; Robert Clyde Tate, oral memoir, August 24, 1972, transcript, 36, and Rebecca Perez, oral memoir,

October 4, 1972, transcript, 14, Mexican American Project, Institute for Oral History, Baylor University, Waco, Texas; Ramos, "The Brownization of Pharr-San Juan-Alamo," 12–13; Rodriguez, *"Obreros Unidos,"* 67–80.

7. This material was gleaned from all of the annual reports between 1943 and 1974 that are cited as American Crystal Labor Agency: Texas Recruitment, Box 14, Labor, RRVSBGA. The pay figures are the only ones this author found. The paper is in an unlabeled file in the above box.

8. Annual Reports, 1950–59, American Crystal Labor Agency: Texas Recruitment, Box 14, Labor, RRVSBGA.

9. Treviño Hart, *Barefoot Heart,* 4–7; Valdés, *Al Norte,* 145; Alvaro Zamora, interview, July 22, 1991, transcript, 13, RRVSBIOHP; Leah Kroger, ed., *The TOKNS Project: An Oral History of Hispanic Immigrants to the Red River Valley* (Moorhead: Minnesota State University Moorhead, 2005), 96; Jesus Sanchez Jr., interview, July 25, 1990, transcript, 13, RRVSBIOHP.

10. Luis Martinez, interview, July 15, 1976, transcript, 14–17, Mexican American Oral History Project, MHS; Annual Reports, 1950 and 1959, American Crystal Labor Agency: Texas Recruitment, Box 14, Labor, RRVSBGA.

11. Stewart Bass, interview, March 23, 2000, transcript, 16–17, RRVSBIOHP.

12. Alvaro Zamora, interview, July 22, 1991, transcript, 9, and Jesus Sanchez Jr., interview, July 25, 1990, transcript, 14, RRVSBIOHP; Treviño Hart, *Barefoot Heart,* 21–22.

13. Annual Report, 1957, American Crystal Labor Agency: Texas Recruitment, Box 14, Labor, RRVSBGA; Statistical Reports, East Grand Forks Manager's Reports, 1958, Box 20, American Crystal Sugar Statistical Records, RRVSBGA.

14. Kroger, *The TOKNS Project*, 92; Treviño Hart, *Barefoot Heart*, 47-50, 59-60; Jesus Sanchez Jr., interview, July 25, 1990, transcript, 5, 16, and Alvaro Zamora, interview, July 22, 1991, transcript, 9-11, 21, RRVSBIOHP; Luis Martinez, interview, July 15, 1976, transcript, 18-19, Mexican American Oral History Project, MHS; Arauza, "The Settlement and Assimilation of Mexicans," 46-47.

15. Coalson, *Migratory Labor System in Texas*, 112-13.

16. Annual Reports, 1950-55, American Crystal Labor Agency: Texas Recruitment, Box 14, Labor, RRVSBGA.

17. "Post Season Agricultural and Food Processing Report," 1957, 9-16, Farm Placement Service Reports, Minnesota Department of Employment Security, MHS.

18. Norris, "Growing Up Growing Sugar," 298-99.

19. Ibid., 301-2; Luis Martinez, interview, July 15, 1976, transcript, 3-4, Mexican American Oral History Project, MHS.

20. Norris, "Growing Up Growing Sugar," 302; "Migrant Worker Welfare Said Problem for Public," FF, April 9, 1958.

21. Norris, "Growing Up Growing Sugar," 302.

22. Ibid., 302-3.

23. Ibid., 303.

24. "More 'Pachuco' Terrorists Suspects Being Turned Up," FF, September 28, 1954; "We Must Thoroughly Uproot and Expose 'Pachuco,'" FF, September 27, 1954; Gutiérrez, *Walls and Mirrors*, 123-25.

25. Norris, "Growing Up Growing Sugar," 303-4.

26. Harold Helmeke, interview, April 9, 1990, transcript, 29-30, and Emmett Gunderson, interview, July 26, 1991, transcript, 17, RRVSBIOHP; Valdés, *Al Norte*, 155.

27. James Gilbert, *A Cycle of Outrage: America's Reaction to the Juvenile Delinquent in the 1950s* (New York: Oxford University Press, 1986), 63-78; Tom W. Smith, "America's Most Important Problem: A Trend Analysis, 1946-76," *Public Opinion Quarterly* 44 (1980): 171-72; Ruth Shonle Cavan, *Juvenile Delinquency: Development, Treatment, Control* (Philadelphia, PA: J. B. Lippincott Company, 1969), 327.

28. Hazel Erskine, "The Polls: Causes of Crime," *Public Opinion Quarterly* 38 (1974): 289-92; William Graebner, "The 'Containment' of Juvenile Delinquency: Social Engineering and American Youth Culture in the Postwar Era," *American Studies* 27 (1986): 81-94; Cavan, *Juvenile Delinquency*, 301-2, 327-28.

29. Norris, "Growing Up Growing Sugar," 304-5.

30. Ibid., 305.

31. Ibid., 306.

32. Norris, "Bargaining for Beets," 206-7; Shoptaugh, *Roots of Success*, 62-65; "North Dakota Farm Labor Report, 1960," North Dakota State Employment Service (hereafter NDSES), 22.

33. "North Dakota Farm Labor Report, 1956," NDSES, 2-3, 26.

34. "North Dakota Farm Labor Report, 1957," NDSES, 26-28.

35. Norris, "Growing Up Growing Sugar," 307-8.

36. Ibid., 309.

37. "Valley Beet Fields Provide Work for Youth under New Program," FF, July 27, 1958; "Job Can Be Satisfying for Children," FF, August 9, 1959; "Beet Field Jobs Available for Youth under YES Plan," FF, June 5, 1959.

38. Norris, "Growing Up Growing Sugar," 309-10.

39. Ibid., 310; "North Dakota Farm Labor Report, 1959," NDSES, 3.

40. "North Dakota Farm Labor Report, 1960," NDSES, 5; "Post Season Agricultural and Food Processing Report," 1960, Farm Placement Service Reports, Minnesota Department of Employment Security, MHS; "5-Year Study Shows Changing Trend In N.D. Crop Acreage," FF, April 8, 1956; "Clay County Farms Low in Sale Value, but High in Cash Income," FF, April 18, 1958; "Average Cass Farm Valued at $60,658 in Land, Buildings," FF, June 19, 1960.

41. American Crystal Statistical Reports, 1955–60, Boxes 76 and 77, Series 15, ACSC/MHS; "Sugar Beet Payments up in 1957," FF, March 21, 1958; "Doubt Vote on Sugar at This Session," FF, May 29, 1955; "Re-Enactment of Sugar Act Needed by U.S. Producers," FF, March 2, 1955.

42. "Clay County Farms Low in Sale Value, but High in Cash Income," FF, April 18, 1958; "Land Value Increases 2 Per Cent," FF, April 29, 1960; "Over 38,000 Drop Indicated in N.D. Farm Population," FF, May 15, 1960; "Average Cass Farm Valued at $60,658 in Land, Buildings," FF, June 19, 1960; "Post Season Agricultural and Food Processing Reports," 1953–60, Farm Placement Service Reports, Minnesota Department of Employment Security, MHS.

43. American Crystal Statistical Reports, Manager's Reports, East Grand Forks, 1955–59, Box 76 and 77, Series 15, ACSC/MHS (direct quote from 1955–56 Campaign Manager's Report); Shoptaugh, *Roots of Success*, 95–96.

44. Annual Reports, 1955–59, American Crystal Labor Agency: Texas Recruitment, Box 14, Labor, RRVSBGA.

45. American Crystal Statistical Reports, 1955–59, Box 76 and 77, Series 15, ACSC/MHS.

CHAPTER 6

1. Shoptaugh, *Roots of Success*, 119–21; American Crystal Statistical Reports, 1959–64, Box 77, Series 15, ACSC/MHS.

2. American Crystal Statistical Reports, 1959–63, Box 77, Series 15, ACSC/MHS.

3. Ibid.

4. Ibid.

5. Shoptaugh, *Roots of Success*, 103–9.

6. "$1.5 Million Expansion Set for Sugar Plant," FF, March 21, 1961.

7. Shoptaugh, *Roots of Success*, 125–30.

8. Ibid., 129–30, 134–35.

9. Shoptaugh, *Roots of Success*, 130–33; "Sugar Beets Afford Glowing Potential," FF, June 30, 1964; American Crystal Statistical Reports, 1963–67, Box 77, Series 15, ACSC/MHS.

10. Shoptaugh, *Roots of Success*, 133–34. American Crystal fieldmen and other personnel were frequently applauded in the reports of the Governor's Migratory Farm Labor Committee published in the "North Dakota Farm Labor Report," NDSES (see especially 1963–67).

11. Annual Report, 1961, American Crystal Labor Agency: Texas Recruitment, Box 14, Labor, RRVSBGA; American Crystal Statistical Reports, "Report of Agricultural Operations Red River Valley," 1961, Box 77, Series 15, ACSC/MHS.

12. Annual Reports, 1962–65, American Crystal Labor Agency: Texas Recruitment, Box 14, Labor, RRVSBGA; American Crystal Statistical Reports, "Report of Agricultural Operations Red River Valley," 1962–65, Box 77, Series 15, ACSC/MHS.

13. American Crystal Labor Agency: Texas Recruitment, Annual Reports, 1962–64, Box 14, Labor, RRVSBGA; "Meet Joseph Axelson," *Crystal-ized Facts,*

Harvest 1964, 30–31, Box 5, Crystallized Facts, RRVSBGA; Stewart Bass, interview, March 23, 2000, transcript, 14, RRVSBIOHP.

14. Hawley, "The Politics of the Mexican Labor Issue," 172–75; "The Migrant Farm Worker in America," in *Background Data on the Migrant Worker in the United States Today* (Washington, D.C.: U.S. Government Printing Office, 1960), 11–13.

15. Annual Reports, 1961–65, American Crystal Labor Agency: Texas Recruitment, Box 14, Labor, RRVSBGA; Mark Edward Erenberg, "A Study of the Potential Relocation of Texas-Mexican Migratory Farm Workers to Wisconsin" (PhD diss., University of Wisconsin, 1969), 12, 16–19.

16. Norris, "Growing Up Growing Sugar," 310–11.

17. Ibid., 311.

18. Ibid.

19. Ibid., 311–12.

20. Ibid., 312–13.

21. Ibid., 313–14.

22. Ibid., 314.

23. Gutiérrez, *Walls and Mirrors*, 181–82; Montejano, *Anglos and Mexicans*, 282.

24. Shockley, *Chicano Revolt in a Texas Town*, 19–23.

25. Ibid., 24–41; Montejano, *Anglos and Mexicans*, 282–84.

26. For an excellent treatment of the farm worker movement throughout the 1950s to 1970s, see J. Craig Jenkins, *The Politics of Insurgency: The Farm Worker Movement in the 1960s* (New York: Columbia University Press, 1985), especially 131–74.

27. Montejano, *Anglos and Mexicans*, 284–85.

28. Rodriguez, "*Obreros Unidos,*" 136–213; Valdés, Al Norte, 184–98; W. K. Barger and Ernesto M. Reza, *The Farm Labor Movement in the Midwest: Social Change and Adaptation among Migrant Farmworkers* (Austin: University of Texas Press, 1994), 52–60.

29. Annual Reports, 1965–67, American Crystal Labor Agency: Texas Recruitment, Box 14, Labor, RRVSBGA.

30. "How's That Again," FF, August 1, 1962.

31. Helen J. Johnson, "An Overview of the Growth and Development of the U.S. Migrant Health Program," *Migration Today* 12 (1984): 13–14; "Health Setup for Migrants Opens in Clay," FF, June 26, 1964; "Worker Health Program Begun," FF, June 14, 1966.

32. Governor's Migratory Farm Labor Committee Report published in "North Dakota Farm Labor Report," NDSES (see especially 1966 and 1967); "Enrollment 210 in Head Start Program," FF, June 25, 1967.

33. "Annual Agricultural and Food Processing Report," 1963, 28–30, Farm Placement Service Reports, Minnesota Department of Employment Security, MHS; Governor's Migratory Farm Labor Committee Report published in "North Dakota Farm Labor Report," 1963 and 1966, NDSES (the quote is from the 1966 report, page 34).

34. "Children Of Migrant Workers Have Lots of Fun at Fiesta in Moorhead," FF, July 21, 1961; "Everybody a Bit Sad as Migrant School Ends Summer Term," FF, July 22, 1962; "Children of Migrant Workers Find Happy Outlet at School," FF, July 4, 1965; "Annual Agricultural and Food Processing Report," 1963, 32, Farm Placement Service Reports, Minnesota Department of Employment Security, MHS; "Worker with Migrants Given Car," FF, July 20, 1963; Valdés, Barrios Norteños, 196–97.

35. "Public School for Migrant Children Planned at Manvel," FF, June 10, 1964; "Community Cooperation Gets Things Done in Manvel," FF, July 17,

1966; "Manvel Club Wins $1,000 in Contest," FF, June 9, 1966; Governor's Migratory Farm Labor Committee Report published in "North Dakota Farm Labor Report, 1964," NDSES, 32; "Labor-Grower Relations," *Crystal-ized Facts*, Spring 1963, 20–21, Box 5, Crystal-ized Facts, RRVSBGA.

36. Norris, "Growing Up Growing Sugar," 312.

37. "North Dakota Farm Labor Report," 1963 and 1967, NDSES (see page 25, 1963; page 18, 1967); "Full-Time Jobs Open to Migrant Workers," FF, March 31, 1967; "Farm Worker, 20, Faces 2 Charges of Murder in Shootings at Argyle," FF, July 9, 1966.

38. Shoptaugh, *Roots of Success*, 135; American Crystal Statistical Reports, 1964–67, Box 77, Series 15, ACSC/MHS.

39. American Crystal Statistical Reports, 1964–67, and "Report of Red River Valley Agricutural Operations," 1956–67, Box 77, Series 15, ACSC/MHS.

40. Herbert Anderson, interview, October 31, 1990, transcript, 21, RRVSBIOHP; North Dakota Department of Agriculture and Labor, *Agricultural Statistics, 1960–66* (n.p., n.d.); "We Can't Afford It, but It's Our Last Chance,'" FF, March 22, 1967, and "Census Gives Close Look at Our Farm Neighbors," FF, July 15, 1966.

41. Stewart Bass, interview, June 6, 1989, transcript, 29, and Herbert Anderson, interview, October 31, 1990, transcript, 19–20, RRVSBIOHP; "Report of Red River Valley Agricultural Operations," American Crystal Statistical Reports, 1965–66, Box 77, Series 15, ACSC/MHS.

42. See roster of committee members in "Reports of Governor's Migratory Farm Labor Committee," North Dakota Farm Labor Reports, 1961–67, NDSES, and Minnesota Farm and Migratory Labor Advisory Committee Reports in

"Annual Agricultural and Food Processing Reports," 1962–67, Farm Placement Service Reports, Minnesota Department of Employment Security, MHS.

43. "Labor-Grower Relations," *Crystal-ized Facts*, Spring 1963, 20–21, and "The Labor Picture," *Crystal-ized Facts*, Spring 1965, 36–37, Box 5, Crystal-ized Facts, RRVSBGA; Herbert Anderson, interview, October 31, 1990, transcript, 20, RRVSBIOHP.

CHAPTER 7

1. American Crystal Statistical Reports, 1968, Box 77, Series 15, ACSC/MHS.

2. American Crystal Statistical Reports, 1969–71, Box 77, Series 15, ACSC/MHS.

3. "Area Ideal for Sugarbeets," FF, July 31, 1967; "Southern Valley Beet Group Says Efforts 'Being Bottled Up,'" FF, July 26, 1968; "Holley Defers Beet Plant Construction Beyond 1970," FF, May 27, 1968; "Corn Sugar Payments Are Made at Mapleton Plant," FF, June 2, 1968; "Mapleton Sugar Plant Won't Operate in '68," FF, April 24, 1968.

4. "Sidewalk Farming," FF, April 12, 1968.

5. "Valley Sugar Beet Growers to Receive 2nd Crop Payment," FF, March 14, 1968; American Crystal Statistical Reports, 1967–68, Box 77, Series 15, ACSC/MHS. The quote is from the 1968 Statistical Report, "Report of Agricultural Operations, Moorhead, Minnesota."

6. "Beet Grower Group Meets Here June 18," FF, June 7, 1968; "Beet Growers Will Establish National Office," FF, June 19, 1968; "Valley Beet Growers to Boost Dues," FF, April 12, 1968.

7. American Crystal Statistical Reports, 1967–68, "Report of Agricultural Operations, Moorhead, Minnesota, Campaign 1967–68" and "Campaign 1968–69," and "Report of Agricultural Operations, Crookston, Minnesota, Campaign

1968–69," Box 77, Series 15, ACSC/MHS; "Moorhead Sugar Plant to Increase Capacity," FF, June 29, 1968.

8. Shoptaugh, *Roots of Success,* 134–35.

9. Annual Reports, 1968–1969, American Crystal Labor Agency: Texas Recruitment, and "Dear Beet Grower," May 4, 1970, Legislation and General Information, Box 14, Labor, RRVSBGA; American Crystal Statistical Reports, 1970, "Report of Agricultural Operations, Moorhead, Minnesota, 1970–71 Campaign," Box 77, Series 15, ACSC/MHS.

10. American Crystal Statistical Reports, 1969–70, "Report of Agricultural Operations, Moorhead, Crookston, East Grand Forks, Drayton, 1969–70 and 1970–71 Campaigns," Box 77, Series 15, ACSC/MHS.

11. Ibid., 1968–69, 1969–70, and 1970–71 campaigns.

12. Norris, "Growing Up Growing Sugar," 314–15.

13. Ibid., 315.

14. Ibid., 315–16.

15. Governor's Migratory Farm Labor Committee, Reports, in "North Dakota Farm Labor Reports," 1967–69, NDSES; "Migrants, Inc.," *Crystal-ized Facts,* Spring 1967, 34–35, Box 5, Crystal-ized Facts, RRVSBGA.

16. Governor's Migratory Farm Labor Committee Reports, in "North Dakota Farm Labor Reports," 1967–69, NDSES; "The Migrants," FF, July 23, 1967.

17. "Migrant Education in North Dakota: Annual Report," 1970–73, North Dakota Department of Public Instruction, North Dakota State Depository Document, North Dakota State University Library, Fargo, ND.

18. Governor's Migratory Farm Labor Committee Reports, in "North Dakota Farm Labor Reports," 1967–69, NDSES; "The Migrants," FF, July 23, 1967; "She

Aids the Migrants to Healthier Life," FF, July 14, 1968; Diebold, "The Mexicans," 104.

19. "Migrant Labor Camp Regulations," Minnesota State Board of Health, 1969, Legislation and General Information, Box 14, Labor, RRVSBGA.

20. Governor's Migratory Farm Labor Committee Reports, in "North Dakota Farm Labor Reports," 1967–69, NDSES; American Crystal Statistical Report, 1970, "Report of Agricultural Operations, Drayton, North Dakota, 1970–71 Campaign," Box 77, Series 15, ACSC/MHS.

21. American Crystal Statistical Report, 1967, "Report of Agricultural Operations, East Grand Forks, Minnesota, 1967–68 Campaign," Box 77, Series 15, ACSC/MHS; "The Migrants," FF, July 23, 1967; Governor's Migratory Farm Labor Committee Report in "North Dakota Farm Labor Reports, 1972," NDSES. The concluding quote in the paragraph is from Chad Richardson, *Batos, Bolillos, Pochos, and Pelados: Class and Culture on the South Texas Border* (Austin: University of Texas Press, 1999), 26.

22. "Southerners Suggest Fargo as Negro Relocation Center," FF, June 3, 1962; "Some Negroes Have Trouble Finding Housing at Forks," FF, May 28, 1963; "Oldtimers Recall Klan Activity in 1920s," FF, April 11, 1965.

23. "'Operation Friendly Town' Brings Children to N.D.," FF, July 21, 1967; "Fargo Area Families 'Meet' Their Children," FF, July 17, 1968; "MSC Faculty Votes to Bring 50 Negro Students on Campus," FF, April 25, 1968; "Racial Prejudice in F-M Area Target of Proposed Committee," FF, May 5, 1968.

24. Gutiérrez, *Walls and Mirrors,* 183–85.

25. The best history of the early period of RUP is Armando Navarro, *The Cristal Experiment: A Chicano Struggle*

for Community Control (Madison: University of Wisconsin Press, 1998), 55–116. See also Montejano, *Anglos and Mexicans*, 285–89.

26. Navarro, *The Cristal Experiment*, 102–7; Montejano, *Anglos and Mexicans*, 286–99; Elizabeth K. Briody, "Patterns of Household Immigration into South Texas," *International Migration Review* 21 (1987): 30–32.

27. Navarro, *The Cristal Experiment*, 303–8; Barger and Reza, *The Farm Labor Movement in the Midwest*, 52–53; Valdés, Al Norte, 187–88, 197–98.

28. Annual Reports, 1969 and 1972, American Crystal Labor Agency: Texas Recruitment, Box 14, Labor, RRVSBGA.

29. American Crystal Statistical Reports, 1968 and 1971, "Report of Agricultural Operations, East Grand Forks, Minnesota, and Drayton, North Dakota, 1968–69 Campaign," and "Report of Agricultural Operations, Drayton, North Dakota, 1971–72 Campaign," Box 77, Series 15, ACSC/MHS.

30. "Field Labor Recruiting," *Crystal-ized Facts*, Winter 1968, 20–21, Box 5, Crystal-ized Facts, RRVSBGA; "Migrant Farm Worker Soon May Disappear from Fields in Valley," FF, July 5, 1968.

31. *Census of Population: 1970, Volume I, Characteristics of Population* (Washington, D.C.: U.S. Government Printing Office, 1973), Part 36, 119–23, 201–5 and Part 25, 229–31, 405–10; Diebold, "The Mexicans," 100, 103; Valdés, Al Norte, 184–85.

32. "South-of-the-Border Delicacies," FF, July 20, 1961; "Tacos Are as Fun to Serve as to Eat," FF, June 15, 1966; "Women Learn Spanish from Mexican Girl," FF, June 2, 1963; "Glyndon Students Find Classroom Spanish Is Adequate in Mexico," FF, March 28, 1967; "Spanish Classes to Begin at YWCA," FF, April 24, 1968; "The Migrants," FF, June 23, 1967; "She Aids the Migrants to Healthier Life," FF, July 24, 1968.

33. Diebold, "The Mexicans," 103; Alvaro Zamora, interview, July 22, 1991, transcript, 26, 30–31; Jesus Sanchez Jr., interview, July 25, 1990, transcript, 27, RRVSBIOHP.

34. American Crystal Statistical Reports, 1968–72, "Report of Agricultural Operations, East Grand Forks, Minnesota, 1968–69 Campaign," Report of Agricultural Operations, Crookston, Minnesota, 1970–71 Campaign," "Report of Agricultural Operations, Drayton, North Dakota, 1970–71 Campaign," and "Report of Agricultural Operations, Moorhead, Minnesota, 1969–70 Campaign," Box 77, Series 15, ACSC/MHS.

35. Eldon F. Synder and Joseph B. Perry Jr., "Farm Employer Attitudes towards Mexican-American Migrant Workers," *Rural Sociology* 35 (June 1970): 244–45, 248–50.

36. American Crystal Statistical Reports, 1964–72, Box 77, Series 15, ACSC/MHS; "Dear Beet Grower," May 4, 1970, Legislation and General Information, Box 14, Labor, RRVSBGA.

37. Douglas Sillers, interview, August 24, 1990, transcript, 24–27, RRVSBIOHP; Richardson, *Batos, Bolillos, Pochos, and Pelados*, 26.

38. Annual Reports, 1967–73, American Crystal Labor Agency: Texas Recruitment, Box 14, Labor, RRVSBGA; American Crystal Statistical Reports, 1971, "Report of Agricultural Operations, Moorhead, Minnesota, 1971–72 Campaign," Box 77, Series 15, ACSC/MHS.

39. Shoptaugh, *Roots of Success*, 124–33, 143–45; American Crystal Statistical Reports, 1968–73, Box 77, Series 15, ACSC/MHS.

40. Shoptaugh, *Roots of Success*, 135–36; "Record Sugarbeet Crop Seen in September Harvest," FF, August 18, 1971;

"Sugarbeet Prospects Still Unsettled," FF, October 19, 1971.

41. "Beet Group Told How Growers Buying Great Western Sugar," FF, December 8, 1971.

42. Shoptaugh, *Roots of Success*, 137–38, 145–58; "Beet Growers Group Opposes Buying American Crystal," FF, April 18, 1972; "Sugarbeet Growers Face $50 Million Gamble," FF, May 28, 1972.

43. "Sugar Quota Increased," FF, January 5, 1972; "Ground Broken for Hillsboro Sugar Plant," FF, September 22, 1972; "South Valley Beet Group Enters into Contract for Plant," FF, July 20, 1972.

44. Shoptaugh, *Roots of Success*, 158–59; "Sugarbeet Growers Approve Merger by Near 76% Majority," FF, February 16, 1973; "Crystal Sugar Co. Plans Moorhead Office Building," FF, March 19, 1973.

45. Shoptaugh, *Roots of Success*, 159–62.

46. Ibid., 163–66, 215–18.

47. "Dear Beet Growers," May 4, 1970, and J. W. Axelson to Stewart Bass, May 6, 1974, Legislation and General Information, Box 14, Labor, RRVSBGA.

48. Migrant Labor Correspondence, 1973–74, Keith Langseth Papers, Northwest Minnesota Historical Center, Minnesota State University Moorhead; Emmett Gunderson, interview, July 26, 1991, transcript, 36, 38, RRVSBIOHP.

49. American Crystal Sugar Company, *A Heritage of Growth: American Crystal Sugar Company and the First Hundred Harvests* (St. Paul, MN: Hakala Communications, 1998), x–xiii, 188–89; Shoptaugh, *Roots of Success*, 163–228.

50. Shoptaugh, *Roots of Success*, 210–11; Arauza, "The Settlement and Assimilation of Mexicans," 82–93, 100–104.

51. Adolfo Aguilar to Stewart Bass (no date, file 1975–76), Correspondence—Recruiters, Box 14, Labor, RRVSBGA.

Bibliography

ARCHIVAL SOURCES

Harry S. Truman Presidential Library (Independence, Missouri)
    President's Commission on Migratory Labor (RG 220)
        Transcripts of Public Hearings
        Staff Studies
    Student Files
        President's Commission on Migratory Labor
        Papers of Steven J. Spingarn
        Papers of David H. Stowe
        Papers of Phileo Nash
Hidalgo County Historical Museum (McAllen, Texas)
    Agricultural Labor Scrapbooks
Lower Rio Grande Historical Collection, University of Texas–Pan American
(Edinburg, Texas)
    Manuscript Collection, Student Papers
Minnesota Historical Society (St. Paul, Minnesota)
    Church Women United in Minnesota, Records 1907–83
        Migrant Reports, Home Missions Council of North America
    Great Northern Railway Papers
        Correspondence of James J. Hill
    Mexican American Oral History Project
        Written Transcripts
    Minnesota County Extension Service
        Annual Reports
    Minnesota Department of Employment Security
        Farm Placement Service Reports
    Records of American Crystal Sugar Company
        Series 2, Annual Reports
        Series 3, Gutleben Historical Scrapbooks
        Series 11, Subject Files
        Series 15, Financial Statements and Statistical Reports
        Series 34, Beet Contracts
        Miscellaneous
        The Sugar Beet (company newsletter)
Nettie Lee Benson Latin American Library, University of Texas
(Austin, Texas)
    George I. Sanchez Papers

North Dakota Institute for Regional Studies (Fargo, North Dakota)
  Council of Welfare Agencies
    Meeting Minutes
Northwest Minnesota Historical Center (Moorhead, Minnesota)
  Kenneth Langseth Papers
    Migrant Labor Correspondence
  Minnesota State University Moorhead
    Department of Education Records
  Records of the Red River Valley Sugarbeet Growers' Association
    Box 5, Crystal-ized Facts
    Box 14, Labor
    Boxes 15–16, Crop Information Reports
    Box 20, American Crystal Sugar Statistical Records
  Red River Valley Sugarbeet Industry Oral History Project
    Written Transcripts
Oral History Project, Baylor University (Waco, Texas)
  Mexican American Project

PUBLISHED PRIMARY SOURCES

American Crystal Sugar Company. *A Heritage of Growth: American Crystal Sugar Company and the First Hundred Harvests.* St. Paul, MN: Hakala Communications, 1998.

Background Data on the Migrant Worker in the United States Today. Washington, D.C.: U.S. Government Printing Office, 1960.

Census of Population: 1970, Volume I, Characteristics of Population. Washington, D.C.: U.S. Government Printing Office, 1973.

Governor's Interracial Commission. *The Mexican in Minnesota.* St. Paul: State of Minnesota, 1948.

Governor's Interracial Commission. *The Mexican in Minnesota.* Rev. ed. St. Paul: State of Minnesota, 1953.

Kroger, Leah, ed. *The TOKNS Project: An Oral History of Hispanic Immigrants to the Red River Valley.* Moorhead: Minnesota State University Moorhead, 2005

National Recovery Administration. *Labor Provisions for the Beet Sugar Industry.* Washington, D.C.: U.S. Government Printing Office, 1933.

North Dakota Agricultural Advisory Council. *Post-war Agriculture in North Dakota.* N.p., 1944.

North Dakota Department of Agriculture and Labor. *Agricultural Statistics, 1960–66.* N.p., n.d.

North Dakota Department of Public Instruction. "Migrant Education in North Dakota: Annual Report." Bismarck, ND, 1970–73.

North Dakota State Employment Service. "North Dakota Farm Labor Report." N.p., 1956–74.

SECONDARY SOURCES

Acosta, Teresa Palomo, and Ruthie Winegarten. *Las Tejanas: 300 Years of History.* Austin: University of Texas Press, 2003.

Alonzo, Armando C. *Tejano Legacy: Rancheros and Settlers in South Texas, 1734–1900.* Albuquerque: University of New Mexico Press, 1998.

Arauza, Yolanda Lara. "The Settlement and Assimilation of Mexicans in Moorhead, Minnesota." Master's thesis, North Dakota State University, 2000.

Balderrama, Francisco E., and Raymond Rodríguez. *Decade of Betrayal: Mexican Repatriation in the 1930s.* Albuquerque: University of New Mexico Press, 1995.

Barger, W. K., and Ernesto M. Reza. *The Farm Labor Movement in the Midwest: Social Change and Adaptation among Migrant Farmworkers.* Austin: University of Texas Press, 1994.

Blegen, Theodore C. *Minnesota: A History of the State.* Minneapolis: University of Minnesota Press, 1963 [1975].

Briody, Elizabeth K. "Patterns of Household Immigration into South Texas." *International Migration Review* 21, no. 1 (1987): 27–47.

Brown, Sara A., and R. O. Sargent. "Children in the Sugar Beet Fields of the North Platte Valley of Nebraska, 1923." *Nebraska History* 67, no. 3 (1986): 265–303.

Carroll, Patrick J. *Felix Longoria's Wake: Bereavement, Racism, and the Rise of Mexican American Activism.* Austin: University of Texas Press, 2003.

Cavan, Ruth Shonle. *Juvenile Delinquency: Development, Treatment, Control.* Philadelphia, PA: J. B. Lippincott Company, 1962 [1969].

Coalson, George O. *The Development of the Migratory Farm Labor System in Texas: 1900–1954.* San Francisco: R and E Research Associates, 1977.

Cottrell, R. H., ed. *Beet-Sugar Economics.* Caldwell, ID: Caxton Printers, 1952.

Danbom, David B. *Born in the Country: A History of Rural America.* Baltimore, MD: Johns Hopkins University Press, 1995.

Daniel, Pete. *Breaking the Land: The Transformation of Cotton, Tobacco, and Rice Cultures since 1880.* Urbana: University of Illinois Press, 1986.

Deutsch, Sarah. *No Separate Refuge: Culture, Class, and Gender on an Anglo-Hispanic Frontier in the American Southwest, 1880–1940.* New York: Oxford University Press, 1987 [1989].

Diebold, Susan M. "The Mexicans." In *They Chose Minnesota: A Survey of the State's Ethnic Groups,* edited by June Drenning Holmquist. St. Paul: Minnesota Historical Society Press, 1981.

Drache, Hiram. *Day of the Bonanza: A History of Bonanza Farming in the Red River Valley of the North.* Fargo: North Dakota Institute for Regional Studies, 1964.

Durand, Jorge, and Douglas S. Massey. "Mexican Migration to the United States: A Critical Review." *Latin American Research Review* 27, no. 2 (1992): 3–42.

Eichner, Alfred S. *The Emergence of Oligopoly: Sugar Refining as a Case Study.* Baltimore, MD: Johns Hopkins University Press, 1969.

Erenberg, Mark Edward. "A Study of the Potential Relocation of Texas-Mexican Migratory Farm Workers to Wisconsin." PhD diss., University of Wisconsin, 1969.

Erskine, Hazel. "The Polls: Causes of Crime." *Public Opinion Quarterly* 38, no. 2 (1974): 288–98.

Fabry, Judith. "Agricultural Science and Technology in the American West." In *The Rural West since World War II*, edited by R. Douglas Hurt. Lawrence: University Press of Kansas, 1998.

Fite, Gilbert C. *American Farmers: The New Minority*. Bloomington: Indiana University Press, 1981 [1984].

Fitzgerald, Deborah. *Every Farm a Factory: The Industrial Ideal in American Agriculture*. New Haven, CT: Yale University Press, 2003.

Fogerty, James E. "From California to the Red River: The Saga of American Crystal Sugar." Unpublished manuscript, Minnesota Historical Society, n.d.

Foley, Douglas E., Clarice Mota, Donald E. Post, and Ignacio Lozano. *From Peones to Politicos: Ethnic Relations in a South Texas Town, 1900 to 1977*. Austin, TX: Center for Mexican American Studies, 1977.

García, Juan R. *Mexicans in the Midwest, 1900–1932*. Tucson: University of Arizona Press, 1996.

García y Griego, Manuel. "The Importation of Mexican Contract Laborers to the United States, 1942–1964: Antecedents, Operation, and Legacy." In *The Border That Joins: Mexican Migrants and U.S. Responsibility*, edited by Peter G. Brown and Henry Shue, 49–98. Totowa, NJ: Rowan and Littlefield, 1983.

Gilbert, James. *A Cycle of Outrage: America's Reaction to the Juvenile Delinquent in the 1950s*. New York: Oxford University Press, 1986.

Gómez-Quiñones, Juan. *Mexican American Labor, 1790–1990*. Albuquerque: University of New Mexico Press, 1994.

Graebner, William. "The 'Containment' of Juvenile Delinquency: Social Engineering and American Youth Culture in the Postwar Era." *American Studies* 27, no. 1 (1986): 81–94.

Gutiérrez, David G. *Walls and Mirrors: Mexican Americans, Mexican Immigrants, and the Politics of Ethnicity*. Berkeley and Los Angeles: University of California Press, 1995.

Hahamovitch, Cindy. *The Fruits of Their Labor: Atlantic Coast Farmworkers and the Making of Migrant Poverty, 1870–1945*. Chapel Hill: University of North Carolina Press, 1997.

Hawley, Ellis W. "The Politics of the Mexican Labor Issue, 1950–1965." *Agricultural History* 40 (July 1966): 157–76.

Hendrickson, Kent. "The Sugar Beet Laborer and the Federal Government: An Episode in the History of the Great Plains." *Great Plains Journal* 3, no. 2 (1964): 44–59.

Higbie, Frank Tobias. *Indispensable Outcasts: Hobo Workers and Community in the American Midwest, 1880–1930*. Urbana: University of Illinois Press, 2003.

Hunt, D. "Mechanizing the Sugar Beet Harvest." *Journal of the West* 30 (April 1991): 78–87.

Jenkins, J. Craig. *The Politics of Insurgency: The Farm Worker Movement in the 1960s*. New York: Columbia University Press, 1985.

Johnson, Helen J. "An Overview of the Growth and Development of the U.S. Migrant Health Program." *Migration Today* 12, nos. 4–5 (1984): 8–14.

Kibbe, Pauline R. *Latin Americans in Texas*. Albuquerque: University of New Mexico Press, 1946.

Kirstein, Peter N. "Agribusiness, Labor, and the Wetbacks: Truman's Commission on Migratory Labor." *The Historian* 40, no. 4 (1978): 650–67.

Ledsma, Irene. "The New Deal Public Works Program and Mexican-Americans in McAllen, Texas, 1933–1936." Master's thesis, Pan American University, 1977.

Longoria, Norma Linda. "The Depression Years for Mexican Americans in Edinburg, Texas." Unpublished manuscript, Lower Rio Grande Historical Collection, University of Texas–Pan American, 1985.

Madsen, William. *Mexican-Americans of South Texas*. New York: Holt, Rinehart and Winston, 1964.

May, William John, Jr. *The Great Western Sugarlands: The History of the Great Western Sugar Company and the Economic Development of the Great Plains.* New York: Garland Publishing, 1989.

McCain, Johnny Mac. "Contract Labor as a Factor in United States–Mexican Relations, 1942–1947." PhD diss., University of Texas–Austin, 1970.

———. "Texas and the Mexican Labor Question, 1942–1947." *Southwestern Historical Quarterly* 85, no. 1 (1981): 45–64.

McCoy, Donald R., and Richard T. Ruetten. *Quest and Response: Minority Rights and the Truman Administration.* Lawrence: University Press of Kansas, 1973.

McWilliams, Carey. *Factories in the Field: The Story of Migratory Farm Labor in California.* Boston: Little, Brown and Company, 1939. Reprint, Santa Barabara, CA: Peregrine Press, 1971.

Menefee, Selden C. *Mexican Migratory Workers of South Texas.* Washington, D.C.: U.S. Government Printing Office, 1941.

Mintz, Sidney W. *Sweetness and Power: The Place of Sugar in Modern History.* New York: Penguin Books, 1985.

Montejano, David. *Anglos and Mexicans in the Making of Texas, 1836–1986.* Austin: University of Texas Press, 1987 [1992].

Murray, Stanley Norman. *The Valley Comes of Age: A History of Agriculture in the Valley of the Red River of the North, 1812–1920.* Fargo: North Dakota Institute for Regional Studies, 1967.

Navarro, Armando. *The Cristal Experiment: A Chicano Struggle for Community Control.* Madison: University of Wisconsin Press, 1998.

Nelson-Cisneros, Victor B. "UCAPAWA Organizing Activities in Texas, 1935–50." *Aztlan* 9 (1978): 71–84.

Ngai, Mae M. *Impossible Subjects: Illegal Aliens and the Making of Modern America.* Princeton, NJ: Princeton University Press, 2004.

Norris, Jim. "Bargaining for Beets: Migrants and Growers in the Red River Valley." *Minnesota History* 58, no. 4: 196–209.

———. "Growing Up Growing Sugar." *Agricultural History* 79 (Summer 2005): 298–320.

Palmer, Phyllis. "Outside the Law: Agricultural and Domestic Workers under the Fair Labor Standards Act." *Journal of Policy History* 7, no. 4 (1995): 416–40.

Pérez, Louis A., Jr. *Cuba: Between Reform and Revolution.* New York: Oxford University Press, 1995.

Ramos, Maria. "The Brownization of Pharr–San Juan–Alamo (1945–70)." Unpublished manuscript, Lower Rio Grande Historical Collection, University of Texas–Pan American, 1993.

Richardson, Chad. *Batos, Bolillos, Pochos, and Pelados: Class and Culture on the South Texas Border.* Austin: University of Texas Press, 1999.

Robinson, Elwyn B. *History of North Dakota.* Lincoln: University of Nebraska Press, 1966.

Rodriguez, Marc Simon. "*Obreros Unidos:* Migration, Migrant Farm Worker Activism, and the Chicano Movement in Wisconsin and Texas, 1950–1980." PhD diss., Northwestern University, 2000.

Romano, Octavio Ignacio, V. "*Donship* in a Mexican-American Community in Texas." *American Anthropologist* 67 (December 1960): 966–76.

Rubel, Arthur J. *Across the Tracks: Mexican-Americans in a Texas City.* Austin: University of Texas Press, 1966.

Ruiz, Vicki L. *From Out of the Shadows: Mexican Women in Twentieth-Century America.* New York: Oxford University Press, 1998.

Saunders, Lyle, and Olen E. Leonard. *The Wetback in the Lower Rio Grande Valley of Texas.* New York: Arno Press, 1976.

Shapiro, Harold A. "The Pecan Shellers of San Antonio, Texas." *Southwestern Social Science Quarterly* 32 (March 1952): 229–44.

Shockley, John Staples. *Chicano Revolt in a Texas Town.* Notre Dame, IN: University of Notre Dame Press, 1974.

Shoptaugh, Terry L. *Roots of Success: History of the Red River Valley Sugarbeet Growers.* Fargo: North Dakota Institute for Regional Studies, 1997.

Simmons, Ozzie G. *Anglo-Americans and Mexican Americans in South Texas.* New York: Arno Press, 1974.

Smith, Michael M. "Beyond the Borderlands: Mexican Labor in the Central Plains, 1900–1930." *Great Plains Quarterly* 1, no. 4 (1981): 239–51.

Smith, Tom W. "America's Most Important Problem: A Trend Analysis, 1946–1976." *Public Opinion Quarterly* 44, no. 2 (1980): 164–80.

Strom, Claire. *Profiting from the Plains: The Great Northern Railway and Corporate Development of the American West.* Seattle: University of Washington Press, 2003.

Synder, Eldon F., and Joseph B. Perry Jr. "Farm Employer Attitudes towards Mexican-American Migrant Workers." *Rural Sociology* 35, no. 2 (June 1970): 244–52.

Taylor, Paul Schuster. *An American-Mexican Frontier: Nueces County, Texas.* New York: Russell and Russell, 1934 [1971].

Treviño Hart, Elva. *Barefoot Heart: Stories of a Migrant Child.* Tempe, AZ: Bilingual Press/Editorial Bilingüe, 1999.

Tweton, D. Jerome. "The Business of Agriculture." In *Minnesota in a Century of Change,* edited by Clifford E. Clark Jr. St. Paul: Minnesota Historical Society Press, 1989.

Valdés, Dennis Nodín. Al Norte: *Agricultural Workers in the Great Lakes Region, 1917–1970.* Austin: University of Texas Press, 1991.

———. "Betabeleros: The Formation of an Agricultural Proletariat in the Midwest, 1897–1930." *Labor History* 30 (Fall 1989): 536–62.

Valdés, Dionicio Nodín. Barrios Nortenos: *St. Paul and Midwestern Mexican Communities in the Twentieth Century.* Austin: University of Texas Press, 2000.

Vargas, Zaragosa. "In the Years of Darkness and Torment: The Early Mexican-American Struggle for Civil Rights, 1945–63." *New Mexico Historical Review* 76 (October 2001): 382–413.

———. *Proletarians of the North: A History of Mexican Industrial Workers in Detroit and the Midwest, 1917–1933.* Berkeley and Los Angeles: University of California Press, 1993 [1999].

Vaught, David. *Cultivating California: Growers, Specialty Crops, and Labor, 1875–1920.* Baltimore, MD: Johns Hopkins University Press, 1999.

Zamora, Emilio. *The World of the Mexican Worker in Texas.* College Station: Texas A&M University Press, 1993 [1995].

Index

Agricultural Adjustment Act (1933), 45

agriculture, diversified, 3, 18

American Beet Sugar Company: *betabeleros*, 28, 31–32; contracts, growers, 31–32; creation of, 21; Red River Valley, 22–23, 35–36; field laborers, non-Mexican, 26, 33; housing for *betabeleros*, 34–35; mechanization of field work, 25. *See also* American Crystal Sugar Company

American Crystal Labor Agency, 7, 71–73, 79–80, 100–102, 109, 117–18, 138, 147–49, 162, 165–66, 169–70, 180, 183–84, 188–90; World War II, 62–65. *See also* American Crystal Sugar Company

American Crystal Sugar Company, 3, 11, 39; contracts, growers, 41, 97, 142; crime, *betabelero*, 129; *Crystal-ized Facts*, 103–4, 106–7, 109, 162–63; employees of, 6–7; factory construction, 69–71, 77–78, 99, 144, 146, 169, 185, 189; Great Depression, 41–42; grower associations, 53, 145–46, 162; growers, tensions with, 144–46, 162–63, 168–70; housing, *betabeleros*, 84–85, 107, 174; illegal immigrants, 100–101; interdependency, growers and *betabeleros*, 11–13, 15, 39–40, 60–61, 87–88, 96, 111, 113, 138, 141–42, 144, 163, 165, 190; labor shortage, 100–102, 105, 180; labor shortage, World War II, 54–58, 60; mechanization and, 102–5, 137, 182; monogerm seed, 139;

New Deal and, 47–51; *patronismo*, 87, 106–7; payment cycle, *betabeleros*, 114–15; purchase of, 4, 12, 184–87; sugar beet production, Red River Valley, 39, 61, 68–70, 78–79, 97–100, 136–38, 141–44, 159–62, 166–68, 187; transportation, Red River Valley, *betabeleros*, 28–29, 50–51; treatment, *betabeleros*, 163; Youth Beet Program (YBP), 152. *See also* American Beet Sugar Company; American Crystal Labor Agency

American GI Forum, 75–76, 115

Annual Plan, 122–23, 158

betabeleros, 4; American Crystal Sugar Company and, 50–51, 100–101; crime and, 80–81, 125, 127–29, 132; discrimination against, 42, 181, 190; education, adult, 172–73; education, children, 5, 66–68, 76, 84, 96, 116–17, 126, 157–59, 172–73; Great Depression and, 39; growers and, 170–71, 182, 189; housing, 5–6, 34–35, 58, 84–85, 93–94, 126; interdependency, American Crystal Sugar Company and growers, 11–13, 15, 39–40, 60–61, 87–88, 96, 111, 113, 138, 141–42, 144, 163, 165, 190; labor, United States, 11, 28–29; labor, shortage of, 100–102, 104–5, 147, 169; New Deal and, 49–51; *patronismo*, 106–11, 183, 189; permanent residence, Red River Valley, 35, 113, 125–26, 160, 164; potato harvest labor, 65; President's Commission on Migratory

Labor, 92–94; recreational activities, 122; seasonal labor cycle, 114–20, 120–23, 125; social service programs for, 65–68, 81–84, 96, 126, 157–60, 172–76; Texas in, 114–17; transportation, Red River Valley, 28–29, 50–51, 93, 118–20; treatment of, 10–11, 35, 61, 110, 162–63; wages, sugar beet field work, 34, 43, 51, 64, 93, 114–15, 121, 137; World War II, 54–58, 61. *See also* Mexican migrant workers
Bonanza farms, 16–17
bracero program, 58–60, 73–74, 88, 95, 102, 116, 135, 148–49, 153, 157

Carver County Sugar Company. *See* Minnesota Sugar Company
Chávez, César, 155, 176, 178
chemical technology, 143–44, 170
civil rights movements, 75–77, 153–56, 176–78
crime: *betabeleros*, 80–81, 125, 127–29, 132; juvenile delinquency, Red River Valley, 130–31; juvenile delinquency, United States, 129–30
Cristero Rebellion (1926–29), 28
Crystal Growers Corporation, 185, 187
Crystal-ized Facts, 103–4, 106–7, 109, 162–63
Cuba, sugar industry, 141, 160
Cycle of Outrage, A, 129

Dingley Tariff (1898), 20
discrimination, *betabeleros* against, 42, 181, 190
diversification. *See* agriculture
Drayton Economic Development Council, 145–46, 184

education: adult, 172–73; *betabeleros'* children, 5, 66–68, 76, 84, 96, 116–17, 126, 157–59, 172–73
Elementary and Secondary Education Act (1965), 157

Emigrant Labor Agency Law (1929), 36–37, 50, 62–63

factories, sugar beet, 22–23, 69–71, 77–78, 99, 144, 146, 169, 185, 189
Fair Labor Standards Act (1938), 48
Farm Labor Organizing Committee (FLOC), 156, 178
Farm Placement Program, 123
Farm Placement Service, 122; Minnesota, 133
farming. *See* Bonanza farms; growers, sugar beet
field work. *See* Labor

GI Forum. *See* American GI Forum
Gilbert, James (*A Cycle of Outrage*), 129
Good Neighbor Commission, Texas, 77
Governor's Interracial Commission, Minnesota (GIC), 82
Grapes of Wrath, The, 66
Great Dakota Boom, 15–17
Great Depression, Red River Valley, 40–42, 45
Great Western Sugar Company, 28, 36, 57, 62, 92, 99, 122, 167, 169, 184–85
grower associations, 12, 39, 52–54, 145–46, 162, 165, 168, 181, 184–88
growers, sugar beet, 3–4, 12, 97–99, 137; American Crystal Sugar Company, tensions with, 144–46, 162–63, 168–70; *betabeleros*, labor of, 91, 102, 146, 170–72, 182–84, 188–89; contracts, American Beet Sugar Company, 31–32; contracts, American Crystal Sugar Company, 41, 97, 142; crime, *betabeleros*, 129; housing, *betabeleros*, 174–75, 183; interdependency, American Crystal Sugar Company and *betabeleros*, 11–13, 15, 39–40, 60–61, 87–88, 96, 111, 113, 138, 141–42, 144, 163, 165, 190; mechanization, 102–5; monogerm seed, 144; New Deal, 47, 54; *patronismo*, 105–11; sugar beet

PHOTOS BETWEEN PAGES 60 AND 61

Photos 1–4, 6–9, and 11 courtesy of the Farm Security Administration, Office of War Information Photograph Collection, Library of Congress.
Photos 5 and 10 courtesy of the Red River Valley Sugar Beet Grower's Association, Northwest Minnesota Historical Center, Moorhead.

PHOTOS BETWEEN PAGE 164 AND 165

Photos 1–6 courtesy of the Institute for Regional Studies, North Dakota State University, Fargo.
Photos 7–13 courtesy of the Migrant Photograph Collection, Northwest Minnesota Historical Center, Moorhead.

North for the Harvest was designed by Will Powers at the Minnesota Historical Society Press, and set in type by Allan Johnson at Phoenix Type, Inc., Appleton, Minnesota. The text type is Miller, designed by Matthew Carter. Printed by Thomson-Shore, Dexter, Michigan.